THE BATTLE FOR DEMOCRACY

THE BATTLE

FOR DEMOCRACY

BY

REXFORD G. TUGWELL

Professor of Economics
Columbia University

GREENWOOD PRESS, PUBLISHERS
NEW YORK

CONTENTS

THE BATTLE
FOR DEMOCRACY

I

DESIGN FOR GOVERNMENT *

THERE is no prearranged field of government which is set apart from the circumstances of those who are governed. Relations here are always interdependent. As the circumstances of the people change, functions of government change. These are trite declarations of principle; I believe they are properly reiterated, however, for they are significant when one undertakes, as I shall, an appraisal of the legal and economic commitments of the new administration. It is a truism, too, to say that what is done by each of its divisions is affected by the whole orientation of the state. Like most truisms, this one contains a kernel of vital truth; it means, as respects ourselves, that executive, legislative, and judicial functions are not unalterably fixed, but are subject to revision. Government, or any part of it, is not in itself something; it is for something. It must do what we expect of it or it must be changed so that it will.

This is true of all institutions. Only the unsound theorist counts upon a static world; he does so, I suspect, in order that his literary generalities may more accurately describe reality. Such theorists, however (and they include many a hard-boiled business man), do not merely prefer to inhabit an unreal, static world; they also accumulate resistance, not always happily, to the recognition of change and the necessities for it. They are, therefore, always ready with criticism because they have a prepared basis for it. It is easy for them to attack any express plans which threaten to create a world

* Address delivered at The Eighth Annual Meeting of the Federation of Bar Associations of Western New York, June 24, 1933.

which is different from their concept of it. It is this sort of criticism which, since it possesses prestige and emotional content, is in the end most dangerous. It seems to me important, for this reason, to begin the building, even somewhat prematurely perhaps, of one of the rationale of recent emergency action.

Upon general social and economic problems, upon fit relations of government to industry, upon the respective functions of the several divisions of government in connection with these relationships, it is the line of least resistance for most of us to affect the attitude of the theorist. And this is true whether or not the consequences appear to be promising for or threatening to our social and economic existence. It is merely a usual process of thought. Our loyalties and affections are apt to attach themselves to instruments rather than to functions. In this instance we are apt to regard the form of a document more highly than the values such a thing produces. We become adulatory and uncritical. Only crisis calls in question our attribution of virtues. We then see suddenly that values attach to these things because they are valuable and not because they simply exist.

The new administration is compelled to reckon with these attitudes of people. In this connection I shall refer to and shall dwell upon two major lines of action which have been taken. I shall attempt to evaluate their constitutional and economic validity; I shall attempt to sustain them against more orthodox theories of government, law and economics. What I can say here and now must be merely the sketch for something which ought to have been longer considered, made more revealing by the inclusion of ramifying implications. There has not been time yet for that. If, however, I can furnish some clues to the rebuilding of a theoretical structure, I may have done something toward closing the gap between theory and reality. There will be sufficient ingenuity, and above all, adequate time, for other minds to follow these directions.

The two major lines of action of the administration to which I refer are, first, measures, such as the National Recovery Act and the Agricultural Adjustment Act, to coordinate and control private enterprise; and, second, measures vesting powers for the execution of laws in the Executive. Is it legally proper, if it is economically wise, for the national Government to assume the leadership of private enterprise; to regulate terms and conditions of employment, including wages; to prescribe permissible trade practices; even, if need be, to interfere with prices? Since these measures are related to the control of interstate and foreign commerce, attacks upon their constitutional validity must be upon broader grounds than that they violate theories concerning the powers of the Federal and state Governments. The doctrinal antagonism is broader than this; in terms of unconstitutionality, the economic theory of "free competition," is employed to attack these measures, this "governmental interference," as we call it. The Constitution is used as a holy of holies within which the ugly practices of free competition can be hid from vulgar eyes.

May I briefly analyze the economic implications of our past competitive economy and prophesy its position under the new measures?

As a matter of early national history, we may admit that unrestrained competition may have been a useful economic creed. Originally, it described our attitudes toward producers, especially producers who wrenched economic goods from sources of natural supply. Nature offered sufficient resistance to the ill-equipped producer to keep the market under-supplied. The problem of overproduction did not exist. The ruthless creed of free competition was appropriate enough to the task of conquering the continent, which necessarily was our great preoccupation during the nineteenth century.

Past circumstances produced needs (or supposed needs) which yielded theories in support of them. Toughest of those theories—so tough that, in the thinking of most men, it became an unalterable fact—was that which made competition a vital necessity, an end in itself, to be preserved at all costs. Competition was assumed to be an inherent part of democracy. Indeed competition and democracy came to be thought of as two aspects of one and the same value: a noncompetitive world was an undemocratic world.

Some two decades ago, it began to be apparent—or should have been—that competition and democracy were not Siamese twins, that they were separable, that in fact the separation had to be carried out if democracy were not to be stifled by competition. Woodrow Wilson evidenced an awareness of this problem in a certain address before the American Bar Association in 1910. But public espousal of this cause was unpopular. In that year the governing technique of industry had not yet been recognized; scientific management had not even been named. It was impossible to foresee the revolutionary impact, upon every institution which it was expected to maintain in the same world, of those productive forces which were then gathering strength. The monster of industry was not yet so pervasive that it could not be ignored. And traditional theory could yet hold its place for a while. Nevertheless, with matters economic developing as they were, the adherence to this policy, expressed in the several anti-trust laws, meant that government was pitting itself against inevitable, unconquerable industrial forces.

Competition, to depart from which was made unlawful,

became a matter of legal compulsion. It meant compelled business confusion. Coöperative impulses, demanded by the current economic trend, were thwarted and repulsed. They expressed themselves only indirectly and unhealthily. What was sound and economically necessary was branded as wrong legally. The nugatory powers of government were just strong enough to frustrate the creative zeal which the situation required. The reason for our insistence in those years on legislation to compel conflict was that conflict was naturally disappearing. Its passing was regarded as a catastrophe. The industry whose contours began to be revealed was an unorthodox one; no one knew what it would be like and therefore it ought not to be allowed to be born. But it was born even though it had to lead a subterranean existence until within a matter of months. And it grew almost as lustily as though it had been nourished with care rather than treated as a pariah. It preyed on its oppressors, however, and so had its own revenge. Its successive victimizations of society became more and more violent until at last there seemed no more possibility of pretense and concealment. It is out, now, in the open; and the hope is that its nature may be tamed to the uses of civilized existence.

But I must insist that our circumstances have changed. The plowman no longer homeward plods his weary way; he rides a tractor; natural resources can no longer resist, with the same effectiveness, our instrumentalities for their exploitation. Our economic course has carried us from the era of economic *development* to an era which confronts us with the necessity for economic *maintenance*. In this period of maintenance, there is no scarcity of production. There is, in fact, a present capacity for more production than is consumable, at least under a system which shortens purchasing power while it is lengthening capacity to produce. In this period of maintenance, the fact, and it is a fact, of dependence of all production upon a monetary market, vitalizes not only problems of transportation, distribution, and exchange, but also the fact of indispensable coördination of these factors of our economy. Even more, this dependence of our total economic life upon the market makes more and more conspicuous the dependence of our economic existence upon the purchasing power of the consumer—upon wages, that is, and protected prices.

This era of maintenance is the era of our present and future existence. The inextricable interdependence of its multiple factors demands a new control, a control designed to conserve their ability to function, a control to conserve and maintain our economic existence. As the Government "interfered," in days of free-competitive exploitation, with bonuses for production, tariffs, grants of natural resources, antitrust acts, and prescriptions for raising two blades of grass where only one grew before, I have felt that the Government must now intervene in other ways to conserve and maintain the industrial system which was developed here. It is a governmental function, not only because this conservation is a matter of public interest, but also because enterprises cannot act collectively for preservation. This paradox is explicable only by reference to the survival of certain competitive licenses when others have been brought under control. Enterprisers are unable to agree by themselves to act coöperatively because of gains which recalcitrant minorities are continually tempted to extort from any great endeavors of this sort. Beyond this there is the final suicidal compulsion which afflicts free industry. It throttles itself by closing off its access to markets.

Must I believe that Mr. Roosevelt's measures are contrary to the "American way," contrary to the public welfare, contrary to the Constitution, when they are measures designed to eliminate the anarchy of the competitive system, to ameliorate the recurrence of our spirals of inflation and deflation? Is his "partnership with industry" so contrary to the spirit of our institutions that it must be forbidden?

This is not an unknown phenomenon in economics. We once had iron laws of wages which we buttressed by the Malthusian notion that war, famine, and pestilence were the natural controls over standards of living. No one believes that any more about population. Shall we continue to believe that panics, deflation, and bankruptcy are our only remedy for overproductivity in industry? Or shall we, by similar ingenuity, control overcapacity and reconstruct the purchasing power of our people? The Malthusian theory did not prevent the one; I doubt if the theory of free competition will prevent the other.

Let me summarize: In this era of our economic existence, I believe it is manifest that a public interest well within the functions of government and well within the authority of government under our Constitution, commands the protection, the maintenance, the conservation, of our industrial faculties against the destructive forces of the unrestrained competition. And certainly the Constitution was never designed to impose upon one era the obsolete economic dogma which may have been glorified under it in an earlier one. For today and for tomorrow our problem is that of our national economic maintenance for the public welfare by governmental intervention—any theory of government, law or economics to the contrary notwithstanding. Hence the National Recovery Act and the Agricultural Adjustment Act of this administration.

I shall now turn to a consideration of the measures enacted in the last special session of the Congress, vesting in the President broad powers for the administration and execution of laws enacted by the Congress. Reference may be made, for illustrative purposes, to the powers granted to the President under the Economy Act and under the appendage to the Agricultural Act which is popularly known as the "inflation amendment." Of what may even the theorist of government, law or economics complain? Has the theory of a republican form of government explicit in the Constitution been violated by the new Democratic President and Congress? Has the philosophy of "checks and balances" within the Federal Government been infringed? These questions naturally arise; they command respect, for they concern our faith in the organization and functioning of our national Government. But must faiths, political more than economic, be preserved at any cost—that is, in disregard of the obviously necessary requirements of the public welfare? May our faiths in "checks and balances" yield to necessity, or even to expediency? If these faiths, and this necessity for more expeditious governmental action, are to clash, must we sacrifice efficiency or shall we establish a new faith?

Let me briefly discuss what the lawyer would call the "merits of the case." The President presumably sought, in asking to be invested with broad permissible powers, to attain a maximum of efficiency in the execution and administration of the laws of the Congress. In view of the complex and multiple aspects of the situation which we then faced, no single statute could be adequate; no series of statutes could be adequate. We had, remember, to repair disaster. The actions called for, if they were to be left to the traditional legislative and enforcement procedures, were manifestly not going to be in time, and were likely not to be sufficiently drastic.

Let me pursue this thought a bit further. The traditional

legislative process is highly spasmodic. Legislation of yesterday may be reconsidered today; it may be amended tomorrow and further altered or repealed thereafter. I might cite, for example, the history of our bankruptcy acts over the past century and a quarter, with which every lawyer is sufficientlv familiar. In other words, the legislature can act and react only by the accumulation of one statute upon another—a process inherently inadequate to meet the necessities of immediate and exigent action on the many fronts of our battle for economic self-preservation. And, of course, it is manifest that mere enactment of a statute, without subsequent executive action, is of little avail. And so the layman's fallacy that legislation becomes effective of its own force had to be disregarded. The subject matter dealt with made this fallacy doubly dangerous. The reform of banking practice or the elimination of racketeering from trade could not be assured merely by posting police. Indeed, the subject matter of the new legislation required little policing, but, instead, much coördinated administration and negotiation. The senior partner in the firm just being formed would need to be something more than a benevolent uncle if order were to be established in an unruly and poverty-stricken household. Such were the necessities, the merits of the case, which confronted the President and the Congress.

To meet these demands for coördinated administration and negotiation looking to our economic resuscitation, the President has accepted the responsibilities which the Congress has vested in him. The laws of the new administration are the laws of the Congress; it lies with the Congress to alter, amend, or repeal them. The President is to execute and administer them. Certainly, I submit, it is not patent wherein our Constitution has been violated, our republican form of government emasculated, or our philosophy of "checks and balances" for the Federal Government infringed. Indeed, I strongly suspect that, for the most part, those who criticize these measures as being unconstitutional dislike them either because of meager understanding or of fear that some protected privilege will be exposed and abolished.

"Constitutionality" is talked about as if it were a tangible fact, undeviating and precise. The wiser lawyers of my acquaintance agree with me in recognizing the folly of such a notion. Constitutional law, at any given time, is the then current theory of what ought and what ought not to be done under the Constitution, a legalistic expression of the prevailing political and economic philosophy.

Thus viewed, the constitutional law of the latter part of the nineteenth century expressed itself not merely in the decisions and opinions of the United States Supreme Court, in legislative debates, in textbooks. It found definite articulation in legislation—notably in the Sherman Act and its family of antitrust statutes. Significantly, in the recent Congressional discussions of the administration's program, some of the elder statesmen frequently approached any proposal to abate the antitrust laws as if that involved a constitutional change. In a profound sense they were correct; such a proposal did mean a change in the theory of the proper use of the powers conferred by that tersely worded paper called the Constitution.

And here let me say that it is my view that what we have done is to rediscover the Constitution, to revitalize the powers it was intended to create, many of which had been obscured in the interest of economic aims and purposes which have now become oppressively obsolescent. Those who wrote that great state paper were wise and bold. The best of them, although they disagreed on details, were struggling to meet a crisis which, in some important respects, was not unlike that now confronting us. They were fighting economic disorganization fostered by inadequate centralization. The Constitution, as you recall, was, in effect, a coup d'état; it was adopted in contravention of the Articles of Confederation because the Government set up by those Articles was too weak, too decentralized, to meet contemporary economic necessities.

The governmental pattern set up by the founding fathers was adapted from the British pattern, but with notable modifications. Among them was the grant of wide powers to the Executive at a time when the powers of the Executive in England were declining. And that American set-up—a strong central government with a powerful executive—maintained itself for years, in spite of verbal protests from one political faction or another. Later, a variety of influences led to the rise of an opposed constitutional theory. And part of that new theory was an increased stress on the idea of checks and balances. That idea, in turn, was based on Montesquieu's false description of the workings of the English government. And Montesquieu's misdescription was, in the interest of this new theory, misdescribed and its errors magnified. It was as if an image in a defective mirror had been reflected in another defective mirror.

The resulting false image of a wise government became the controlling design for government in these United States. Governmental action was considered as, at best, a necessary evil. To check and balance government to a point just short of inaction was the desideratum. The prevailing constitutional theory, and therefore the constitutional law, of course corresponded to this prevailing economic outlook.

At the center of this constitutional law was the conception of government as policeman. Government was to stop flagrant abuses, but not, in any circumstances, to do more.

It was to be negative and arresting, not positive and stimulating. Its rôle was minor and peripheral. It was important in this one sense: It was to prevent interferences with the competitive system. Behind that system (so it was said and thoroughly believed) was an invisible hand which beneficently guided warring business men to the promotion of the general welfare.

The jig is up. The cat is out of the bag. There is no invisible hand. There never was. If the depression has not taught us that, we are incapable of education. Time was when the anarchy of the competitive struggle was not too costly. Today it is tragically wasteful. It leads to disaster. We must now supply a real and visible guiding hand to do the task which that mythical, nonexistent, invisible agency was supposed to perform, but never did.

Men are, by impulse, predominantly coöperative. They have their competitive impulses, to be sure; but these are normally subordinate. Laissez faire exalted the competitive and maimed the coöperative impulses. It deluded men with the false notion that the sum of many petty struggles was aggregate coöperation. Men were taught to believe that they were, paradoxically, advancing coöperation when they were defying it. That was a viciously false paradox. Of that, today, most of us are convinced and, as a consequence, the coöperative impulse is asserting itself openly and forcibly, no longer content to achieve its ends obliquely and by stealth. We are openly and notoriously on the way to mutual endeavors.

And there is the importance of the rediscovery of the Constitution. We are turning our back on the policeman doctrine of government and recapturing the vision of a government equipped to fight and overcome the forces of economic disintegration. A strong government with an executive amply empowered by legislative delegation is the one way out of our dilemma, and on to the realization of our vast social and economic possibilities.

I have spoken of the resurgence of the coöperative impulse. It has long struggled for more active expression. That struggle might have been unsuccessful. But it is our great good fortune that at the moment when the failure of that struggle would almost surely have meant total collapse, there came into the presidency a man deeply moved by the coöperative impulse. And, above all, it is our good luck that that man was one whose integrity is beyond question.

That point cannot be overemphasized. The success of the new spirit demanded a restoration of power to the Executive. The executive branch of the Government is not a piece of mechanism, it is a body of men. If the new program is to succeed, those men must be wise, able, ingenious and honest. The shift to a new design for government would be a total failure if they were otherwise.

President Roosevelt is establishing, at this most critical period, an enduring pattern of administrative conduct. A lesser man, a self-aggrandizing, humorless one, a person less gifted with administrative talent and less eagerly hungry for wisdom, a dogmatizer without the experimental attitude, would merely have aroused false hopes which his accomplishments would have destroyed. The new design, with its unavoidable stress on vigorous governmental administration, possesses promise of endurance because it found precisely the right man. He is creating a lasting standard of administrative conduct below which none of his successors will dare to fall.

It is rather common to hear praise and criticism in one breath these days. The program is deplored because of its departures from tradition; the shaper and administrator of the program is praised because he embodies all those traits which we like to think of as American. But this is an antithesis which cannot be allowed. If praise is due for what he does, praise also is due for the program which permits the doing. The Executive is inseparable from his program—not any single part of it, but the total attempt to meet exigencies as, he has said, the football quarterback meets them, with power to do the expedient thing, to advance or to withdraw, creating strategy as the need for it appears.

There is nothing in all this which violates the spirit of our Constitution. As Mr. Justice Brandeis has said, "We do not need to amend the Constitution, we need to amend men's minds." And Mr. Justice Holmes, following in the footsteps of Marshall, has reminded us to remember always that it is a Constitution with which we are dealing and that "The Constitution was not designed to establish for all time any particular economic theory, whether of the organic relationship of the individual to the state or of laissez-faire." It is an experiment as all life is an experiment. We shall follow resolutely wherever the dictates of our minds propose. In the noble language of Mr. Justice Brandeis, "If we would guide by the light of reason, we must let our minds be bold."

II

THE SENIOR PARTNER

O N the night the Industrial Recovery Act was passed by Congress, one able Washington correspondent wired the news to his paper with the words, "At half past ten tonight, the Senate ratified the action previously taken by the House and abruptly departed from the economic system which had grown up without change during the entire existence of the Nation."

I am not sure that I know how much territory this correspondent intended to take in with the phrase, "the economic system," but aside from that, I believe he described what had happened accurately as well as dramatically.

Clearly, the greatest departure from our customary procedure in all the new legislation is the new governmental relation to industry which is embodied in both the Agricultural Adjustment Act and the National Recovery Act.

The old principle had been official since the nineties; it was expressed in a whole series of antitrust laws. The idea behind this was that competition protected all interests. Consumers were protected by competition among sellers which tended to drive prices down. A nice balance among all competitors was thought to balance all interests as well as it could be done.

The real reason for the passage of all the antitrust legislation was that competition in many areas failed to operate as it was supposed to do. The weaker among business men, consumers, farmers, workers—all suffered disadvantages.

It might have been said at that time that competition had had its chance and that some new kind of protection was needed. But instead, an earnest attempt was made at enforcement to restore competitive conditions where they had disappeared and to maintain them where they still existed.

There are differences of opinion as to whether it was wise to attempt to compel businesses to accept this condition of conflict. For a long time, however, there has been a growing distrust of conflict as a sufficient principle of organization. Part of this distrust came from observing many businesses growing bigger and stronger in spite of attempts at repression, and finding ways to do the very things it was thought they would not be able to do under the antitrust laws.

But part of it also came from the notion that efficiency was being so restricted that consumers and workers might have more to gain from an entirely different kind of attack on the problem. People who felt this way began to ask how it would be if certain businesses were allowed to coöperate as they wanted to do, instead of competing, and if an earnest effort were made to insure that such advantages as came from cooperation were secured for the public.

Many variations of this idea have been put forward in recent years. The great growth of trade associations was a definite movement toward it even while the antitrust laws were in universal force. Businesses, through these associations, could coöperate in everything except price-fixing and the division of the market. By the time the new legislation came to be written, there was little left to do except to recognize these associations for what they were, make them openly legal, and require that they should not be used in such a way as to injure the public interest.

This is the philosophy behind those sections of the Agricultural Adjustment Act and the National Recovery Act which have to do with the recognition by the Government of "agreements" in the one case and "codes" in the other. The first step has been for the various units in an industry to find substantial agreement among themselves as to what they want to do. They then present this for recognition. At this stage the Government is able to examine the situation it represents from the point of view of the public interest, and through its power to withhold recognition, on the one hand, and its power to impose conditions, on the other, it can determine the standards which are to be maintained.

The public objectives to be gained are fair wages and working conditions for the employed, fair prices for consumers, and, under the Agricultural Act, fair prices for the producers of farm products. No agreement or code need be recognized which does not meet these tests.

In the preliminary stages all this is voluntary on the part of industry. Yet Government recognition endows such an agreement or code "with the force and effect of law," so that any small recalcitrant group within the industry, which chooses not to meet the standards, can be subjected to the severest discipline. It is further provided, however, that if any whole industry should be reluctant to set its house in order, the Government may require any concern doing an interstate business to obtain a Federal license in order to continue. The obtaining of this license will be conditioned on the meeting of such standards as can be given governmental approval.

Industries are asked to do what they have always professed a desire to do: carry on their operations with fairness to the whole community. If this is done, there will be no restraint other than a code of decency to be arrived at among themselves. But if any small group among them, or any whole industry, fails to come into the civilized majority, it can be made to do so summarily.

This will perhaps explain what President Roosevelt meant

when he spoke of this new system of relationships as governmental partnership with industry. The phrase is precise. The Government, however, is the senior and controlling partner. And it should be, since it represents no interest save a general one, and has no objective except that of establishing a "concert of interests."

For the first time in our history industry can now be organized to express its technological possibilities. It can move forward with a vast productive program without destroying its own market by cutting wages and raising prices. What each produces, the workers in every other will be able to consume. And we may thus find a more secure basis for prosperity, one which we may hope will last beyond the few months or years involved in the speculative fever of a boom.

We ought always to remember that potentially, in resources, in the training and spirit of our people, we are the richest nation on earth. We have only to consolidate our already great gains on nature. The chance we are taking in these new arrangements is very slight indeed, compared with what is at stake for our people.

III

AN EXPERIMENT IN RECONSTRUCTION

THE Tennessee basin offers as pretty a picture of waste and opportunity as could be found anywhere on this continent. What unguided self-interest can do to an originally generous provision of natural resources within a few generations is wholesomely demonstrated there for all who have eyes to see. The lesson is written on a page of twenty million acres, spread from ridge to ridge of these lovely southern mountains.

The basin is on the way to ruination, what with the massacre of its forests, the overcropping of its lands and the washing away of its soil into the big river. The wastage has been caught none too soon and yet not too late. There is the possibility still of a laboratory demonstration in conservation which, if it succeeds, may furnish a new pattern for civilization. If planning can succeed anywhere it ought to in the basin. Yet the difficulties are very great. Nature has been grievously hurt and man is as yet unrepentant. The problem is a double one of repairing the damage and of conviction of sin.

If the two million people within the basin can be brought to see that their poverty has its source within themselves and if they prove willing for once to coöperate in a joint enterprise in which a few do not share at others' expense but which is calculated to benefit all alike, then a new kind of American life can rise out of what threatens to be desolation.

Of the twelve million acres of farm land, for instance, only six million ought to be farmed. The rest ought to be returned to forests. Otherwise the streams will continue to run yellow with precious soil and the reservoirs will fill with silt. Moreover, agriculture and industry will have to submit to remarriage after their long divorce. For power lies close to the heart of the Tennessee plan. And power makes possible the decentralization of industry.

A vision of villages and clean small factories has been growing into the minds of thoughtful men, and they foresee the first considerable embodiment of their vision in this valley. Efficient farming, they say, is not a year-round enterprise. Linked to industry, however, its great virtue is saved. Farming makes homes and these we regard as something good beyond argument. Also the rural slum is less likely to perpetuate itself if the double opportunities of farming and industry can be made available. Perhaps some of the difficulties which torment both city and country can be resolved in this way.

It does not do to be naïve about this. Many of the industrialists like the decentralizing scheme because it fixes their workers on a patch of ground from which escape is difficult. It makes them satisfied with a lower wage, and less vigilant concerning the conditions of work. The domestic system of manufacture which prevailed in the seventeenth century was something less than utopian, and on the surface this scheme seems to have many of the same characteristics. But if the power of these streams can be made freely available and if farms and little factories can be united without subjecting the workers to a new kind of serfdom—however contented—the way of life which is promised seems altogether desirable.

There is need, evidently, for the development of a kind of industrial democracy to which the South has hitherto not taken kindly. But this again is one of those elements in the experiment which it will be interesting to see engaging the administrative talents of Arthur Morgan. Hidden away in the coves and valleys of this region and living in cities and villages along the streams, there is a stock which carries those traditions which are genuinely our own. These are Americans in the truest sense. And what will come of the Tennessee basin enterprise will be an illustration of what it is that Americans can do.

The project is appealing to the imagination. The arrest of erosion—our greatest enemy—the re-creation of forest resources, the harnessing of a great pool of power and turning it to use, the remaking of homes and factories—all the elements are there which appeal to the practical imagination. I do not think, however, that anyone who has studied the situation believes there is more than one chance in five that it will succeed.

The power companies already operating in that region are deeply intrenched. There is required a complete permissive program of legislation from the states which are involved and, judging by the experience of the western states where this fight has been going on for several decades, this will not be easy. The old cries of government competition with private business will issue loudly from many well coached throats. There will be a great show of righteous indignation over the invasion of private rights.

These specious appeals to a tradition of individualism will carry a lot of weight—at least they always have. It will be difficult for Mr. Morgan to show his constituency what cheap power can mean to their standard of living; how the grandchildren of this generation will bless us for a heritage of deep soil, husbanded forests and clean-running streams; and to find his way through the maze of power and real-estate interests which may block his path at every step.

His success, if he should succeed, will be a demonstration to the whole country. It will mean that region after region will follow the pattern he has created. He and his associates are pioneers. Their job is not to conquer the West, but to conquer the East, with all that implies. I, for one, wish him well.

This work of his carries more significance for the future than any other single attempt of the administration to make life better for all of us. It is in no sense emergent, as so many other actions have necessarily been. It did not have to be done to stave off financial panic, to avert war, or to relieve distress. It is a deliberate turning toward the future, a commitment to an ideal. Its success can depopulate cities, destroy a thousand intrenched privileges, invalidate a whole tradition of single-hearted self-interest.

IV

OUR WEIGHT IN GOLD

THERE is a legend telling how the nations of the world, in a moment of inspiration, settled the gold question once and for all. They shipped all their gold to an uninhabited island in the Pacific, and left warships to guard it. Once a year the agents of each country assembled at the island to tally the gold supply, and to report the reassuring news that the gold was still there. One year, however, the routine was interrupted. The island had disappeared. The agents were horrified. Should they rush back and report the fact to their governments? Profound discussion left them agreed that that would never do; they must make their customary report. Returned to their capitals, they reported as usual. The new routine went on, year after year. The world, according to this historian, wagged on.

But, of course, that is a legend. The nations of the world still have their gold. They probably have, among them, monetary gold worth $10,950,000,000. Against this, are currency and liabilities of central banks amounting to $24,500,000,000.

The situation exists in the United States in exaggerated form. We have only some $4,000,000,000 of the precious metal, yet on June 30, 1932, there were in circulation some $5,000,000,000 of paper currency which called for payment in gold; some $19,000,000,000 of government obligations, some $30,000,000,000 of state and municipal bonds, and a large but uncertain amount of urban mortgages and real estate bonds which might bring the total up to $70,000,000,-000 or $80,000,000,000.

Obviously you cannot pay $75,000,000,000 with $4,000,-

000,000, and yet, on the face of it, this was what we were pretending we could do. The only reason why this was possible for a moment was that no one ever thought of asking gold for the obligations which theoretically demanded gold payment. As long as no one asked for gold, we could believe that gold would be given if we asked for it. In this way, and only in this way, was it possible to maintain a "gold standard" and to comply with the Parity Act of 1900, which provided that all forms of money issued or coined by the United States should be maintained equal to 25.8 grains of gold nine-tenths fine.

Money, after all, though, is only an instrument of value, "a thing" of paper or metal which is accepted by the people of a nation in exchange for their goods or services. It is both a thing of value and a rod of measurement. This the writers of our own Constitution tacitly recognized when they provided that "The Congress shall have the power . . . to coin money, regulate the value thereof, and of foreign coins, and fix the standards of weights and measures." That is, in one clause, money, weights and measures are all treated as one.

In the latter half of 1932 and the first few months of 1933, the burden of debt had become unbearable. Compared with 1926, it now required twice as many bushels of corn, pounds of bacon or cans of tomatoes to equal a dollar. More and more people found dollars hard to get and fewer and fewer debts were paid. This, and the strain of three years of depression, unemployment, governmental inaction, the bankruptcy of business, and the failure of 11,000 banks, explain why both foreigners and Americans demanded immediate redemption of their claims in gold.

The liquidation movement reached a crisis in March. Everyone wanted his share before the whole supply should be exhausted, and everyone wanted to hoard it. On the sixth,

President Roosevelt declared that no bank might pay out gold coin. Three days later Congress in the Emergency Banking Bill granted the President formal powers of control. He at once ordered recent withdrawals of coin returned to the Treasury. This action on the part of the President was also made into law by a Senate resolution on June fifth. The justification for this was that gold was no longer obtainable. It seemed absurd, therefore, to keep up the fiction that any large number of debtors should be required to pay it out. From then on all obligations, whether they promised payment in gold or not, were treated alike. All coins and currencies of the United States were made legal tender for all debts, public and private.

These measures have brought about a quiet, unheralded advance toward social justice. For fifty years it has been possible for certain individuals who could come into the possession of gold to set themselves aside from the rest of the community during periods of uncertainty. Obviously only the well-to-do could protect themselves in this way; those whose incomes had to be spent as they were earned lived at the mercy of the fluctuating prices. They had to meet their obligations, buy goods, pay wages, in the ordinary currency whose value rose and fell with good and bad times. It is one of the achievements of this administration that all monies are now made equal and that gold has become the exclusive possession of the Government rather than of a favored group. All of us now have an interest in the general stability of currencies which is not related to our possession of gold. We may all try harder to maintain security and equilibrium now that it is made certain that, so far as currencies are concerned, we shall all suffer alike.

Another effect has been that the dollar has fallen relatively to other currencies. We no longer suffer the disadvantage of having a currency which is hard for foreigners to acquire. A merchant in Italy or Germany who now wants to buy dollars with his own money can buy more of them than he formerly could; he can therefore buy more American goods which have to be paid for in dollars. Some pick-up in our foreign trade ought to help in the struggle for recovery.

The whole gold action looks toward freedom from an orthodox myth: it promotes equality and it will force us in the years to come to search for a really satisfactory medium of exchange—which gold never was and never could be.

V

BANKING FOR THE PEOPLE

BANKING in this country has always been considered a field of business properly and exclusively reserved for individual initiative and competition—an attitude which lies deeper in our traditions than is usually thought and so is more uncritically accepted. What we now call banking was once done by goldsmiths who kept other peoples' gold in their strong boxes. Gradually their customers, instead of bothering to ask for the metal whenever they wanted to pay a debt, grew accustomed to using goldsmiths' receipts. Pieces of paper thus passed from hand to hand, while the money changers' gold coins lay quietly beside his brooches and bracelets. They were our first bank notes.

This function gradually became more profitable to the goldsmiths than their craft and they assumed the name of bankers. Instead of issuing bank notes on the basis of gold in their vaults and then lending the gold to others, they merely told a borrower that he could have so much money and marked up his name and the amount lent on their books. The borrower would then, without asking for gold or currency, draw checks and pay off his obligations with them. Bank credit is manufactured in this way. It is obvious that, so long as people will accept checks in payment for goods, the bank has created something of as much value as dollar bills. We have always controlled the issuance of dollar bills and are planning to control them still more strictly, but we have never really dared to touch these goldsmiths' receipts called checks. The situation is anomalous.

It is more anomalous today than ever. The speculative

boom of 1929 was largely financed through abuses of a system of credits, which was thus loosely conceived. It is impossible to detail here the complex nets of finance which were woven through the old laws. Banks which could not themselves speculate with depositors' funds, discovered the elaborate fiction of affiliates through which it could be done. Securities could be created, sold back and forth, and manipulated at will by the use of depositors' funds and to the immense profit of speculators who pretended to be bankers. All this has to be brought under some kind of control if any progress is to be made in mastering the forces of modern economic life. The world was not made for bankers—a lesson they have had to be taught by legislation.

Parts of the new law were adapted from English and Canadian banking customs; parts represent a fresh approach to the problem. In general, however, the attack has been concentrated on three fronts: control of speculation; strengthening of the internal structure of the entire banking system; the protection of investors, of depositors, and of home owners.

The attack on the first front has been written into the act in definite terms, the Federal Reserve Board being ordered to ascertain "whether undue use is being made of bank credit for the speculative carrying or trading in securities, real estate, or commodities, or for any other purpose inconsistent with the maintenance of sound credit conditions." To prevent undue speculation, the Board has been granted broad powers which include the withdrawing by the Board of its credit facilities, limitations on the amount of loans made by the member banks which are backed by securities, and strict control over the amount any member bank may loan its investment affiliate. Even excessive investment in a bank's own premises has been brought under limitation, and discretionary authority given the Federal Reserve Board to supervise all negotiations with foreign banks or bankers.

On the second front, two forms of attack have been provided: first, the close alliance of ordinary commercial banks with their stock affiliates has been brought under more control. Each member bank will now for the first time be required to furnish the Federal Reserve Board with reports on the financial conditions of its subsidiary and the Comptroller of the Currency can periodically examine their activities. Furthermore, if any director of a member bank is judged, after due hearing, to have violated any law relating to his bank or to have continued unsound business practices after a warning has been given, the Comptroller has the authority to require the removal of that director.

Then also the ability of the banks to help themselves has been strengthened, for it was realized that fundamental soundness in financial conditions has to be self-created, not imposed. In furtherance of this, the initial capitalization of national banks has been raised from a minimum of $25,000 to $50,000. Banks in all cities of over 50,000 will have to have a paid-in capital of at least $200,000. Every director, now, must have a share in his bank of at least $2,500. Private banking houses can no longer accept the people's deposits and yet escape examination and control. The double liability clause, an obligation which has always been more of a hindrance than a safeguard, is repealed. And, finally, it has at last been permitted national banks to expand, when they are strong enough to expand, by establishing branches within those states which specifically permit it. All these provisions are intended to strengthen individual banks and yet to make their activities so open and definite that indispensable control may be maintained and extended.

The attack along the third front was forced by the

hardships and misfortunes which millions of depositors have undergone since 1929. The administration has resolved that these people's suffering shall not have been entirely in vain. A Federal Deposit Insurance Corporation, entrance to which is to be allowed only under strict regulations, has been established. This Corporation will have a capital of about $500,-000,000. With this, and with authority to issue debentures to three times that amount, and to require a further contribution from member banks of $175,000,000, it should be prepared to guarantee the deposits of the subscribing banks in the following degrees: 100 percent, deposits under $10,000; 75 percent, deposits between $10,000 and $50,000; and 50 percent, those over $50,000. The real significance of this is implied in the clause requiring that before any bank shall be admitted to the facilities of the Corporation, a "thorough examination" must show that "the assets of the applying bank are adequate to enable it to meet all of its liabilities to depositors." This will probably attract business to the banks which have publicly been approved as sound; but it must be understood that the provisions of this section apply for only a three-year period and that deposits are "guaranteed" in only a provisional sense.

By the Home Owners' Bill a corporation is created with the power to issue $2,000,000,000 of tax-exempt, interest-guaranteed bonds. The proceeds of these are to be used in refinancing mortgages on homes valued at less than $20,000 and in recovering homes already lost. It gives the Federal Home Loan Bank Board the opportunity to function really effectively.

The program is not a perfect one. It does not go the whole way in creating a consolidated, national banking system, and it still leaves a practically free hand to private bankers. It restricts, but does not abolish, affiliates; it hinders, but cannot absolutely prevent, irresponsible management, speculation, and bank failures. It is a great step forward, however, and a necessary adjunct to a program of delicately balanced adjustment among economic forces which the administration's industrial and agricultural bills contemplate.

VI

TRIAL AND ERROR

SAGEBRUSH and greasewood grow where nothing else can
survive. Where America's inland empire tapers off from
fifteen to ten or even to eight inches of rainfall in the year,
the brown land still produces a crop. True it is a useless one,
save for its bare, clean beauty; but agricultural engineers say
that its product is an unfailing index for the future. Where
the sage grows sturdily, the soil is sweet so that when it can
be brought under water it will yield prodigiously. But where
the greasewood grows, there is black alkali. The warning is
as plain as that of the rattlesnake's castanets. Water here will
dissolve the salts and defeat any intentions men may have to
make it useful.

Driving through these hundreds of northwest miles, from
cold dawns to blistering noons, I found myself wishing that
sagebrush and greasewood grew in Washington corridors. If
only we had, I thought, an index as old and as unfailing, we
might know which of these complex social soils we now hope
may be productive will raise black alkali and so defeat all
our hopes for a prosperous crop. We should know what can
and what cannot be done, so saving ourselves much grief and
raising our efficiency; we might concentrate on real rather
than unreal possibilities. Lacking it, we have to fall back
still, in spite of our developing arts of forecast, and in spite
too of our leader's genius for reading public opinion, on the
oldest method of contrivance—trial and error.

I see no reason why I should not report in these columns
that the neighborhood of Puget Sound still is the best place

to eat this side of Cherbourg. One, surely, of the elements of Utopia we Americans presumably are striving for is good food; and here it exists—cheap and plenty. There are, for foundation, these rich northern valleys where it rains all winter—a soft rain broken by weeks of May in January. Vegetables grow every month in the year, discouraged occasionally by frosts but never wholly kept from market.

Such vegetables they are, too! They have not been forced on hot, light soils; they have not been packed, chilled, shipped a thousand miles, auctioned, repacked, distributed by truck and sold at 300 percent advance. They have had an easy journey from some bungalow-owning trucker's "ranch" to the best public markets I know of, there to display their quite spectacular charms before a highly critical audience of housewives, who, in person, choose them with discretion and lug them home in their own automobiles.

But the Puget Sound vegetable, incomparable as it is, is only the beginning, a claim to distinction where distinction is most difficult. There, also, are the food resources of the Sound itself, to say nothing of Alaskan waters for which the Sound cities are home ports. The Dungeness crab shames the Chesapeake (these notes are made in Washington State, not Washington City); indeed, it is one of the more remarkable of this nation's products. And everyone, I suppose, appreciates the quality of fresh-caught King Salmon, of halibut and cod, to say nothing of numerous minor salt-water fish. But, to add to this piscatorial wealth, it has to be remembered that a person standing on any of the seven hills of Seattle can see mountains on several sides; where there are mountains there are streams; where there are streams there are fish. So, Seattle, Tacoma, and Everett are particularly rich in this way too.

I might add that there is a range country just beyond the

mountains which lie within sight to the east of here, whence comes feeder stock which has not traveled a thousand miles before death and another frozen thousand afterward. Nowhere do steaks and chops always seem so full of flavor; nowhere are there nobler roasts and stews.

Besides all this, and just to make my eastern lament complete, I have to report that the beer is excellent. After trying a famous Milwaukee brew on draught alongside a local one, I voted honestly for the home product. And I might say that a group of us walked openly into a large, clean, and shining place, stood at a bar with respectable folk all about us, and drank large helpings at ten cents. It was all, to my mind, as it should be.

I find as I reflect on what has just been put down here that I have come close to describing one of those fishing-farming economies which have been the basis for so many civilizations. And that, of course, is what this is. The mountains seventy-five miles to the east are a real barrier; they turn these people's faces toward the sea. Across that sea lies the undeveloped Orient, and in it lie comparatively unexhausted riches. There is bound to be here, in the far Northwest, something unique, perhaps valuable or beautiful.

If only these people lived as easily on their land as older peoples do! Candor, however, compels the observation that they are self-conscious, defensive, and insistent on being typical. For myself I do not enjoy the Northwest more because it is praised nor because its people value an exaggerated usualness. It is the special quality, the distinctive flavor which ought, it seems to me, to be cultivated. The basic materials of this Northwest all lie exposed; and they are more than half developed, as its arts of cooking are. But like its cooking, so much of its civilization is something borrowed, rather than built on the really excellent local foundation and followed through in independent and imaginative fashion.

The unwillingness of Americans to be culturally indigenous is notorious. The New England poets borrowed the English lark and imposed on our sour, reluctant eastern April the borrowed adjective "halcyon"; somewhere in these states we make every "type" of cheese—Camembert, Roquefort, Gruyère—no special kind of milk or refinement of cure is sacred from adaptation. The goat and the sheep are blithely confused with the cow; and the cow's own quality is lost sight of in a general insanity of imitation. Having been raised in a hill county of New York, I am prepared to defend an old New York cheese against the world. But I know men who, without compunction, divert the milk of our honest cow from this intended use to the making of inferior Muenster. We ought not to be like that.

It is curious that these imitative Americans who show their fear of usualness in so many ways should be, in so many others, ingenious and even daring. Our national capital may illustrate a slavish copying of classical forms; but the American automobile is sufficiently unique; here in Seattle, too, there are some intimations that the Chicago exposition architecture was not without some basis in existence. And within recent memory, a whole hill was moved out of the city's center and used to make land in the bay. It is not the size of any enterprise that stops us; it is what may be said of it by the inexpert and the tasteless. These very Americans who enter so reluctantly on any rigorous adaptation of form to function are the same people who object so strenuously to governmental interference. They call it "regimentation," as though every aspect of their lives would not lead to the belief that sameness is a weighty consideration.

It is part of my hope, at least, for the New Deal that it will strengthen those elements of uniqueness and difference which are so natural to our diversified land, that we shall become less rather than more alike. This has nothing to do with the management by the government of those functions which belong to it, nor has it anything to do necessarily with standardization as an industrial principle.

As Cornelia Parker once said, "I don't care who designs the drain pipes of my house so long as I can choose my own hats." And this seems to me a classic distinction. There is room yet for vast extensions of governmental activity before regimentation will appear; it may even be that an extension of governmental activity is necessary to prevent the great industries from making robots of us all; and I might point to the Tennessee Valley and to the Columbia Basin projects as examples directly in point.

Having visited the Grand Coulee and the Columbia Basin country, I think I can understand why people out here have clung so many years to the hope that some day the Columbia Basin would be "put under water." It is about a twenty-five-mile drive off the main road between Spokane and Seattle to the Grand Coulee and the site of the proposed Columbia River dam. It is, in August, a hot, dusty drive, through thousands of acres of wheat, and then, near the river, between steep hills desolated by old lava flows. Sagebrush grows there, and I suppose rattlesnakes; certainly little else. The road down to the river drops about a thousand feet in a steep grade. The dam site, where it is proposed to build a power dam with Public Works funds, is interesting as showing how engineers can see, in a powerful river sweeping through desolate country, the embryonic muscles of civilization. It will be hot, wearing work, building that dam; but the achievement will be proportionately great.

Where the river now curves to the north, the Grand Coulee begins—a broad valley between cliffs twice the height of Niagara. This was once, until some geologic phenomenon occurred to turn the river in a broad swing to the north, the channel of the Columbia, roughly paralleling the present one for about a hundred miles. It is as if the Hudson River had been diverted by some cataclysm of nature from its present channel past the Palisades, and it were possible to drive an automobile down the river's present bed from Albany to New York. In the main portion of the Grand Coulee, perhaps twenty-five miles long, a few ranchers are trying to grow a little wheat, and to find pasture for live stock; but mostly the floor of the valley is sagebrush and slowly crumbling basalt rock—and dust.

Some day, when the high dam planned for the Columbia at this point is built (the low dam is already approved, but that is only for power), it will be possible to build earthen dams at both ends and pump water up from the Columbia to form a huge artificial lake, storage for irrigating the vast stretch of level land in the basin to the south.

Past attempts at dry farming in this country are only too evident. Every mile displays a tragedy of enterprise. Some few ranchers hang on; but their lives must be miserable. Yet the country has a magnificent sweep, fertile soil, a rich future— if water can be got into it.

In years past it would have been heresy for anyone connected with the Department of Agriculture to speak kindly of a new irrigation project. It is not so now, in view of the new administration policy that for every acre of fertile soil brought into cultivation by reclamation, the Government has the obligation to see that an area of submarginal land equivalent in productivity shall be removed from competition and given a long, long rest.

This settlement of an old governmental controversy is so sane that it seems incredible it had not been hit on before. We have millions of acres of land, worn out by our careless methods of farming, which can never again provide a living for anyone, no matter how high the price of produce may be. Erosion and soil-mining have destroyed it. We must take it out of cultivation, if necessary return it to the public domain, plant it to trees and grass, and allow it to recover what fertility it can. For this marginal farming we can substitute, in so far as we need to, the intensively managed sort which may be seen in some of these western valleys.

If we pursue this policy far enough we shall reduce the use of sweated acres and locate agricultural production where it belongs, on the richest, most unexhausted lands we have. At present, of course, we simply have too many farmers and too many acres; but the surpluses they produce are temporary. Our old dependence on the land has been minimized for the moment, perhaps, but we shall always need better management of agricultural resources. And this is a step that way. The Columbia Basin cannot arrive at development for a decade, at the earliest. By that time, if the new land policy develops smoothly, we shall, unless I am mistaken, be in need of it.

It is my belief that this million acres of Columbia Basin land will some day be put to work. Certainly any reasonable person would prefer its rapid utilization to the laissez-faire policy which would hold it in reserve until another generation of farmers had starved it into use. We have, in the past, shied away from viewing this sort of project reasonably because we lacked the clear objective which we now possess; and also because of the emotional fog which has always surrounded any proposal that the Government do this or that. The fog seems to have lifted; it is now possible to propose without recrimination that the Government—state or Federal, or both—move directly to utilize a great natural resource for the common good.

It is not meant to imply that the Columbia Basin project, or any other comparable one, is exempt from critical examination. We are still ignorant in many particulars about the soil of the region; all sorts of problems of farming under irrigation will come up for study; what crops ought to be grown there and how they may affect other areas which grow them must be decided quite frankly. Above all, 90 percent of the land in the basin is privately owned, and much of it is held by mortgage and insurance companies.

Also, the speculator in real estate is no more absent in the State of Washington than in Tennessee or anywhere else. This cannot be a project for the relief of land speculators. Some way will have to be found to make sure that the land's average earning power is the measure of its selling or leasing price; the object, in utilizing this natural resource, must be to establish pleasant and profitable homesteads for the many, rather than speculative profits for the few.

In the settlement of America there was too much exploitation both of land and of farmers. It must not happen on these new lands, and the means of prevention may not be found short of condemnation and leasing. But there is a chance here which is good enough, in spite of the many difficulties, for a resettlement of some few Americans, at least, in a local area with great farming and industrial potentialities.

There will be cheap power for industry and plentiful water on fertile soil for farming. These, after all, are the basic requirements for civilization. It will be, to all intents and purposes, man-made and man-controlled. There is now good soil and assured sunshine; the worst hazard of industry—cheap, unfailing power, and the worst hazard of farming

—the weather, will both be immensely reduced. There will
be new problems, as there are now in the Wenatchee and
in the Yakima Valleys, but most of them will be known from
the beginning and the means for their solution will be organized.

VII

FREEDOM AND BUSINESS

THE N.R.A. and A.A.A. are about to enter their second phase—one much more difficult than any heretofore encountered. Codes and agreements are rapidly going into effect. But these arrangements have been made swiftly and without the complete knowledge which will come to administrators as the results are registered in practice. Each of the emergency administrations is excellently equipped with facilities for knowing exactly what is happening. The best statisticians and economists in the country have been called into this work. The results of their running analysis will be available to administrators constantly.

The information thus collected will have a greater influence on coming policy than might at first be thought. Facts are stubborn. Windy representation cannot prevail where facts occupy the ground. Whether business margins are too high or too low; whether employment is increasing or decreasing; whether wages are going up or down—all these things will be known, and the problems underlying them will have to be dealt with.

The blanket-code phase of the recovery effort is now nearly completed. As much, I think, has been accomplished by it as was expected. Industry has been put through a first phase of reorganization. Government has asserted its right to require order in industrial processes. There is no doubt, also, that there have been real accomplishments. But the crucial times are yet to come. The working out of day-to-day relations, the actual requiring of businesses to do what seems to them against their own interests—these will be less spectacular than the N.R.A. campaign. But in this daily procedure there will be built up a new law and a new governance for industry.

One test of the goodness of business is the lowness of its prices. This is an unfashionable kind of economics just now; but it is a maxim we ought to hold to. It ought not to be stated flatly, of course, because low prices achieved by cutting costs are not always desirable. The easiest costs to cut are often labor costs, and if these are reduced by lowering wages the purchasing power of the workers is reduced. This kind of economy returns to torment its inventors.

But the history of American industry in the last decade and a half pretty consistently illustrates another kind of economy. It also illustrates the kind of difficulty we get into when economies are not translated into reduced prices. The greatest gains in efficiency ever registered in a similar period have accrued to our industry since the years of the War. New ways of using power, new processes of manufacture, better control over operations, enabled us to turn out more than a third more products with the same effort than we were able to do fifteen years ago. This meant that costs were steadily, almost spectacularly, reduced. Prices were reduced somewhat, but by no means in proportion to the reduction in costs. The result of this disparity between costs and prices was that profits rose enormously. These profits were used, generally speaking, to make more improvements and to enlarge productive capacity. But toward the end of the period the inevitable results of such a policy began to register. Consumers had not been allowed to share in the gains from the efficiency movement and so the demand for the goods produced began to fail.

The failure of demand was concealed for a few years by certain new devices. Consumers who could not buy out of their current incomes were given installment credits. But when debts had piled up to unprecedented heights it began to be clear that they could never be paid, and so lending was stopped. There is nothing wrong with consumer credit if its volume is not greater than the expectation of income to pay it off. But if it outruns ultimate ability to pay, it merely postpones the inevitable day of settlement. In a way the depression of 1929 can be described as a stoppage of industrial operations to permit consumers' purchasing power to rehabilitate itself.

It seems clear enough that if purchasing power had equaled the price required for our goods there would have been no failure of demand. And it is a curious paradox of progress that the situation should have been intensified by gains in efficiency. Good public policy seems to require such a management of this matter in the future that a better relationship between costs and prices is maintained. Otherwise we shall have more and worse depressions in the future, rather than fewer and more moderate ones.

The question immediately arises: What can the Government do to protect industry against itself in this respect? I say protect industry against itself rather than protect consumers, because the interests here are ultimately identical. Industry cannot operate permanently and continuously unless it adopts the policy of relating its prices to its costs. It was with a realization of this background that certain sections of the Agricultural Adjustment Act and the National Recovery Act were framed. It was conceived under both these acts that industry might control its own prices if adequate public remedies were reserved for enforcement. The agreements under the farm bill and the codes under the recovery act give industry its first opportunity to meet this problem. If, in general, industries are willing to admit that the policy of relating costs to prices is a necessary one, it will now be possible to prevent recalcitrant business men from wrecking a program of stable prices. For these agreements and these codes are given in the new legislation the force and the effect of law.

More attention, so far, has been given by business men to the prevention of price cutting. This also is one of the difficulties which can be met, but it is a more immediate and obvious one, and not anything like so important as this other one of relating prices to costs and reducing the margins of profit. The whole effort looks toward stability and many industrialists recognize both sides to the problem. But even if they should be reluctant to see that their interests must at last be brought into consistent relationship with those of consumers and workers, the Government does not lack power for persuasion. The codes and agreements, in order to have the force and effect of law, have to be recognized by the Government; and wise administration requires that business shall not be given charters for exploitation of workers and consumers, but rather charters of responsibility to perform social tasks in a new and more coöperative way.

The operation of these new acts is sometimes forecast as the end of laissez faire in business. However one may feel about the desirability of this, it is clearly not true, except perhaps in a very limited sense. These new measures will reduce the scope of freedom. An employer will no longer be able to operate a sweatshop; certain retailers will no longer be able to ruin their competitors by price cutting; industries will no longer be able to exploit their individual markets without relation to the future. But there is plenty of scope left for initiative; there is still freedom for inventiveness; and there will be plenty of reward for business men who exhibit these virtues. The danger is, perhaps, that there will still be too much freedom and that rewards will be allowed which are out of proportion to service.

The time is here which will furnish the test of administration. It is one thing to write laws; it is quite another to administer them—and especially laws of this sort, which pass on to the executive officials most of the really crucial decisions. It will be necessary to have an informed and alert public opinion following these decisions from day to day. The support which rallied to the President as the legislative program was being perfected will be even more needed as his helpers proceed to put that program into effect. If any of us who are officials fail to guard the public interest we ought to be checked immediately and forcibly.

It will not be easy for us to require the coöperation of reluctant businesses in any case; they have been used too long to going their own way without regard to any general program. Consistent pressure and wise guidance will be necessary at every step. They will have the smartest lawyers and accountants available—ones whose salaries are ten, perhaps fifty, times those which can be paid to government servants. They have shown a preliminary willingness to go along, having fallen into so serious a state of late, but they have never disguised their hope of using the new legislation for their own selfish purposes. They can be got not to persist in this, and they can be brought to see that their own interests will best be served by merging them with others; but these results will follow only from the wisest and firmest guidance at Washington.

VIII

PRICES AND DOLLARS

NOTHING could be more severely logical than the development of the President's monetary policy. He stated quite clearly in his note to the London Conference that his intention was to see to it that the dollar should have substantially equal purchasing power from one generation to another. His recent action in preparing to buy and sell gold was the first implementing step necessary to this intention.

To be on gold means having a standard of weight rather than of value; the dollar has been defined as a certain weight of that metal. The difficulty with this standard is that gold is a commodity and that its value fluctuates, and that rather rapidly since there is so little of it and since, in troublous times, there is considerable competition among countries and among hoarders to get what little there is.

The real reason gold has been used as a standard up to now is not that it is a good medium of exchange—the world's commerce outgrew gold long ago—but rather that it furnishes what economists call a "store of value." It is a convenient retreat for the monied. Their holdings can be converted into gold and held. They are thus made immune to social changes which might otherwise affect them. Those who are owed by others are always conservative on this question; but those who owe—the debtors—as well as those who desire a better medium of exchange and a more equitable store of value, have long felt that a commodity so scarce and so liable to fluctuation ought to give way to some other monetary medium.

There have been many suggestions for an alternative.

"Managed currency" and "commodity dollar" have become the phrases most used by those who wanted change. It is not yet clear whether the President will adopt other commodities as a basis for the dollar; but he has given notice that he intends to manage the currency in the interest of an overwhelming majority of the people.

The present step recognizes that gold is still the orthodox international medium and that managing the dollar in relation to foreign currencies requires that our gold supply shall be under the control of our Government. With this weapon at command our dollar can be made to serve our own domestic purposes and can be put beyond the reach of foreign manipulation.

Present policy requires that the commodity price level shall be raised; this is equivalent to saying that there shall be a fall in the value of the dollar in relation to other commodities. But this policy can be carried out only if it is impossible for foreigners to buy and sell gold at will, thus determining the price and with it the value of dollars.

The bankers, most of them, the creditors, the monied group in general, will not like this policy and will resist it. It favors debtors, people of low income, the farmers. These last will favor and support it. And doubtless they will want the President soon to go on to the next logical step—the creation of a commodity dollar which will separate the monetary medium altogether from its present basis on a certain weight of gold. They will not, for instance, favor devaluation, for this would reinstate gold as a medium, only reducing the amount of it in the dollar. They will want it recognized that gold is only another commodity like wheat, silver, or iron. And they will press for a dollar based perhaps on an index number which expresses the relationship of all commodities to one another.

Such an index, it will be argued, is quite feasible with our present statistical resources. With its use the dollar can be kept constant in general purchasing power, because not gold alone is exchangeable for other goods but each commodity is exchangeable for every other. This would furnish a stable price level and would also give us a dollar which would represent a store of value constant "from generation to generation." This point of view will be vigorously opposed by those who are roughly described as advocates of "sound money."

Even a stable price level is not enough, of course, if we are looking for an ideal instrument for exchange purposes as well as something which will keep purchasing power constant. In fact we had a stable price level, or one which was substantially so, from 1923 to 1929. And at the end of that period we had a debacle. The difficulty was—and it might happen again—that many savings were made in costs of operation so that profits grew at the expense of consumers' incomes. Purchasing power suffered a steady attrition throughout the period. Surpluses went to build new factories, to make unrepayable foreign loans, to proliferate middlemen's services, to finance speculation. Workers' and farmers' incomes should have been enlarged as efficiency and capacity grew. Only in this way could a permanent system of exchange have been built up.

To avoid a recurrence of this situation recognition will have to be given, in considering monetary policy, to the increasing efficiency of production. There are two ways to do it. One would be by a progressive raising of farmers' and workers' incomes. The other would be by a progressive lowering of the price level as efficiency increased.

Theoretically, a commodity dollar could be used to accomplish this purpose. Practically, there are great difficulties, the most important of which is that it would make always

more difficult the repayment of debts because they would
have to be discharged in dollars which were more valuable—
and thus harder to get—than those which had been borrowed.
Still there may be ways around this difficulty, such as the
periodic scaling down of debts. And the supreme importance
of constant purchasing power to a mass-production economic
system is more and more clearly recognized as time goes on;
eventually ways must be found—whether or not they are monetary—to insure it.

IX

THE PROSPECT FOR THE FUTURE *

LAST year was long, long ago. Each day's news brings a rush of developments which only a few months back would have seemed incredible. Forces of change long pent, deflected or ignored, are now released to be governed as best we may. We are reaping the whirlwind we inherited and trying to make it turn the mills of a capitalistic society, hastily re-ordered.

Thus far we have managed to live within the existing structure while alterations are in process; and it seems more likely now than it did a year ago that we shall be able to go on that way. If we can keep our heads; if we can work out of our system little by little the venom of unrestrained competitive greed; if, before it is too late, we can come to see that class advantages are illusory and in the end destructive— then we can continue making revolutionary changes without violence. But these are tremendous ifs. Abruptly we have become a nation bereft of comfortable certainties; and—perhaps by the same token—a nation come to life.

Threatened from within by a multitude of maladjustments, forced at the same time to consider a gathering of thunderheads on world horizons, our national life today is a life of conscious risks. Only an astrologer or an instinctive charlatan would venture with certainty to predict the outcome. In choosing, then, to speak to you of new destinations, I mean only to indicate possibilities, and not to prophesy. I do not say, "This is what we shall be or do"; but merely,

* Address delivered at the Chicago Forum, October 29, 1933.

"This, from our present start, is what we *may* be and do, if we have courage, patience and sense enough."

I think that we have new reasons for hope. And hope is manlier than the spiritual paralysis which has afflicted us ever since we took up arms and crossed the sea. Our national catchwords since that time have reflected a callow disillusionment unworthy of adults. In the A.E.F., when any statement of fact or principle was made to the troops, *"You* tell 'em, while I mark time," said the boys. Now that, in view of everything, expressed at the time a perhaps not unsuitable skepticism, and a sane attempt at detachment from murderous events. But the feeling that there is somehow merit in a flat, wholly unreflective disbelief in everything, carried over to dim the ecstasies of our postwar commercial boom. To any warm, impassioned statement of thought and purpose, "What of it?" we said. Later, when men dared dream and speak of alternatives to what we were becoming, the note of derision became sharper: "So what?" And with lean days upon us, doubt became a snarl, voiced in the stricken, childish cynicism of, "Oh, yeah?"

Perhaps you will agree that nothing on earth can seem more impervious to reason than the weary cynicism of immaturity. If your experience is like mine, you will have been confronted in these years just past, with the glazed and chilly eyes of children determined to be hard-boiled. That look was not born of itself; we older people put it there. The eyes of our young reflect the state of this world we brought them into, as they have seen it in their time.

Consider the America known to the Americans now enrolled in our secondary schools and colleges. Drums were beating when they were born. Their earliest perceptions were formed in the years between 1914 and 1919, in a world given over to slaughter and waste, with all that in time of peace is wrong acclaimed as right and glorious. And their next ten years, from 1919 to 1929, were marked by almost as mad a confusion of values. It was a time of easy money, conspicuous consumption, defiant and stealthy excesses, un-exampled greed. A decade of empty progress, devoid of con-tribution to a genuinely better future—except, of course, in a technical sense. And our technique served only to leave us at the end a nation with too much of everything; nothing important to do; nothing of worth to believe in; on the make.

Sometimes I wonder if we do not blame too much on the War. We have had other wars, and periods of exploitation afterward; enormous spurts of free enterprise, privilege, and economic manslaughter, in time of peace. The difficulty this time was not so much the War itself, as the conditions under which we carried it on. The country was about filled up; its natural loot was spoken for. Its more obvious resources were beginning to be pretty well picked over, even before 1917. Without conscious dream of empire, but with a pioneer lust for continued internal expansion, we were headed for an awakening, anyway. Sooner or later a people, in a new coun-try, like any one of us, must bow to limits, stop grabbing and grow up. Our exciting and terrible adventure beyond the water; the false spell of prosperity and forced expansion that we managed to pump up afterwards, in the face of world cloture of markets against our goods, enormous structures of old debt and the subsequent catastrophe, may all have served as hastening shocks in bringing us to the end of a prodigal national childhood. "We have swarmed over this continent like demanding, thoughtless children," said M. L. Wilson in a recent address on public policy. Now we must settle down, put our lands in order, rid our hearts and minds of the bar-baric notion that unlimited economic conflict leads somehow to universal balance and plenty, and learn to live together as a civilized people should.

I think that in no other land was a deification of individual initiative and freebooter enterprise ever carried to such a pitch as it was with us during all the opening years of the present century until March 4, last. By the opening of the century it had become apparent that competition and democracy were separable; that, in fact, the separation had to be carried out if democracy were to survive. For years we refused to recognize that. As fast as coöperative combinations appeared, we cried them down as trusts, passed laws against them, called for the Big Stick to put them out of business. But the thing could not be stopped. The result of our mandate was simply to stem, and drive into subterranean channels, what might have been open combinations of industry, openly regulated for a common welfare. Our prohibitory maneuvers against the coöperative instinct of man bore results strangely similar to that of our efforts to prohibit the taking of a social glass together. It brought on a speakeasy age of industrial combinations, an era of legal and illegal evasions. We forced business to be lawless, or when not actually lawless, hypocritical. We compelled confusion. Instead of business combinations regulated for the common benefit, we encouraged a concentration of vast corporate powers, interlocking, and operation entirely for private benefit, in the dark.

This made possible vast concentrations of wealth in one place, with areas of dire want elsewhere. It made necessary a touching faith that if the big men of the country only be permitted to pile their holdings high enough, they will shower down smaller blessings upon the little fellows and make us all very happy. As we know now, when the sky of business turns gray, that is just the time when the big fellows cease to shower down. Let there but appear a cloud the size of a man's hand, and they tighten their purse strings, and brood in splendid isolation, figuring wage cuts, dickering with price schedules, sustaining dividends, and practicing saying "No." They are inaccessible and, within wide limits, accountable to no one. They were not born that way. With our strange and twisted insistence upon the holiness of free enterprise, and the sin of large-scale coöperative operations, we made them so.

Our present effort is to bring business combinations into the open, sanction them fully, coördinate and control them for the public good. We are trying to show that the competitive system which requires heaped-up corporate surpluses and an overconcentration of wealth is not the life of trade, but the death of trade. Incomes must be transformed into larger wages and higher prices to farmers, not simply stacked up in sterile hoards of capital if wealth in any large and gratifying sense is to breed again.

You will say that these things have not been done; you may say that the start which has been made is scarcely perceptible. That is true. But the process of reconstruction in the midst of a more exigent effort for recovery on any basis is not easy. The rules of the game have not yet been greatly revised; businesses have not become so enlightened overnight that they are willing to sacrifice much for a better future. We are just now in the midst of another crisis caused by failure to appreciate the need for instantaneous and generous coöperation. I refer to the advantage taken of the possibilities of increasing individual prices at the general expense. The advance of prices at a more rapid rate than the expansion of purchasing power—which it was hoped might be prevented—has again threatened to kill the goose from which, like children, we expect a magic flow of golden eggs. Many of us still appear to

believe that we live in a kind of economic fairyland where
cake can be eaten and also kept; either that, or the impulse to sacrifice the certain general good for a doubtful
particular advantage has once more overcome our better
judgment.

The present crisis throws new light on some old theories.
They might have been thought to have been exposed before;
but we are incorrigibly resistant to painful truths. Perhaps
the most popular of all the presently prevalent theories of
recovery among the business men of my acquaintance was
succinctly stated the other day by Sir Josiah Stamp. "Make
sure of a profit," he said, "and we can go along." This theory
runs as follows: to set things going again we must insure
businesses a profit. Only with this assurance will they begin to
borrow, to expand their operations, and to give employment.
What is holding us back, it is said, is uncertainty—uncertainty that goods made can be sold at a gain, uncertainty that
these gains can be invested in further enterprises, which will
make further profits, ultimately, I suppose, to be salted down
in bonds redeemable in gold.

The theory, it will be seen, demands the familiar program
of deflation—reduced governmental budgets so that taxes may
be low, abandonment of the program of higher wages and
farm incomes, a declaration of intention to preserve a sound
dollar at all costs—and so on—all, of course, the familiar ingredients of orthodox government pronouncements before
last March.

The election was a mandate of repudiation, it might be
supposed. If it repudiated anything it must have been the
administration which lived by these attitudes. It seems to
me demonstrable that this was a thoroughly sensible mass
revulsion. And those people who would have us crawl back
to the old ideas, like a wounded animal to an abandoned den,

misread the temper of the people as well as the intelligence of the present government.

If, I should like to ask, we guarantee profits, in the terms of their interpretation, to all businesses, who is to buy the goods on which the profits are made? It is elementary that purchasing power must equal retail prices if activity is to be maintained. This is not consistent with the kind of profits contemplated under the theory I have mentioned, and the kind to which many businesses are attempting to help themselves under the sheltering wings of our Blue Eagle. For when prospective buyers are lacking, this fact also is obvious to those who distribute credit. They will refuse to lend because then also their loans may not be repaid. The wherewithal for expansion cannot be had until we have definitely and with honest commitment gone over to the low-price, large-volume program. That was contemplated under N.R.A. Nothing but higher wages and farm incomes, together with moderated retail prices, can redress the maladjustments which continue to exist in the structure of our prices. Profits will have to follow from new efficiencies. To put them first is to put the cart before the horse. In fact the best guarantee of profits is capacity operation at low costs and prices; this involves the preservation of purchasing power, the conservation of markets. It may mean smaller earnings at once, but it ought to insure their steady continuance.

A change in monetary ideas has its place in the new economy we are trying to create, but it cannot take the place of honest readjustment through the management of prices. And as to "sound" money, this is quite evidently a phrase which means different things to different people. The soundest dollar, I should say, is the one of which President Roosevelt said it would have a substantial equality of purchasing power and debt-paying power from one generation to another. This is not what is meant by those who are coming forward as critics of the present program. They mean gold. And with it they mean a Shylock's collection from debtors, which can be stored away and made safe from the vicissitudes of less cautious or less lucky people. It seems to me a mistake to provide islands of safety in a changing world to which some of us may retreat clutching certain sterile goods. And especially that this retreat should be particularly designed for the protection of the gains which are got from the sabotage of recovery.

I need not point out to you the significance, in any survey of the prospect for the future, of the possibility that purchasing power may be protected. This involves a whole category of blessings we have hitherto been resigned to doing without. It means relief—at least partial—from the specter of depression and unemployment. It means the possibility that we may at last turn our backs on those philosophies of despair which have emasculated many of our best efforts. I refer to the theory, which is so prevalent, that there is only a limited amount of work left to be done in the world and that much of the energy of each of us must be given to withholding both efforts and goods so that our competitive situation may be protected.

Meaning these things, it also means ultimately the release of vast technical and human energies from which economists and engineers have always ultimately expected the physical transformation of our society. That we should sit slothful and supine, facing unmoved the challenge to human intelligence presented by a world sunk in misery and degradation, has seemed to them an intolerable confession of ineptitude and weakness. The source of our paralysis has been known for long enough, but its defenses have seemed invulnerable. They are being challenged now at the very heart of their strength. We may at last hope for that freedom which will furnish scope for the work we all of us are longing to do, motivated by a call to service, and rewarded by a sense of contribution to the public good rather than by the hope of speculators' winnings.

There are unexplored springs within the human heart which have been choked by the sand of distorted appeals. The old competitive commercial system asked of us only that we make life profitable for ourselves. We might do it by altogether antisocial actions, by checkmating one another, by withholding and by creating scarcity values for the goods and services we controlled. These are not the appeals which speak to the deepest responses of men and women. And they have called out characteristic grudging responses. If we can create this single change, so that motives can function on the higher level of service to the common good, we shall be astonished at the response we shall get. Those of us who work to create such institutions will not have to change the world or even to create the designs for it. Indeed we are unfitted to do so by our training and our affiliations. But those who succeed us will do it after their own fashion and we shall at least be credited with having taken the first step toward the release of thoroughly human possibilities. We have no need to change human nature. We need only to give it a chance.

I speak of the necessary reversal of attitude not as one inclined to blame, for the stricken and empty years of our postwar decade, our men of wealth alone. Their dreams and thoughts were pretty much our own. We were all more or less in the same boat, or, at least the same kind of a boat, spiritually and mentally in those years. The main difference was that they had the bigger boat and the right of way down the best channel. During the Morgan hearings in Washington, an acquaintance of mine, whose tendencies are occasionally radical, remarked that he hoped the day would come when people would not brag of knowing billionaires, but tactfully avoid reference to it. I answered that the actual model, a billionaire, in the flesh, would seem to me, though I had never had the honor, rather more worth knowing than most of that mass of petty billionaires of the spirit that one met everywhere, in banks, behind the ledgers of plantation stores, at clubs, in church, and on Pullman smokers, during the final decade of our national adolescence. It was a period of arrested spiritual and mental development. Everybody was out to be rich and what was called successful at the expense of everybody else. That cannot be done. We all know how it ended.

In far more ways than show in the tabled indices of business, I think it may be said now that the tide has turned. The nation has come of age and turned from a confused and wishful appeal to the past to confront the future. It would be hard to say whether we have ruled events thus far as much as we have been ruled by them, but at least we have lifted our heads and taken hold.

I am not here to anoint my chief with biased praise. The occasion is unsuitable, but this much, quite apart from partisan considerations, may be said: He has restored belief in government, renewed faith and courage, and established a new mood. In an almost perfect state of chaos, with the national ship foundering, we saw that one man at least had courage. The wave of gratitude for this much of new faith was reinforced a hundredfold by the discovery also that he knew what to do. He summoned Congress and asked permission to act. It was his purpose that the Government should assume responsibility for recovery. It was his conception that the leadership which had failed and was now discredited should be shown a way to regain a balanced prosperity and to maintain it. In a series of classic messages to Congress and the people, his program was submitted piece by piece.

The administration has barely started on that program. From March to November is a very short while. But already we are far enough along with it to glimpse possibilities undreamed of a year ago. Certain of the steps already taken may be thought of as commitments, if the present line is followed, to further steps and far destinations. This is particularly true of our basic program with respect to the use of the land.

Faced with the fact that we have been planting some 40,-000,000 or 50,000,000 acres of land in staple crops to be sold in foreign markets now largely closed to us, we have moved to take those 40,000,000 or 50,000,000 acres out of cultivation and put them to other use. Nine-tenths of our cotton planters coöperated this year to take out 10,500,000 acres of cotton, more than a quarter of the entire American acreage in that crop. Next year, they will reduce the national planting of cotton from 40,000,000 to 25,000,000 acres. Our wheat growers, operating in accord with a world wheat agreement, will reduce the national sowing some 9,000,000 or 10,000,000 acres this fall and next spring. Moving in the same manner, coöperatively, through county production control associations, our corn and hog growers will remove in advance from next year's market, by not seeding it, between 12,000,000 and 15,000,000 acres of corn, and will make a corresponding reduction in pork production.

In all, we have already moved to take out of export crops, which, dammed up behind tariff barriers, have been choking our markets and killing trade, an area in excess of the entire cultivated area of Japan proper. These are all key crops. To alter the proportionate seeding of any one of them over the 1,906,000,000 acres of the continental United States as a whole is to alter the basic pattern not only of our agriculture but perhaps of our national life.

To begin with, we have made acreage cuts pro rata, on the basis of existing plantings, but anyone who has ever considered the question knows that we must push on from that to more selective and more permanent adjustments. Many of our farmers are working land which ought not to be farmed, but rather planted to trees, or grass, or diverted to recreational or residential purposes. And a large part of our non-agricultural population is living in the places manifestly unsuited for the best life and the best work.

The President has announced a new land policy which I believe in time may be looked back upon as of equal importance with the Homestead Act. He has said that as fast as good new lands are brought into cultivation by drainage and irrigation, a correspondingly productive area of inferior land will be taken out of cultivation, and kept out. The attempt will not be to match acre for acre. An acre, or area of rich new land brought in, may mean three or more acres—or areas —of poor soil retired to more suitable uses.

The land is our basic wealth. We have misused it shamefully. To hold what we have, we shall launch at once numerous soil-erosion projects to protect from further ruin about a million acres which are washing or blowing away. As time goes on, we shall probably take whole ridges and blasted semi-arid areas out of farms, and try to induce the people there to move to places where they may make a better living. And we shall certainly discover in the mountains, and by sea and lake shore, areas unfit for extensive farming, but delightful places for people, sustained by decentralized industries, to live and to cultivate gardens.

All this suggests a gradual resettlement of America, and a changed appearance of great stretches of our country now bare and overfarmed. I believe that we shall plant in our middle and more western areas far more trees, perhaps wide belts of them to turn the wind and temper the climate, and many a sheltering grove around farmsteads and workers' garden homes. The country will be better looking. Farms in the valley, larger farms, probably, than we have now, more closely tilled, and more easily, with greater machines. But we shall have as a whole, I think, less land, rather than more, broken and cultivated. We have so much land that we are beginning to see the need of working only the best of it hard; keeping the rest of it in trees or grass; and returning on a wide scale, and modern methods, to more pastoral methods of culture. It takes three or four times as much land to feed a cow on grass as it does to grow grain and feed the cow with high-pressure feed mixtures. A cow on grass, with supplemental rations, will not give as much milk as a cow pressed on into high production by grain feeding; but we have too much milk as it is, and too much land; and milk produced on a grassland economy over wider areas is much more cheaply produced. Much the same thing is true of meat production. I believe that considerable areas of rolling country, now broken to the plow, will tend rather rapidly toward sward culture; and become in appearance more and more like the beautiful "Green Counties" in southwest England.

With improved transportation one may note already a tendency for farmers to bring their houses together, and to go out from town or village, as reversed commuters, to their work. In flat country, this seems especially the trend. Already, in places, we see the basic pattern of a new design for country living: the houses gathered with large lawns and pleasant shade around a modern communal center, the school. But the same mobility which makes it possible for the people of the dusty plains of Kansas, for example, to cluster, makes it just as possible for people to get out of the over-crowded cities and suburbs of our thronged industrial re-gions, seeking space and solitude in small homes, supported often quite apart from farming, by the sea, or lake shores, or in the hills.

Various new designs take form from the pressure of the things men most long for there, and lack. I do not think that we should be so arbitrary in our blue-print plans for a new design as to try to fit the resettlement of America into one pattern. But we can plan, in each region of resettlement, to make the country more beautiful.

It is not merely a fond pastoral hope to say that we are marching, without changing base, toward a land of greener fields and bluer streams. For reasons wholly practical, which I have named, our present trend in acreage adjustments is from cultivated crops to meadows, lawns and pastures; and the steps we are taking to prevent erosion will tend to clear our running waters.

As we bring better order into our use of land, it will be not only crops that will move. People will move out from the cities. It may even be that the partially empty office sky-scrapers and tenements of New York and Chicago will never fill up again. There is no longer need of our living jammed together. We can look toward an interweaving of the rural and urban. The development of electric power and with it the new arts of road-making and motor-building, make it possible in increasing measure to move industrial workers into the country, and their work with them. Here they may live apart from the fearful stress and the pinch of all those costs which congestion multiplies. Our system of distribution can then move in shorter circuits, with less waste. Quite as important, in another way, is a renewal in modern terms of an old American dream: that citizens should be given access to this soil, and allowed, in their various ways, to live in homes of their own, in peace and security. These are the aims, at least, which make profoundly stirring our crop-adjustment program, our experiments in decentralization—a land in order, wisely used, with the hills green and the streams blue.

The natural concomitant of a reordered countryside is a city life which also has been reordered. We can hope, for instance, that the cities' present severe case of elephantiasis may be cured by some decentralization. Outright manufacturing can be deleted from their functions without injuring them as market and control centers. And this ought to be done by various persuasions. In fact the loft and the sweatshops ought to be transformed and moved bodily to become the nucleus, along with the schools, of our projected farming villages.

Heavy industry has not now usually an urban location. It frequently requires, however, a regional concentration because of the interrelations of such materials as coal, iron and other minerals in manufacture. But the land is wide enough for that without the intolerable crowding we permit at present. A factory, even a great one, is not necessarily a devastatingly ugly thing—as numerous examples even now go to show. And homes do not have to be huddled into their shadow. Sun and air are listed in the textbooks as free goods; we have made them more inaccessible than gold for most men and women, a fault we ought to be at work to repair.

The new organization of industry under N.R.A. makes this vision of a better future more possible. Competitive pressure can now be removed from access to the good things of life. Standards can be set at levels limited only by our power to produce them. For the first time we are honestly and generously searching out the forms and charters of industry which will reduce it to civilized criteria. This may seem visionary to one who sees only the rather confused and troubled processes now taking place in Washington. But out of that effort of learning by doing, something of what I have sketched for you can quite possibly take shape. It will come more quickly if the mirror of the future is held up occasionally for a steady look.

Some rigorous changes in financial methods must make these improvements possible. The new, the unexpected, cannot be welcomed and given place so long as the debt-load of past improvements has not been written off and the way cleared. Our habit of carrying every incurred cost forever in the rate and price structures which consumers are expected to meet must in some way be reformed.

A magazine correspondent not especially enamored of the New Deal made to various people in our Department, on a recent visit there, a complaint of this sort which seems to me reasonable and stimulating. He said that in our plans for recovery we do not make enough allowances for the unexpected development. More than once in our past some new burst of invention or enterprise has come into the picture and altered the whole design. The steam locomotive and the building of railroads across the country was one such development. The subsequent rapid development of the automotive trades, and the construction of a national network of paved highways, was another. We have been looking to the sky for signs of a new era of transportation, and a nation again made over. But the time for that, it seems, is not yet. Examining other possibilities, I wonder if our next great spurt of common endeavor will not be to see America rehoused.

In part, I suppose, this will accompany resettlement, and in part be a matter of rebuilding where we are. I recall Gilbert K. Chesterton's remark at the end of his first visit to

America. Noting with wonder our wooden and archaic shelters, spread at random, he described us as a nation camping out. In large measure, we still are. In country and city alike, it seems to me, air-conditioning, which we are now beginning to demand in communal places and conveyances, will be individually demanded, as time goes on. But that is only one, and possibly a minor factor, in our general need of rehousing, planned for dignity and permanence. Farmsteads, villages and slums; offices, churches, factories and schools, need widespread overhauling and replacement. It is possible that even before we conquer the airways we shall get around to making ourselves better houses.

I have spoken of the case of arrested development that afflicted our national spirit during the dying years of the Old Deal. In concrete progress, too, it seems to me, we have suffered a curious lapse of daring and enterprise. Perhaps we were too well satisfied with things as they were. The railroads, for instance, have seemed until recently to provide an almost perfect example of arrested development. This summer I traveled some ten thousand miles by rail. Thinking back to the first train ride of my extreme youth, I found it strange to reflect that for three decades or longer our trains and schedules have remained substantially unchanged. Out West, not once but constantly, I saw $600 cars slipping at sixty miles an hour by lumbering limiteds making thirty-five miles an hour.

But now there are notable changes pending. It is as if, in railroading, sources of ingenuity and inventiveness, long and mysteriously damned, had been reopened. Trains gratifyingly unlike the cindery, rumbling, and stiffly cushioned vehicles we have known all our lives, are projected. Schedules will be speeded, with ease and safety. The comfort of the passenger is at last being taken into account. I am told that on one of our greatest railways, light, torpedo-shaped trains of modern design will be put into service within the next few years. These trains will have an ordinary speed of about two miles a minute. They will have pneumatic tires and move with a smoothness said to exceed that of any other means of locomotion yet developed on earth, or in the air. The contemplated schedules will beat the present flying time of planes on the shorter hauls, especially if one counts the time now spent in getting in and out from airports. I speak of this neither to deride the railroads for belated improvements nor to praise them for waking up; but merely to indicate possibility that in many other fields of effort we may, after long lapses, be on the point of new and unimagined strides. Enlivened means of transport will help to make of this nation a single neighborhood. With our good roads and cars, we may seem to have come a long way in that direction; but I believe that we are only at the beginning of ease and speed in travel.

A consciousness of great events is stirring the nation. We feel ourselves caught up in the sweep of momentous changes. We would be dolts indeed if we remained intellectually unmoved and spiritually inert. No longer barren of hope, irrevocably committed no longer to fruitless designs and conflicts, there is perhaps some danger that we may form excessive expectations of the morrow, demanding a changed new world to accord with yesterday's change of heart. That never happens. It will be a long trek. We shall have to be contented with a little progress at a time, to count the way by steps and not by leagues. Reforms technical, financial, administrative, are taking place everywhere; but it has to be done rather stolidly, slowly, carefully.

But here what I have said about changes in methods of capital allocation and more rapid writing off of capital commitments is in point. I believe it accurate to say that no railway bond was ever retired—at least few of them ever have been. Yet we have come to a time of impending change in that industry which will make its old capital obsolete. Shall we have to go on paying for it? And this is an example which is just as true of other industries. Everywhere old charges prevent the entrance of new techniques.

Release from the false gospel which regards dull toil as an ennobling and necessary burden; debt a necessary prelude to owning things; advance to the concept of wages dissociated from production; and a social sharing of abundance, fully; general, not competitive standards of consumption; all such shining destinations are far beyond present attainment. But we are headed that way.

Let us meanwhile take faith and comfort in smaller sanities and advances already established: the spectacle of a free people drinking beer or wine in the open, not gin in toilet rooms; an increasing number of factories swept with light, with no children working there. In our open country, fewer foreclosures, and the strong growth of a feeling that men must farm together hereafter, not against one another if they are to get along. In our cities, a beginning at least toward higher pay and greater leisure. In many places we have changed directions and made a start.

I have waited until the last to speak of schools, and the educational implications of our new mood and purposes. My theme, restated, is that we have passed as Americans from years of infantile and greedy yearnings to something larger, that we are a people come to life. The schools and colleges must be brought to life also, to the common life, and the common problems of our workaday world. I speak in dispraise of dusty learning, and in disparagement of the historical technique. At a great university with which I was lately connected, it once became my task to survey the courses we were offering, and it was depressing to note how many teachers sought to validate their facts and assertions by solemn statements that such and such happened very long ago. Often there was no apparent connection between the historical precedents presented, and the current teaching; the precedents were simply dragged in for the sake of safety and respectability. The facts adduced meant nothing. But they were facts; no question about that; if you doubt it you could look in hundreds of other books, and there it all could be verified.

The past is nailed down. Nobody can deny it. There it is, and if you add plenty of footnotes, you, in turn, may become an authority. It is necessary now to break with the past. Education in the active mood, present tense, and the future conditional, must be invented if the training of youth is to be tuned to the more resilient, experimental attitude now prevailing generally, if students are to be allowed to form new opinions without salaaming to discredited precedents. The right kind of teaching today must show people how to use real things and how leisure may become creative. I am not speaking for propaganda, but for intellectual free play, and intellectual gallantry. I form that phrase from the remark of a wry old bystander and critic of the national scene, with whom I recently talked in Washington. "I'm a Tory," he said. "I don't believe in these new ideas. But never in my life have I seen a more gallant performance!"

Are our plans wrong? Who knows? Can we tell from reading history? Hardly. The only way is to try and see, to test out opinion in the press of actual events. Was the opinion wrong? Then alter it. Try another approach. We have been too long inert. And always we must remember Dewey's dictim, "We learn by doing." It will save us much discouragement and it will keep our energies alive.

As a group whose chief interest is adult education, I suggest that you consider the magnificent experiment set going very largely by persons without pedagogical experience, I mean the Civilian Conservation Camps. They have been successful, because their teaching, born of need, goes directly toward fitting the individual for significant and necessary work. Those boys are in the national service, yet they are free men doing something for the country. I have never seen more remarkable transformations of spirit and purpose than those which abound in these camps, after only a few months' work.

Much of the same new spirit is observable in Washington. Something has happened when young men in white collars leave good jobs and labor obscurely for the Government at a money sacrifice. Many such are now in Washington, not to have a job, but to do a job. Youth, speaking generally, seems by no means as hopeless as it thought itself this time last year.

Let me reiterate; I do not foretell the future. Prophecy implies certainties and there are no certainties today. The old assurance that snugness and a fat, fixed future for all of us lay just around the corner is now lacking. I, for one, want no such assurance. Just around the corner lies a new country, vast uncertainties, endless problems. Let us take them as they come. I am even against planning too rigidly in advance. Like educators, many national planners desire too ardently, I feel, to anticipate experience in detail. The need is rather for a point of view, resilience, courage, willingness to learn, humility before research.

In detail, the march is multifarious and confusing, but the general direction is clear. It is a march renewed, as a nation, to landmarks which in our earlier pioneer neighborhoods stood always plain. Common neighborliness. Common decency. In a recent talk to his neighbors at Hyde Park, the President made that plain.

Men do not want to be hard on one another and to do one another harm. As the old neighborhoods broke down, men began to exploit each other impersonally, helplessly in the dark. Life lost meanings which we are now regaining. We may yet fill the United States with the world's most pleasant neighborhoods. And if we find their right relationship to one another, giving each an economic, a social and a moral reason for being, that will be a sufficient task for our time, and our generation can pass with some confidence that our children will find our work good.

X
LATER MORAL EQUIVALENTS

THERE is widespread, among many people, the fear that some nation in the world may, at any moment, furnish the occasion for war. There seems to be nothing definite to which this fear may be pinned, no situation in which compromise is impossible. There is no doubt, of course, that at the end of these long years of depression there is disillusionment and discontent. It may be true also that gradual relief from distress will bring disorder. Rising levels of living gradually free people from utter despondency, revive their vision of better things, arouse new hope and courage. When they gain a renewed sense of personal worth and integrity, of being some use in the world instead of merely dependent in it, old grudges begin to be paid off and new sources of expression begin to be explored.

In such situations a call to arms is difficult to resist. The seductive music of military drums can loose forces which cannot be touched by any appeal in the midst of depression. Something like this occurred in Italy in the early days of Fascism; something of the sort always occurs in great revolutionary movements.

The masses move out of a slovenly past, out of submergence in misery toward the prospect of a new discipline and a new outlet for the irrepressible human spirit. The ardor and imagination of the American people make it ridiculous to say that nothing of the sort could happen here. There need only be a cause and a leader with classical notions concerning power and force. We could have men marching in the streets to the same music which has always called them out. It is tampering with dynamite to minimize the possibility of this.

Suppose the present epidemic of strikes should suddenly become focused on some one great industry whose relationships ramified into many others; and suppose the paths to compromise should be closed by vindictive employers; suppose, also, a leader of the proper ruthless sort, with an understanding of the mechanics of power and the uses of force, should undertake the organization. There might be a mass movement here, the end of which would be wholly unpredictable.

It is important, therefore, as we emerge from depression, that we should again explore the possibilities of what William James called the "moral equivalents" of war. This conception implies that the recovery of the human spirit can find an outlet for its renewed energies quite as well in a discipline which may count for construction as in one which may lead us all over the cliffs of destruction.

On going back and reading this essay of James's, which was written in 1910, I find some of the reasons why war could happen a few years later, and why also it might happen again now. The occasion for that war seemed trivial; the occasion for another need be no more momentous, provided we are ready for it. The advocates of peace are no wiser; the military mysticism is just as prevalent; the dead hand of misery has lain even more heavily on the world. There is a sense of black injustice abroad, also, which can add itself to the monotony and the confining of spirit which characterize the long years of unadventurous industrialism.

We never need the moral equivalents more, if war is to be avoided, than we need them in this hour. The gallant spirit smothered, pent up within men's souls, requires to be let loose. We need new causes of action, a marching toward understood goals, shoulder to shoulder with our fellows.

James put it this way:

If now—and this is my idea—there were, instead of military conscription a conscription of the whole youthful population to form for a certain number of years a part of the army enlisted against Nature, the injustice would tend to be evened out, and numerous other goods to the commonwealth would follow. The military ideals of hardihood and discipline would be wrought into the growing fibre of the people; no one would remain blind as the luxurious classes now are blind, to man's relations to the globe he lives on, and to the permanently sour and hard foundations of his higher life. To coal and iron mines, to freight trains, to fishing fleets in December, to dishwashing, clothes-washing, and window-washing, to road-building and tunnel-making, to foundries and stokeholes, and to the frames of skyscrapers, would our gilded youths be drafted off, according to their choice, to get the childishness knocked out of them, and to come back into society with healthier sympathies and soberer ideas. They would have paid their blood-tax, done their own part in the immemorial human warfare against nature; they would tread the earth more proudly, the women would value them more highly, they would be better fathers and teachers of the following generation.

Not all of James's conception can be carried out; not any of it, perhaps, in just his terms. Organized labor prevents the competition of drafted men—still on the fallacious theory that there is a limited amount of work to be done and that, in what is done, they have a vested interest. And James speaks of "gilded youths"; but our concern is not with them in this crisis, but with the more genuinely disaffected, the unemployed workers. Still the thought is sound. It has worked like a leaven throughout these two decades; and it is surprising to total up the phenomena of the New Deal which might answer to his tests.

There is first the C.C.C., in which 300,000 youths are for

the first time learning what it is to do a job which looks beyond their generation into a better future. They are having those experiences of camp life and campaigning which the militarists value so highly and they are under discipline of a sort—and a good sort, I should say, less rigorous than war would impose but more suited to a return to civil pursuits.

But there are a number of other projects in the air which may shortly come to reality. Disease, for instance, can be exterminated; filth can be cleaned up; noxious plants can be eradicated. Already they are at work on the white pine blister rust and the black stem rust of wheat. And they are working in thousands on country roads. Just on the horizon is a campaign against malaria, typhus and spotted fever, all diseases which can be stamped out—one by the same means which made heroes of the Americans who conquered yellow fever in Cuba and Panama, another by the extermination of rats, still another by killing ticks. Less dramatic, perhaps, but useful for the purpose of equivalents, are such things as the war against the gypsy moths, the completion of our survey of the country's physical features, and the demolition of great slum areas.

These could easily be dramatized. These men who, yesterday, were standing in bread lines, or sitting despondent in their precariously-held homes, can, tomorrow, become a part of the armies of peace, setting out on a great adventure in reconstruction. The effort can make the world safer, not for democracy, but for common men. It ought to be looked at this way.

XI
THE ECONOMICS OF THE RECOVERY
PROGRAM *

I N the midst of the cross currents of activity in Washington, it is necessary from time to time to stand apart and recall the general outline of the program which is expressing itself in a day-to-day detailed activity. Only as it is considered as a whole will the apparent paradoxes be reconciled and the total effort be comprehended.

The general objective is clear and easily stated—to restore a workable exchangeability among the separate parts of our economic machine and to set it to functioning again; and beyond this to perfect arrangements which may prevent its future disorganization. This means that we must insure adequate income to the farmers, adequate wages to the workers, an adequate return to useful capital, and an adequate remuneration to management. What we want, really, is to provide the opportunity for every individual and every group to work and to be able to consume the product of others' work. This involves a creation of buying power which is coördinate with the creation of goods. We shall not rest nor be diverted to lesser things until that minimum is achieved.

But to outline an objective in such broad terms does not take us far in understanding specific undertakings. What constitutes a workable relationship among income to farmers, wages to workers, and a return to useful capital? Here is a question which we can answer only when we have considered why they are now inadequate.

* Address delivered at the Institute of Arts and Sciences, Columbia University, November 16, 1933.

That they are less than our productive capacity entitles us to, there can be no doubt. Consider what our economic machine could have produced if it had been working in the last four years at the same rate as in 1928 and 1929. If all the labor and equipment which have been idle during the depression could have been converted into houses, every second family in the country could have had a brand new $5,000 house; or we could have scrapped the whole American railroad system and rebuilt it three times over. Such is the waste of the last four years; the waste caused by the failure of the economic machine to function properly, a failure to produce and distribute, which makes inadequate the income of nearly every group in the community. So long as the economic machine fails to operate at its potential capacity the income of each group will continue to be insufficient. So long as our economy provides vastly less to each group in the community than our resources in men and materials make possible, the incomes of everyone will be inadequate.

Consider the reaction of the country to the first three years of depression. Down and down went the curves of business activity. Longer and longer grew the lines of idle workers and the rows of idle machines. The whole constituted a challenge to the American people to act *as a body,* to remedy a ridiculous situation which had developed out of their *acting separately.*

Why was this challenge to American intelligence and action not met in the first three years of depression? We have grown up in a tradition which says that if economic forces are let alone all will come out right in the end. In the past we have regarded social interference in the interest of economic continuity as highly improper. This supremely crucial function we abandoned to private initiative, operating through the price system and controlled by competition.

Such a system had worked in the past—haltingly and after a fashion. In the first year of the depression there may have been justification for waiting for recovery in the interest of protecting this principle. In the second year, was there justification? In the third year, with more than a quarter of our working population out of work and agricultural income reduced to a third its former size, had not the time come for positive action by the community as a body instead of by individuals alone?

A year ago the people of this country voted on precisely this question. And with an overwhelming majority they chose a President with a mandate for positive action; and he assumed his delegated duty with a gallantry which the whole nation unmistakably approved. The change involved in this was of major importance in the development of this country. It meant a shift from laissez faire to positive effort. It implied an effort by the community through its government to restore exchangeability by positive action. It placed directly on the shoulders of the new administration the responsibility for bringing about recovery from one of the deepest depressions this country has ever known.

The immediate reasons for this popular demand for positive action are clear. The terrific waste of depression, the hardships suffered by individuals through no fault of their own, the failure of business leadership to cope with the forces of depression, these all led to the insistent demand for change, a demand which would respect no allegiance to theory or preconceptions. How this demand was to be carried out, what action was to be undertaken, was not clear; but a policy of laissez faire was no longer to be countenanced.

What positive measures could be undertaken? Preliminary to their understanding is an assessment of the underlying developments which led to this general demand for governmental activity. This takes us directly into economic analysis. Those people who have so extravagantly praised the beauties of laissez faire have always done so on the assumption of highly flexible prices and a degree of freedom in competition. Actually the breakdown came at a time when our economy was a spotted reality of competition and control—with the control entrusted to irresponsible trustees. In 1929 we did not have a system of free competition and flexible prices. True, in some areas, like farming, we have had highly flexible prices and a considerable number of individuals actively competing in both production and price.* If prices throughout our economy had been as flexible as those in the farm area were, it is quite possible that the 1929 depression would have been of minor consequence. The truth was, however, that an important part of our economy had prices which were not responsive—as theoretically they should have been—to changes in supply or demand. At the furthest extreme are railroad and public-utility rates, steel rails and many other goods and services whose prices were fixed over very considerable periods of time. In such occupations and areas, the whole impact of changes in demand are taken in the form of changes in production without any changes in price.

Intermediate between the extremes of flexible price and fixed price, lies most of industry. In this area prices are fixed for shorter periods of time but are periodically revised over longer periods of time. Thus, in varying degrees, changes in

---

* This flexibility in prices received by the farmer, however, has not been permitted to reach the consumer, so to be reflected back to the producer as an accurate, prompt thermometer of demand. Rigid freight rates, rigid interest charges, and relatively rigid wage rates and dividends of the processing and distributing trades have intervened. From 1929 to the first of this year, prices paid to farmers fell 61 percent, but retail prices paid by consumers for food fell only 36 percent. The classic virtues of flexibility become slightly soiled by such facts as these.

demand are met by changes in production, and more slowly and over a longer time only, by changes in price.

This matter of temporary or more permanently fixed prices is vitally important. This fixity is a major disturbing influence in a system which is theoretically competitive. Consider a concrete case—the production of automobiles. The manufacturer of cars will set a wholesale price on his cars at the beginning of the season. Presumably he will set a price which he expects will sell as many cars in the year as will make his total profits at that price as large as possible. Once the price is set, any drop in demand for cars will result, not in a drop in price, but in a drop in production. Men will be discharged and machines will become idle. Because of lessening employment and lessening incomes, there is likely to be a further drop in demand for cars. If this condition were typical of all industry the resulting condition would be one which we describe as depression. It is, of course, true that once or twice a year the prices of cars will be revised. But in the intermediate periods, prices are fixed, and changing demand is reflected only in changing production, with a direct effect on the income of consumers. It is this fact which is of major significance. It is this price inflexibility which causes an initial drop in demand to induce unemployment. In this manner, the rigidity of some prices and the flexibility of others tends to make production in our system unstable, deranging the balance between prices and production in different fields. We have a choice, if the situation is to be remedied, of really restoring competition or of extending the areas of rigidity until they include all prices of real social consequence.

Notice how differently the depression has affected different parts of our economy. In the agricultural area, in which prices are highly flexible, the drop in effective demand during the depression has caused a great drop in prices, while production has declined little. The farmers are working as hard as ever, but they get less for their product. Throughout most of industry, the effect of the depression has been essentially different. Prices have dropped relatively little compared to the drop in agricultural prices. The fall in demand has been met for the most part by reduced production. The income of the workers as a body has dropped as rapidly as that of the farm group, not primarily because wages were lower (though that has been important), but because of being out of employment. Thus, while the cash incomes of farmers as a body and of wage workers as a body have fallen off to an almost equal degree, one has fallen because of a fall in prices and the other because of a fall in production.

This difference in the effect of the depression in agriculture and in industry is of great importance because it suggests that quite different methods for restoring balance must be applied in the different fields. Restoration of balance would require a lowering of production and a lifting of prices in agriculture, but a lifting of production and in some cases even a lowering of prices in industry.

This difference in the effect of the depression on prices and on production is of vital importance. It is the key to many of the apparent conflicts between the agricultural and the industrial programs. Even for different industries the relative effect on prices and on production has been different; some with fatally flexible prices and maintained production, others with rigid prices and flexible production. Perhaps the picture of the depression is best portrayed by thinking of all the different economic activities distributed along a scale according to the amenability of prices to change. As has been suggested, most agricultural activities and certain industries are at one end of the scale and at the other extreme are certain more or less monopolized trades. Between these extremes are ranged the bulk of industry. If we think of the prices and production of different commodities as having been roughly in balance in 1926, the effect of the depression was to reduce prices at the flexible end of the scale and to maintain production there, while at the other end prices were being maintained and production was dropping.

To restore exchangeability in such a situation we can do one of two things: we can lift the flexible prices to the level of the rigid ones, and simultaneously increase production in the fixed-price areas; or we can reduce the rigid prices to the level of the flexible ones, and reduce production in the flexible-price areas.

The advantages of the first path toward the restoration of exchangeability are clear; and it is this path which has been taken by the administration. The major advantage of lifting prices—of lifting most those which have fallen most and lifting not at all those which have not fallen—grows out of the burden of debt created at the old price level. To lower all prices to the level of those which had fallen most would be to overburden the debtors in the country and to endanger the solvency of our many great debtor institutions. Elementary justice thus required a lifting of the flexible prices to parity with the prices which had not dropped, rather than the more difficult course of revising downward those which had remained fixed.

Here, then, is the more immediate objective of recovery: to raise prices in the area of flexibility, to raise production in the area of rigidity, and raise both prices and production in the intermediate areas of industry until all groups attain the ready exchangeability which they once had. How is this immediate objective to be reached? From here on we must take up each element of the recovery program separately, remembering that each element is essential and that each depends for its success on the development of the other parts of the program.

The agricultural program may be considered first. Here the immediate problem is to increase the farmers' incomes by asking the industrial population to pay a fair exchange price for food. The exposition of the way in which the industrial population is to be enabled not only to pay more for food but also to consume more of its own products is deferred here. For the present, notice that the intention is to perfect a synchronized program which will increase the farmers' incomes by approximately the amount which the industrial populations' purchasing power is reduced. I say "approximately" because it is hoped that some of the farmers' increased incomes will come from a reduction in spreads and margins. Such a shift in power to buy might seem to involve no net advance toward recovery; yet two benefits should be noticed. First, no recovery can occur until the farmers are able to buy industrial products on an ample scale; therefore, the raising of farm income even at the immediate expense of the urban population would be a definite step forward if it secured for farmers a more adequate income. Second, there would be a direct expansion of purchasing. Since the increased purchasing of the farm population would be exactly counterbalanced in the initial stage by decreased power to purchase on the part of the industrial population, a net gain in total purchases would arise only as the increased prices for farm products induced a more rapid expenditure of the forty billions of dollars involved.

It is believed that a greater expenditure would be induced by giving farmers more income than by saving it for consumers. If this is true a definite increase in business, in total expenditure, and in total income, would result. So the farm program, by raising prices, on the one hand restores price balance, and on the other hand induces increased total expenditure.

The methods being employed in raising farm prices are foretold. It is well recognized by economists that in the area in which prices are highly flexible, as in agriculture, it is possible to raise prices only by reducing supply or by increasing demand. The total recovery program involves both, though the A.A.A. program, taken alone, involves mostly a reduction in production. The need for this reduction is greater because of long accumulated surpluses traceable to the shift of this country from debtor to creditor status during the War. This shift involved such a reduction in our agricultural exports as to unsettle all the relationships which had been established during our long history as an exporter of raw products. Nor can we count on any immediate change. Combined with a positive program for reducing farm production, and as an aid in bringing about reduction, the processing tax has been employed as a means for raising the price paid by the consumer so that it constitutes more nearly an adequate remuneration for the farmer. The proceeds of the processing tax have been distributed in a manner to insure the reduction of crop acreage. So supply is limited to demand.

The third part of the program involves an effort to increase farm exports, a difficult program and a program on which little reliance can be placed for dealing with the existing crop surplus. However, no opportunity is being overlooked, such as furtherance of world commodity controls. Not much can be done of a permanent nature, however, unless we are willing to admit on far easier terms than are at present in force upwards of half a billion dollars in foreign commodities in exchange for our agricultural goods.

Still another element in the recovery program is of a long-run nature; the effort to remove some 40,000,000 acres of land from cultivation, an effort which has beneficial incidental results, such as the arrest of erosion and the conservation of the soil. The relation sought in this way between farm and industrial activity is of a permanent sort and belongs not in the category of emergency action but of long-time planning of land and population.

All this agricultural effort ought to increase farmers' incomes; and if the industrial program is carried on adequately the whole community must benefit. At the same time success in raising prices to the farmer necessarily rests on the corresponding success of the industrial plan. Through the action just described the supply of farm products is being reduced. Complete success, however, demands that we also increase the demand. If the unemployed population can be returned to work they will be in a position to buy more farm products. This is the farmers' interest in the spread of employment and increased wages. The two are inextricably related.

When we come to the industrial sector of the recovery program, the immediate objectives are almost exactly the reverse of those in the agricultural sector. The main problem is, in some industries, to raise volume of production and volume of pay rolls without increasing price; in other industries, to raise volume of production and volume of wages with an increase in price but not an increase at all commensurate with the increase in the price of agricultural products.

At first thought you will ask how the wage bill can be increased by an industry without increasing the prices charged. This is the very crux of the recovery program. It was by reducing production and wages in some industries, without a corresponding drop in prices, that we destroyed exchangeability. To restore it the process must be reversed. In many industries the declining volume of production in the last three years has increased overhead costs per unit of product.

In order to meet this increasing cost, the industrialists have, on the one hand, maintained prices at nearly their former level, and, on the other hand, have reduced wage rates and employment. In this way they shifted the burden of reduction to the workers, brought on unemployment and destroyed purchasing power.

To regain exchangeability, it is necessary that the increased direct costs of operation attributable to paying higher wages should be absorbed by profit takers without any increase in prices. This involves spreading overhead and increasing wages so that the increased volume of production can be purchased by workers, or in part by workers and in part by farmers who receive more from the workers for the commodities they supply.

It must be recognized, of course, that there are many industries which fall between the two extremes of price flexibility and price rigidity. In such industries, the regaining of exchangeability requires that only part of the increased costs due to increased wages be absorbed by the industry through a wider spreading of overhead costs, while the remainder of the increased costs is passed on to the consumer. In still other industries in which prices have fallen very greatly over their earlier level, a return to an economic balance would undoubtedly require that the whole of the increased costs be passed on to the consumer. In such cases, the worker would be directly benefited at the expense of the consumer, a condition properly parallel to that in respect to agricultural products.

Many important industries should have regarded themselves as belonging in the first two classes, in which the whole, or an important part, of the increased labor costs would be absorbed in the expectation of an increased volume of activity. Unfortunately for the rapid progress of the recovery program, most industries have acted as if they belonged in the third class, and have passed the whole of the increased labor costs to the consumer. Indeed, in many cases, it looks as if more than the increased costs had been passed on, at least in the primary areas of production. For this reason, the recovery program may be slowed up; in fact if the raising of prices beyond the increased costs is widely pursued, the recovery program will be seriously impaired.

It will be seen that the most important consideration in all this is that increased payments should be made to workers without a corresponding increase in charges made to the consumer. The reverse of this has taken place during the depression. Less and less money has been paid out in pay rolls, while the prices of industrial products have shown no corresponding decline. The reversal of this process is necessary to recovery.

Because of the importance of this, it would seem that insufficient attention has been given to classifying industries according to the extent to which the increased costs could be properly passed on to the consumer and the extent to which they ought to be absorbed by the industry. To the extent that industry effectively supports the present program, the increased wages paid out will represent new purchasing power, a net gain in the demand for the products of industry and agriculture, and a real step forward toward recovery. To the extent that a lifting of prices out of proportion to increased costs occurs, we will have retarded progress. The balance of gain or loss from the industrial sector is the responsibility now of industry itself. The opportunity has been provided. If there is failure it will be yet another example of the inability of industry to coöperate; and this time there will not even be the excuse of antitrust restrictions. If further and more drastic controls become necessary it will be because industry has demonstrated its inability to conceive and carry out, even under the best auspices, that program of enlightened self-interest from which laissez-faire economists have professed to expect so much.

There are certain considerations which should be held to firmly. Even if all the increased costs from higher wages should be passed on to consumers, so long as no increases in prices beyond this were imposed, there would still be some net gain. The raising of prices would undoubtedly increase total expenditures. It would do this by inducing some of those who now hold part of our forty billion dollars to expend not only their current receipts but part of their savings, thereby increasing the flow of money and causing a net increase in the demand for goods. This would be a step in the right direction, though it might not carry very far or very rapidly. In essence, the industrial effort will have been a failure if the wages paid out by industry do not on the whole increase more rapidly than the prices charged by industry as a whole. In the hurly-burly of code-making, this fact has too often been lost sight of.

So far we have covered the agricultural and industrial programs. A third major factor consists of public and civil works. Through these programs, it is intended that a large volume of new purchasing power shall be created. By these expenditures, workers are given increased power to buy. This power to buy means that the money paid out for these purposes will go directly for the purchase of goods. The public-works program is getting under way. There have been difficult problems of organization. Like any effort of this sort results are slow to appear in the early stages. But a formidable momentum is now apparent. An increasing volume of funds is going out each week and will soon come to significant result. I often think, in this connection, of the slump which preceded the War. It takes about as long to build up a program of peace construction as it does to organize for war. The efforts are similar; and the time required cannot be greatly shortened.

These, then, are the main features of the program. The complete success of each depends upon the success of the others, carried on as parallel drives in the grand strategy. They constitute a reasoned whole which should bear us to success. The failure of any one of these three attacks to attain its objective means the partial failure of the others, and the necessity of beginning anew. There are other things being done which play into and strengthen these major elements: attempts to expand credit; the bolstering up of existing credit so that it will not be a depressing influence or cause hardship while the machine is set in motion; encouragement for the expansion of private construction, a process which will put purchasing power into circulation without adding to the goods which come immediately to market; the protection of consumers so that their choices can be carried out on a basis of reflection instead of in a welter of conflicting and exaggerated claims; the protection of the debtor against the worst consequences of threatened dispossession; relief for the unemployed, which amounts by now to a characteristically American form of unemployment insurance.

The success or failure of these will not jeopardize the whole. The success or failure of the three great branches of the program—reducing production and raising prices to the farmer, increasing production and raising wages to the industrial worker faster than industrial prices are raised, and the putting into circulation of a new flow of buying power—these are the central core of the recovery drive conceived to be undertaken by the community as a whole. It is, I believe, adequate. It is in many ways unorthodox. It runs counter to the accepted notions of the doctrinaire—convinced believers in laissez faire like it no better than communists. It is tentative, but still carefully hammered out of the iron of reality. We believe it to be the instrument of our present salvation; but we believe in no part of it so fanatically that we are unwilling to change. And this, of course, is the reason for proceeding through permissive powers with a calculated avoidance of any commitment whatever to doctrine.

The sheer hard economics of the situation in which we find ourselves makes certain demands on human nature from which recoil is natural. Sacrifice is demanded. Promise is also offered, of course, but the sacrifice seems much easier to concentrate on than the promise; and those who are squeezed give themselves whole-heartedly to opposition. All the old shibboleths, behind which vested interests have always hidden, are trotted out to do their stuff. The noise is tremendous and all the faint-hearted are quickly intimidated. To pursue a considered program in the midst of this welter of recrimination and special pleading is the task to which we have now to give ourselves.

There is no reason to suppose that our measures are unsound or that any of the experimental procedures have yet failed. They have not achieved utopia; but no one who was intimately concerned with their fashioning supposed that they would. Only the hangers-on, and those whose hopes outrun their intelligence, believed that results would be seen before the causes of those results had become operative. There is complaint from many sources; and no administrator can be deaf to it. But what it was hoped to do in two, four or six years, none of us expected to see in eight months. Yet we have, I think, in all modesty, some reasonable ground for pride. The organization necessary to our eventual aims has been, if not perfected, yet set up in measurably competent fashion. And the long-time effort is being pursued by it with singular energy and determination. Besides this, however, it is only just to say that the immediate demands of a population hungry, cold and in despair have been met. We have not turned aside from any responsibility; we have not asked anyone else to do what it seemed possible for us to do.

The most captious critic, I believe, after careful assessment of the efforts of this administration, would be forced to admit that such an outpouring of loyal and devoted effort has seldom before been seen. I wish it were possible for me to describe for you, in any adequate words, the phenomena of sacrifice, of self-imposed discipline, of giving everything which was possessed by heart and hand and brain, which I have seen so intimately among my colleagues in these past months. I have no lack whatever of confidence in the results to come when the time is ripe for them to come; I have, however, a miserable feeling of the inadequacy, in this case, of the test of results. I wish my fellow citizens could have seen the ordeal, got something of its feel and color, so that adequate honor might be paid where it is due. I do not speak of any of those whose names you may have seen in the press or of whom you may have heard reports. It is truly the unknown servants of the Republic who have deserved well of their country in this crisis.

I have called some of them to Washington myself. Others have called more. They have come with fresh minds, clean motives, and unselfish aspirations. Numbers have come from this university at sacrifices known only to themselves. And their only reward will be unspectacular: the personal sense of having served in a crisis to re-create the gigantic strength of America. Those who have come from this and from other universities have come quietly and gone to work in prosaic ways. They have found that what they had to do was really only an extension and an intensification of what they were used to doing. But under the lash of need they have been driven almost unbearably.

I have had a chance to see the truth of the saying that ours is a government of men. The fiction that it is a government of laws would, I think, never have attained its great prestige if the right men had been called to govern. Much has been said lately of the new institutions which have been invented, of the changes which have overtaken hitherto accepted arrangements. It is possible to overemphasize this idea. In fact, a careful examination of the new legislation will disclose that its novel characteristic is its provision of freedom for action by those who have to do the acting. The powers granted are mostly permissive; the rules written are mandates for performance. Everything depends on men.

The center of the present storm is in the economic field. It is natural that economists should be our greatest dependence for guidance as well as for skillful administration. This university and others have not finished their task by thinning the existing ranks and making temporary loans to government. The end of the demand is not in sight; perhaps it never will be. Perhaps it must be assumed as a regular burden from now on. This requires, of course, a return from economics to political economy as the needed discipline. Economics belonged to laissez faire; the world has turned its back on that. The danger is that universities may not find it out, but may continue to turn over and over the sterile dust of free-competitive principles. Men trained in this kind of thinking are handicapped now; it is the greatest single difficulty with economists in government that they can think only of ways to emasculate the government in its dealings with economic phenomena, because they carry in their heads a formula of noninterference. Political economists are what is needed, men not ridden by preconceptions, careful analysts who recognize logical needs and dare to follow them across their concepts to conclusions in simple operating arrangements, even if this requires the government to do novel things. I say this because for a long time I have been saying it and the event has proved the necessity. Some important part of the effort of our universities has gone to stuffing students with preconceptions which are shattered the moment they meet the economic realities of everyday life. The departments of political economy in our universities are not yet conceiving their problem in the terms to which they must ultimately come—or else go the way of the academic classics with which they really belong.

The most grudging consent to our recovery program comes from these departments of economics; they appear to have forgotten how little they liked the logical alternative when they were living with it a year ago. Seemingly they would rather have us fail than to succeed in unorthodox ways. People who find themselves in such a frame of mind belong with the Bourbons, the Malthusians and other historical diehards after whom deluges have come.

It is quite impossible to predict the shape our newly invented economic institutions may take in the future. That seems to me, in any case, unimportant. What is important is that we have undertaken a venture which is theoretically new in the sense that it calls for control rather than drift. In the years to come much ingenuity will be needed in the effort to isolate and strengthen the nerve centers of industrial civilization. We have yet to discover in determinate fashion what efforts are naturally those of common service, and so require a high degree of socialization, and what ones can safely be left to relatively free individual or group contrivance. We are turning away from the entrusting of crucial decisions, and the operation of institutions whose social consequences are their most characteristic feature, to individuals who are motivated by private interests. It will take a long time to learn how this may be done effectively. But the longest step toward its accomplishment was taken when the new and untrod path was entered on. It is my earnest hope that the university which has been my home during so many active years, and from whose encouragement I and others have drawn strength, may enter on these tasks with courage and determination. The link between this institution and that one which I am at the moment serving in Washington is a natural one. The university is a place for learning and for renewal. It is the source on which government must depend for inspiration, for criticism, for expert service; the source, also, of that political economy out of which the new industrial state must be forged.

XII
FREEDOM FROM FAKES *

EVER since the introduction last spring by Senator Royal
S. Copeland of the bill revising and revitalizing the
Food and Drugs Act of 1906, there have been distant but very
distinct roars and rumbles from the direction of the propri-
etary-medicine interests, which become more and more
ominous and threaten to break into a veritable barrage when
Congress convenes in January. The opposition has enlisted
the support of at least some food manufacturers and, although the cosmetic industry has thus far remained neutral,
it will not be at all surprising if some of them are persuaded
into the ranks of the disgruntled before the campaign has
progressed much further. This has made things difficult for
advertising agencies who handle food and drug accounts;
there seems to them an economic threat in the new law which
is hard to swallow; and many editors, publishers and broad-
casters find themselves in the same position. The line-up is
public interest against private ones; and the strain on the
"spirit of service," which is so much talked about, is almost
too great to be borne.

It promises to be a stirring siege with battle cries of "Defend freedom of advertising!" and "Preserve the public's in-
alienable right to self-medication!" But what these users of
high-sounding slogans seem unable to grasp is the fact that
the enemy is lurking in their own camps; and that what it
is proposed to do is in their own interest, long-run if not
immediate.

The new food and drugs bill is not directed against the

* Article published in *Today*, Nov. 17, 1933.

manufacturer of legitimate patent medicine, the purveyor of healthful food, the producer of safe and sanitary bottled beauty, the well intentioned, truthful advertiser. If some of them have stooped to questionable practices within the last few years—and there is no denying some of them have—it is recognized that competition is a fierce, unrelenting opponent and profit a powerfully effective salve for consciences. But on the whole, their interests and those of the consumer are identical, and the Food and Drug Administration has been the first to recognize that fact.

The purpose of the bill * is to wipe out that contemptible, degraded race of fakers, quacks and poisonous nostrum-makers which is conceived in the slums of public ignorance and nourished by the pain and obsessions of the diseased and the ailing; and most certainly ethical manufacturers have nothing to lose and everything to gain by the annihilation of these parasites.

The Food and Drugs Act of 1906 attempted to protect the consumer against leechery of this sort and it has done a good job—as far as it went. But with the intervening twenty-seven years since its passage, it has become an anachronism; its

* Senate Bill 2800, the proposed new Federal Food and Drugs Act now pending action (September, 1934) is primarily designed for the strengthening of the provisions of the present Food and Drugs Act of 1906, which have been weakened, and, in some cases, made obsolete by the passage of time and changing conditions. The two outstanding additions are the sections controlling the sale of cosmetics and prohibiting false advertising.

The control of the manufacture and sale of food is strengthened by provisions in the new bill

Making dangerous foods illegal and proscribing the use of poisonous containers,

Providing for the issuance of standards of identity and a reasonable standard of quality for foods,

Preventing slack filling and the use of deceptive containers for foods,

Requiring unstandardized foods to bear labeling disclosing the names of the ingredients, except coloring and flavoring, which may be declared simply as such, authors were naturally unable to foresee the tremendous changes which have been made in the production and marketing of foods and drugs and in the field of advertising; also the great growth of the cosmetic industry has come mostly since that time.

It has sufficiently controlled labeling but its control is negative and full of yawning gaps; it applies, not to what must appear on the label, but to what must not. And the burden of proof that a label claim which is false is *also* fraudulent—that is, that the person who makes the claim *knew* it was false when he made it—lies with the Government. And so any Tom, Dick, or Harry can make an unpalatable stew of weeds, label it as a cure for any or all of the ills to which mankind is heir, sell it at a convincingly exorbitant price, and the Government will have to go through all sorts of legalistic gymnastics to prove that he *knew* it was worthless before he sold it. Meanwhile, thousands of credulous

---

Requiring informative labeling of dietary foods,
Requiring foods to be prepared and handled under sanitary conditions;

and the manufacture and sale of drugs by provisions

Prohibiting traffic in drugs which are dangerous when used according to directions,
Making more rigid requirements for official drugs used in medicine and setting up special protection against drugs liable to deterioration,
Making non-official drugs illegal which are more potent than their labeling claim,
Making ignorance no longer a defense for unwarranted therapeutic claims and prohibiting drugs sold for self-medication being represented as cures unless they are cures,
Requiring that habit-forming drugs bear warning labels,
Requiring explicit directions for use and appropriate warnings against the consumption of drugs which in certain conditions are dangerous,
Requiring truthful labeling of antiseptics, disinfectants and similar substances.

Finally, permission is granted the Federal Government to immediately detain imminently dangerous foods, drugs and cosmetics, to control by license traffic in foods, drugs and cosmetics when public health cannot otherwise be protected, and to impose increased penalties for infractions of the law.

souls may be taking the concoction in all good faith and getting no better or perhaps even dying from it.

Perhaps a good example is a patent medicine called "B. & M." which it has taken the administration eleven years to stamp out. This was a Satanic mess of ammonia, turpentine and eggs, which purported to cure a list of thirty ailments ranging all the way from tuberculosis to insect bites. Legal action was taken against its sale in 1922 on the basis of false label claims, but the case was lost because it could not be proved that its manufacturer *knew* it would not cure these things. The mixture continued to be sold and to take its yearly toll of lives while officials lost case after case and wrung helpless hands in despair. Finally, last spring, by proving that the manufacturer bought false testimonials, the administration won its case and "B. & M." was banished from the list of proprietary medicines. But it took eleven years, countless lives, and cost the public thousands of dollars in lawsuits, to do, under the present law, what the revised law could do in one court action.

The Food and Drug Administration, by enforcing the provisions of the Act of 1906, has been fairly successful in forcing these products off the market, only to have many of them sneak in again through the back door by transferring their outlandish claims from the label to their advertising, over which the present act has no control.

Under the same general heading of self-medication are the fiendishly conceived mechanical devices which guarantee to make short men tall, pug noses classic, bald heads hairy— all outside the scope of the present law because it contains no specific definition which applies to them.

Surely it is as much to the advantage of the reliable drug manufacturer as it is to the consumer to oust these ruthless and unfair competitors from the field.

The cosmetic industry was in its infancy when the present act was passed and so its abuses have not been provided against except in those rare cases where labeling bears medicinal claims. As a consequence the market is replete with hair dyes which forever uncoif their users, eyelash preparations which blind, poisonous depilatories which disfigure and maim, and bleaching creams which take off freckles *and* skin. Does it add to the good will and profits of reliable cosmeticians to allow those scandals to continue to occur within their industry?

Because the present act has given the administration no authority to promulgate legal standards for foods, marketing for the housewife has become a costly and not-very-amusing game of chance. She may be able to afford the best foods but it is a toss-up whether or not she gets her money's worth in quality—often she loses. Shopping for jam, she may buy a bread spread with a trick trade name, containing a multitude of berry seeds in a bottle of sugar and water, and is unprotected by law because the "distinctive name" provision of the present Food and Drugs Act affords a loophole through which manufacturers can escape the requirements as to honest and informative labeling. Such products as these are imitations and although they may be, and often are, perfectly wholesome and the purchaser may prefer them to the original products, she should at least have the right to make a deliberate choice. She may purchase flavoring, for instance and, hoping to get the most for her money, choose the largest bottle at the price she can afford—only to find on closer examination at home that it is mostly bottle and very little extract.

Can it be that manufacturers and canners of wholesome, truthfully represented foods are anxious to protect these unethical competitors? I think in their hearts they are not;

and I believe that many of them realize the necessity of new legislation for the protection of their own interests. But of all the questionable practices made possible through the impotency of the present act, that most familiar to all of us, because we have had it thrust down our throats in such generous doses, is the sleight-of-hand advertising to which we've been subjected. This ranges all the way from claims for dangerous, death-dealing concoctions and devices forced off the market by control of labeling and now relying for their existence solely upon the vulnerability of the public to false advertising, to the ballyhoo for really authentic products which fills radio programs and the pages of some of our most widely circulated magazines and newspapers.

An instance of this sort of fraudulent evasion is the case of a nationally advertised vegetable preparation purporting to cure and prevent every conceivable type of female disorder including such serious conditions as ulceration and falling of the womb. These claims were made on the label until prohibited by the enforcement of the false and fraudulent provision of the Act of 1906. Then they were transferred to the advertising, which now plays up the symptoms of the diseases formerly itemized in the labeling, while the label itself bears the very innocuous, lamblike legend, "For conditions to which this tonic is adapted."

Not so universally harmful, perhaps, but nevertheless wholly indefensible, are the advertisements for obesity remedies which are nothing but common Epsom salts sold at ridiculous prices; for mineral waters, good old-fashioned Glauber's salt laxatives, more frequently used as horse physic than anything else, so beatified in radio sermons that we begin to wonder whether a dose wouldn't raise the dead; for antiseptics, recognized as being effective in local, temporary control of bacteria, but which are palmed off on the public as cures and preventatives for all sorts of internal infections.

Witness the totally useless, high-priced rejuvenators, of which a good case in point is one merchandized by the producer of several obesity cures, which depends for its sale upon advertising emphasizing the reputed mystical, youthifying effect of the "rare" fruits it contains, and is a pure, unadulterated example of economic fraud, for it has no more rejuvenating effect than a good glass of water.

Then there are the tooth pastes, useful and reliable products when used for the purpose for which they are intended—cleaning teeth—but so extravagantly and ridiculously advertised that the representation defeats its own ends. We have all heard so much, for instance, about pyorrhea that it has become almost an obsession. Is there a soul who breathes and reads advertisements who has not at one time or another had a sneaking suspicion that perhaps he might be one of the "four"? And when, on comparing his condition with the symptoms the tooth paste ads assure him are those of pyorrhea, he becomes convinced that he is a victim, does he dash off to the nearest drug store for a tube of that marvelously effective tooth paste—or does he hotfoot it to his dentist?

These products would be able to stand on their own quality without exaggerated representation if it were not for the competition to which they are subjected. There is no denying that advertising plays an active and essential part in the efficient marketing of food, drugs, and cosmetics, nor that it assists the consumer to make intelligent choices. But it has been so badly used and so extravagantly overdone that consumers no longer have confidence in it. And without consumer confidence, appropriations for advertising become just so much useless expense.

Editors and publishers have themselves recognized this

fact and have made praiseworthy efforts to clean up their copy; but the total of their achievements up to now has been a mere drop in the bucket. The field is much too extended, competition too cutthroat, and chiselers too squeamish about the loss of revenue to admit of private regulation.

Telling the truth would be an effective "line" in advertising after these many years of pettifogging fiction. Certainly the public has shown no disposition to object to trade puffing nor does advertising have to be mawkish slush just because it's truthful. Several of the most widely-known makers of medical supplies have been almost severely truthful in their advertising; yet their popularity has mounted steadily. There is a lesson in this which others could learn. And the very law would go a long way toward protecting their efforts at reform. I cannot believe that manufacturers will not welcome the opportunity of placing their products on markets free from the ruthless competition of a chiseling minority which resorts to cheap, illicit advertising to keep its head above water. And if, by the right to self-medication is meant the privilege of the poor and the ailing to poison and disfigure themselves and to spend their hard-earned dollars in pitiful attempts to cure incurable diseases with worthless nostrums, then it belongs to the age of witchcraft and has no place in the modern scheme of things.

XIII
NEW STRENGTH FROM THE SOIL *

A NATION does not take a new direction overnight. There will be years of pressure accumulating; there will be an eruption, into plain view, of facts that can no longer be ignored; forces, the existence of which has been suspected only by the more discerning, will rather slowly come to the surface; there must follow, finally, the discovery of the institutions which fit the times. I shall explore with you some of these irrepressible facts and forces as I see them; and some of the institutions which are taking shape slowly in answer to newly revealed needs.

I am asked to speak of that part of the national recovery program which has to do with agriculture, and it may be more useful to begin by identifying some of the pressures, which for many years have been accumulating and which now seem to compel a new national direction.

Perhaps the most insistent pressure, the most determinative fact of all, came into existence during the World War, when the United States was transformed from a debtor to a creditor nation. For generations, Europe had had a great deal to do with the financing of our railroads and of new industries. We paid our debt in goods, and particularly farm goods. Annually, before the War, we were paying some $200,-000,000 on interest account; and we were paying an important part of it in wheat and pork and cotton and tobacco. The Old World was hungry, willing and able to pay at least something for food; our new lands and rapidly developing efficiency seemed particularly appropriate for the task. The

* Address delivered at Swarthmore College, Nov. 26, 1933.

added requirements of the War served to induce intensified efforts among our farmers, led them to visualize an insatiable world desire for the products of our fields, and concealed, unhappily, the delusiveness of that demand, the underlying changes which were accumulating beneath the surface of trade.

Yet we were changing very rapidly, during these war years, from Europe's debtor to Europe's creditor. We went into the War owing $200,000,000 a year on interest account, and we came out of the War being owed $500,000,000 a year on interest account. Our farmers could go on producing for this market, other things being equal, only if we permitted Europe to pay her debt to us and pay in the form chiefly relied upon, that is, goods. The tariff barriers we raised made that increasingly difficult. European purchasing power for our farm products, formerly derived from her exports to us, declined first slowly and then sensationally. We hid the decline, up until 1929, by forwarding huge loans. But all the time we were making it more and more difficult for payment to be made. The cumulation of stresses reached a breaking point finally. Loans, in a profit system, will not continue to be made after it becomes perfectly clear that no means of payment exists.

When the cloak of foreign financing was torn away, the true nature of the world demand for our farm products was revealed. And there began a period in which Europe had to forego buying from us because she could not sell to us. What she needed, she was compelled to produce herself, so far as possible; what else she needed, she obtained from nations other than the United States. Our exporters, sitting astride our own high tariff walls, saw even higher walls across the water. The compulsion involved in our policy was one, at least, of the causes which led to that determined agrarian nationalism which has now developed everywhere on the Continent and has effectually closed to us the markets we once had. For practical purposes, this situation has to be treated as permanent. Certainly, our efforts at modification have had little result so far.

Our foreign customers now became our competitors. The drive for nationalistic self-sufficiency was on, and I suppose no nation had more to do with speeding it onward than the United States, in its tariff and financial policies of the post-war years. The consequences were most immediately felt by agriculture. Wheat and pork and cotton began to back up on American farms, beginning as long ago as 1926. It was not only that Europe had higher tariffs and was producing more of its own raw material; there was the added fact that the newer countries—Canada, Australia, the Argentine, and others—had come into the world market with a tremendous volume of commodities raised on new and unexhausted lands at low cost. The pressure of events was compelling American farmers to look more and more toward the domestic market, and less toward the foreign market. This was fairly obvious a dozen years ago; but national administrations either couldn't or wouldn't see it. No doubt the alternative of providing the machinery of adjustment for agriculture frightened them even more than the prospect of losing foreign markets.

Our national policy, ever since the War, has been a policy of drifting. We were a great creditor nation; the implications of that position required us to invite imports, if we expected our debtors to pay us, and if we hoped to continue to do any exporting. But we continued to behave as if we were still a debtor nation, and our leaders, by their inaction, refused to admit that anything had happened to our relationships with the rest of the world. The results of so terribly mistaken a foreign policy have been unfortunate for all of us, but for farmers the results have been peculiarly severe. In the decline of foreign trade they had more to lose than others, and they lost it.

When the farm problem was taken seriously, after the election in 1928, the conditions of solution were not really met. Stabilization operations were undertaken, which, because they sought to raise prices, without controlling supply, aggravated an already impossible situation. The Government's excursions into the market merely resulted in an increase in the supply of those very commodities which might have been reduced if prices had been allowed to fall—an awkward and expensive process for all concerned, but the best a completely laissez-faire system has to offer. But we learned something for the $500,000,000 the Farm Board spent. This administration has refused to attempt price stabilization without that fundamental planning of supplies which is its necessary concomitant. Farmers like to be limited in their operations even less than other business men; and pressure on them to do the one thing needful was undertaken with natural reluctance. But like all tough problems, the toughness has proved not to be so formidable on close contact. We have measurably succeeded.

The decline in foreign trade has been only one of the pressures operating upon American agriculture. Forces of great significance have been at work within our own boundaries. The agricultural map of the United States has changed many times. It has changed considerably in the last twelve years even, for within that period the wheat and cotton belts have shifted westward. Mechanization, by substituting automobiles and tractors for horses and mules, has thrown more than 30,000,000 acres out of the production of feed crops and into the production of cash crops. More efficient farm practices have also, in effect, enlarged our crop land area by 25,000,000 acres.

Meanwhile, the number of customers and their need for farm products have by no means kept up with the supply. The Malthusian thesis of a population pressing upon the food supply has become, for the time being, at least, a food supply pressing upon the population. The Malthusians feared scarcity, for they could not visualize its conquest. Yet in our generation we have seen scarcity vanquished, and our ever-present fear, so far as agriculture is concerned, is a fear of overabundance. We wish, if not for scarcity, at least for relief from price-depressing surpluses.

The pressure of efficiency, illustrated in new machines and in improved farm practices alike, has operated to such an extent that the volume of output per farm worker increased by 40 percent between 1910 and 1930. Furthermore, this merely continued a trend which has persisted as far back as the records go, and which presumably will continue, in one form or another, as long as human beings entertain notions about progress.

Fewer farmers are therefore needed today, to produce food enough for all of us, than ever before. In 1800, at least three-quarters of all workers were farmers, and only 5 percent of the people lived in towns and cities with a population as large as 8,000. In 1880, farmers and farm laborers represented only 44 percent of the gainfully employed. By 1930, the percentage of all workers on farms had shrunk to 21. We can say, therefore, that to produce the food and clothing for 10 families, 8 had to be farmers in 1800, 4 in 1880, and only 2 in 1930. It is quite within the realm of possibility that even this proportion could be widened to one family in 10, even with present technique.

Another force which, though it does not represent progress, nevertheless tends to mean fewer farmers and fewer acres in production, is the force of tax delinquency, of particular significance in what we call the submarginal farming areas. Relatively unproductive soil or uneconomic location; relatively high taxes and other fixed charges; dispossession, breakdown of community institutions, and complete failure of human efforts in the affected regions—these are the elements all too easily noted in great areas of the South, the cut-over regions of the Great Lake states, the Appalachian counties, and parts of the semiarid West. To a lesser extent, the same forces have operated even in the richest agricultural areas, but there as a product of the depression, and in large part to be corrected as we work our way out of the depression.

Against these long-time trends which suggest increasing productivity per worker, there are other trends of equal importance. One of them is soil erosion, which has already ruined, beyond hope of recovery within our lifetime, more than 20,000,000 acres, and which is making dangerous inroads on another 100,000,000 acres of our land in farms. The total of all land in farms, incidentally, including woodland, pasture land, and crop land, is not quite 1,000,000,000 acres.

But a more obvious pressure on agriculture is that which comes from the millions of men and women who are out of work. Industry, at the moment, cannot take care of all of them; in the opinion of some, it never will be able to. Where is their opportunity to earn a living?

The answer that has always been given in past depressions has again been given in this depression. There is—so the answer runs—land to be had, almost for the asking; on the land there is food and shelter, or so it is usually assumed; so the cry is "Back to the farm!"

As a temporary expedient, a great deal of this sort of

movement has been going on since 1930; but of what promise is it for the longer future? Even for the immediate present, the movement back to the farm may be merely transforming an urban relief problem into an acute rural relief problem. In such rural states as Oklahoma and South Dakota, for example, 27 and 22 percent, respectively, of all the families in the state are on the public relief rolls. These percentages are, of course, higher than for most rural states, but they are also much higher than for any of the industrial states.

It may not be possible to say, with any assurance, that the trend from city to farm will be reversed when industry gets back to predepression activity. It may be that machinery has displaced, at least for a number of years, an impressive number of city wage earners. If the city holds no promise for them, will the country? Certainly if the inevitable trend in commercial agriculture is toward fewer farmers and fewer acres, there would seem little opportunity for them in commercial farming. And the same thing may be said, of course, of the millions of farmers, young and old, who have not the makings, for one reason or another, of efficient commercial producers of farm stuffs.

You will notice that I refer to these trends with some tentativeness. They are trends, not dogma. Nevertheless there is a good deal of evidence that the number of commercial farmers will become smaller, and there is likewise a good deal of evidence that industry will not reëmploy all those now idle unless there are some rather radical changes in our machinery for the distribution of industrial income.

It is important, in this connection, to keep in mind an outstanding difference between agriculture and industry. As a whole, the demand for industrial products is elastic, while the demand for farm products is relatively inelastic. The ability of the population to consume industrial products is apparently unlimited—given the income to buy with. Consider the needs of the people today, for example; not merely millions but billions of dollars might profitably be employed in building new houses and repairing old ones, in making over our railroad system, and in providing all the people with all the tools of education and entertainment which they really crave. Certainly the saturation point is a long way off, and it was a long way off even in 1929—the provision being always that purchasing power must be related to production.

But for farm products, with a few exceptions, the outlook is different. Once every individual in the country has been given not only all he can buy but all he needs—plus what can be sold abroad—what virtue is there in producing still more? There are growing uses of farm products in industry, but the growth has come very slowly; there are shifts from one crop to another, and these shifts may indicate higher dietary standards; but by and large the human stomach is not elastic, and our consumption of farm products does not increase any faster than our population, if as fast.

Output per worker, I have said, has increased both on farms and in factories. The implication is that as industrial output per worker increases, more and more can be disposed of, and more and more people can be employed—always provided industrial income is properly distributed; but as farm output per worker rises, there must be fewer workers lest more be produced than can be disposed of.

Meanwhile, there are millions looking to the land for relief; the trends I have spoken of operate slowly, and the task of obtaining a balance between purchasing power and industrial production is not one to be accomplished overnight. Furthermore, out on the land now there are millions whose standard of living is tragically low, has long been low, and threatens always to be low, because their land is unproductive. If you are tempted to think that these submarginal farmers are at any rate better off than the urban unemployed, you might recall the fact that many, many thousands of them are on the relief rolls, that for many of them there are neither schools nor any other community institutions, and, finally, that their hope of the future cannot be brightened much even by higher prices.

To recapitulate: we have an array of pressures on agriculture, as on our urban economy, accumulated through the years and exposed to public view by the depression. Some of them conflict with one another; there is no simple means of relief, but it is first of all important that we begin, without further delay, to apply long-time remedies and corrective devices. These may grow out of our present emergency measures, or they may not; the point is that any further delay in correcting long-standing maladjustments would be indefensible.

I am thinking particularly of national land policy, in which package we have wrapped so many of our more persistent problems of agricultural and human maladjustment. For at least a dozen years the problem of land utilization has been under study by the Federal Government, and there have been scores of thoughtful resolutions passed recommending this or that procedure. The Department of Agriculture had a large part in crystallizing such public opinion as there was two years ago in a national land-use conference at Chicago. The problem, at least, was recognized; it was admitted generally, what had long been observed by students of the subject, that laissez faire was a source rather of confusion than strength, if an intelligent, national land policy was to result. And only a national policy, properly coördinated with state and local needs and responsibilities, would suffice.

Since that national conference of two years ago, two national land-utilization committees have been studying important phases of the land problem, and giving the benefit of their research and judgment to Congress and to the general public. Nevertheless, it was difficult, if not impossible, for their conclusions to be translated into action. There was needed an agency or agencies properly equipped with men, with money, with adequate information, and with power to do the job.

I believe we now have, or soon will have, such agencies in the Federal Government. One of them is the new Erosion Control Service. Another is the new Subsistence Homesteads Division. A third is the Land Management Company, an independent agency, the organization of which will, I hope, be announced very soon.* Another, of course, is the Tennessee Valley Authority. All of these, let me emphasize, are for the long pull, and their final relationship to the emergency organizations has yet to be determined.

The Erosion Control service, by coöperative arrangements with state and local authorities, and with individual land-owners, is launching ten or twelve erosion control projects to protect against further ruin about a million acres of naturally good land which is washing away and losing fertility at an alarming rate. These projects will serve as a demonstration of what man can do to save his most precious natural resource—the land itself—from irreparable damage. To spread the results to other areas, and to attract the interest of the individual landowner, should not be an insurmountable task.

The program of the Subsistence Homesteads Division is likewise more of an experimental and a demonstration program than an attempt to solve, all at once, the problem of the

---

* Legal obstacles blocked the formation of this company. Its functions, however, have since been performed by other governmental units.

submarginal farmer and of the unemployed factory hand who yearns to get back to the land. You have perhaps read of the first project to be approved in West Virginia, where some 200 miners and their families will be given an opportunity to start out afresh, earning a decent wage in a small factory, and having a small acreage upon which to grow some of their living and upon which—above all—to live.

Obviously this will not cut a very wide swath this year or next. We have to feel our way along. Many mistakes have been made in earlier land-settlement projects, and we should prefer to profit by them. But surely in such an experiment there is hope. It takes account of the trend toward industrial decentralization, and it may amount to a significant force as cheaper power, lower transportation costs, and lower raw material costs lend their help. At the same time the formation of subsistence homesteads—or homestead gardens—will not come into any important competition with commercial farming.

In some respects the Land Management Company will be the most significant of the new land agencies, for it promises to be the chief implement of a new land policy announced by the President last summer. Up to this year, such national land policy as we have had has stemmed from the Homestead Act of 1862 and the Reclamation Act of 1902. The object has always been to encourage expansion, and in our pioneer period that object was pretty well attained. It might have been attained in other ways, in ways more conducive to sound land use and to the welfare of the general public; but all that is history.

Today we face a period of resettlement, mostly upon land already in use, and we desire it to be a rational resettlement. The individual good was not necessarily the general good in the romantic days of pioneer settlement, and it is no more likely to be the general good in these days of resettlement.

In consequence President Roosevelt has announced the first significant departure from our pioneer land policy. He has said that as fast as good new lands are brought into cultivation by Federal reclamation, or other means, a correspondingly productive unit of poor submarginal lands will be taken out of cultivation, and kept out. That may mean retiring several acres of bad land for one acre of good land. And there is no reason why the retirement must stop at that point, if the stability of our agriculture requires even greater contraction of the crop-land area.

The mechanism for such an operation is the new Land Management Company. Under our present agricultural adjustment operations, designed primarily for the emergency, good land as well as bad goes out of use in any horizontal acreage cut. But for the longer future the only sound procedure is to keep the best crop land in crops, and keep out of cultivation the poorer lands. If there comes a time when these marginal areas are needed, they can easily enough be put to the plow; but meanwhile, given intelligent management, their fertility and their power to resist erosion will have been built up. That is the sort of thing the Land Management Company should be able to do. It can become one of those balancing mechanisms which our economy so badly needs.

There are other tasks awaiting it, too. In the erosion-control projects, for example, it is necessary to withdraw from the possibility of private use some of the land in each project area. If there are people trying to squeeze out a living there, they ought not to be disturbed, unless voluntarily. The Land Management Company, however, can help provide homestead gardens as the alternative to their starvation farming, and at the same time it can acquire and manage the eroded parts. Similarly, lands can be acquired by the company for proposed new forest areas, for expansion of the more crowded Indian reservations, and for such public purposes as are necessary in the Tennessee Valley.

These are the first tentative moves to bring order out of chaos in the use of our land. These new mechanisms can, I believe, hasten the day when every acre can be put to its optimum use; when a region which grows grass more economically than wheat, will be permitted to stay in grass; when thin soil that ought never to be farmed at all, will be put to uses more in keeping with its potentialities. Slowly but surely, I believe, we are on the way to correcting long-standing maladjustments in our civilization by a new and well implemented emphasis on putting the earth to its right uses.

There will be some contribution to the solution of these more chronic problems by the emergency organizations such as the Agricultural Adjustment Administration, but it is too early to do much more than guess at what form that contribution may take. The immediate task of these emergency organizations is a different one, and at times they have to move in a direction and with a method which can be supported only by reason of the urgency of the immediate need and the absence of any practicable alternative. Nevertheless our hope is that out of these emergency efforts will come a sufficient security for agriculture so that we may continue with the long-time program uninterruptedly.

Coming now to a consideration of the emergency efforts to help agriculture out of the depression, it ought first to be recognized that almost every phase of the recovery program has some implications for agriculture. Renewed industrial activity and higher factory pay rolls mean increased purchasing power for farm products. A monetary policy designed to lessen the great and tragic injustices as between debtor and creditor, has special significance for farmers. Help in refinancing their mortgages at fairer appraised valuations, and at reduced interest rates, is giving many a desperate farm family new courage and new hope. This evening, however, I can do no more than mention these things in passing, and restrict myself to that part of the recovery program for which the Agricultural Adjustment Administration is responsible.

Earlier I listed some of the accumulated pressures on agriculture, compelling a new national direction. Foremost I named the pressure of a changed world situation, dictating a contraction in that part of our acreage devoted to production for export. At the same time, there has been the pressure of technology, shoving more and more commodities on the market; and there has been the necessity for farmers to maintain production, no matter what the price level, in order to meet fixed charges. With the arrival of depression, the effects of these and similar forces are intensified a hundredfold. A sharp drop in effective demand, both at home and abroad, conflicted with the persistent pressures for a maintained, if not increased, production. If there were no national concern for the farmer, per se, at least there had to be some for the farmer as a purchaser of city goods and services. You may recall the statement that this nation cannot endure, half boom and half broke.

Of the 14,000,000 unemployed last winter, probably half owed their unemployment either directly or indirectly to the drying up of farm buying power. Here in one common distress were the two major producing groups of the nation— the farmers and the wage earners. And here also were the two chief groups normally capable of that mass consumption so necessary to mass production. The purchasing power of both groups had to be increased, and with some dispatch, if recovery was to come.

The absurdly low prices for farm products had to be raised. The only sound way to accomplish that was to get at the cause of their lowness. With such products as wheat and cotton and tobacco and pork, it was clearly a case of overproduction; with other products, notably dairy products, it seemed to be a combination of overproduction and underconsumption; with still others, the difficulty was underconsumption. The attack, therefore, had to be varied enough and flexible enough to meet the variety in the problem.

In any case, it was early recognized that the only satisfactory way of raising the price of a particular commodity was by making a fundamental adjustment in either supply or demand, or both. Price-depressing surpluses had to be cut down, and new surpluses kept from appearing. But starvation diets in the midst of plenty had also to be a thing of the past. If private enterprise couldn't feed the hungry, or didn't know how to distribute what had been so bountifully produced, then the Government would. The attempt, you see, is for balance, not for scarcity; the drive against wasteful overabundance is in fact a drive against the paradox of want in the midst of plenty, and it goes to the very heart of our economic system.

Left to themselves, farmers were helpless to adjust production. They could be forced to it, of course, by the slow working of such forces as continued low prices, high fixed charges, and virtual retirement from our money economy. But that would take another ten years, in all probability, and the result would be as painful for the cities as for the farmers.

An individual farmer might have reduced his production, but this would have resulted only in reducing his own gross income without affecting the general situation. With prices dropping, the individual incentive was to increase production so that income might be stretched as far as possible toward meeting expenses. The fact that the welfare of farmers as a group called for different behavior, did not and could not have much reality for the individual and his immediate personal problems. Some mechanism had to be found which would permit individual and group incentives to work as a team rather than as opposing forces.

The Agricultural Adjustment Act, with its processing taxes and its benefit payments, however crude a piece of social machinery, has this result. It makes it possible to reimburse the individual farmer for his individual loss in reducing production; it permits him, for the first time, consciously and unhesitatingly to contribute to the group good. It identifies individual and social motives without depending on a changed human nature.

In a few short months the program of agricultural adjustment has been advanced to an extraordinary extent. This spring the economy of the South sagged under a cotton carryover two and a half times the normal, and a price less than half of fair exchange value. The situation was desperate; only a drastic operation could help, distasteful as the idea might be to all of us. In a remarkable campaign the farmers of the South retired more than 10,000,000 acres of the growing cotton crop, reduced a prospective 17,000,000 bale crop to a 13,000,000 bale crop, and saw their income increase by $300,-000,000 over last year's. The South breathed easier, and is a much brighter spot on the economic map. Nevertheless, another average cotton crop in 1934 would wreck things, despite all that can possibly be done to stimulate demand. Next year, however, it will be possible to avoid the drastic surgery of plowing under; there will be time, and machinery, to prevent the planting of excess acres. Admitting that we cannot control the weather, there are still plenty of factors in supply and demand which we can control and which, when controlled, ought to provide a sufficient leverage for success.

A similar program has succeeded with growers of certain types of tobacco, likewise confronted by unsaleable surpluses. The wheat acreage reduction campaign did not involve this year's crop; nature had done an effective job there, although the carryover even now is nearly twice the normal. The wheat campaign calls for a 15 percent reduction in the crop to be harvested in 1934, in line with the world wheat agreement, and nearly 600,000 wheat growers have agreed to make such a reduction. In return for their pledge, a portion of the benefit payments due them are going out to the wheat belt now.

In the tremendously complicated corn-hog enterprise, a campaign is now under way to reduce corn acreage and hog numbers in 1934 to somewhat nearer the quantity demanded by our own needs, plus what can be sold abroad. Benefit payments will go out to producers as soon as contracts can be signed and approved.

Meanwhile, the second major device of the Adjustment Act—the marketing agreement—has been utilized in raising prices to producers by agreement between producers, distributors, and the Adjustment administration. This has been applied to a number of minor commodities, and more notably to the marketing of milk in many of our major milk sheds. I think it ought to be admitted that there are enormous difficulties in the effective use of the marketing agreement, and that we have by no means disposed of them. The chief problem is to protect the consumer against undue price increases, and to make sure that efficiency rather than inefficiency, both in production and in distribution, is encouraged. We have a long way to go, and the going is rough; but that is no reason for quitting.

The efforts I have been describing affect the supply of farm products, and seek a balanced production. There have also been efforts to increase the demand, for it is a fact that some of our low prices are due more to underconsumption than to overproduction. You are doubtless familiar with the formation of the Federal Surplus Relief Corporation, organized last summer and directed by Harry L. Hopkins, administrator of Federal emergency relief. This corporation, and the emergency relief organization in general, goes to the heart of the problem of temporary underconsumption by transferring surpluses from those who have them to those who need them. Millions of pounds of pork and beef, of butter and of milk, of many another necessary farm product and even nonfarm product, are now going to augment the meager diets of families on the relief rolls. These items are in addition to the cash or other allowances previously granted.

Besides providing a direct attack on both overproduction and underconsumption, the creation and work of the Federal Surplus Relief Corporation constitute an interesting commentary on the effectiveness of our traditional economic order. I find it not widely appreciated that the Surplus Relief Corporation is, both in theory and in fact, direct unemployment relief quite as much as farm relief. It transfers unsaleable surpluses from those who have them to those who need them, and thereby cuts to the core of the modern paradox of want in the midst of plenty. It operates, of course, outside the profit system, and it is conceivable that in some cases it can provide a useful comparison with the existing machinery for distributing goods.

I have already indicated that these new mechanisms are in many ways crude and inefficient; that was to be expected in a nation where the invention of social machinery has always been discouraged. There have been mistakes, and there will be more, but I hope we shall always be quick to locate them, correct them, and move forward. The important thing, in the long run, is the conscious striving for new national directions, and the substitution of realistic guidance in economic affairs in the place of romantic—and tragic—rugged individualism.

The immediate results of the agricultural recovery program may be less significant than the residue to be carried over into the years when our long-time national policies for agriculture are in the making. Surely there is some significance in the fact that through these adjustment programs millions of farmers are for the first time made aware of the effect of their activities on their neighbors, and the effect of their neighbors' activities upon them. The same result can reasonably be expected, I think, from all the important occupational groups, as they learn the practical and individual meaning of the term "interdependence." Please do not misunderstand me; I do not wish to be romantic about this; the hoped-for result, it seems to me, can come simply because men learn by doing.

If this is true, if this new sense of interdependence is really the residue of all or any of our emergency efforts, then there is genuine hope that America will turn in a new and more promising direction, and that this depression will not have been endured in vain.

XIV

SENATOR PROGRESSIVE

SENATOR PROGRESSIVE is back in Washington for the first time since Congress adjourned in June and, since he counts me among his friends, he came in to sit by my fireside out in Georgetown for an evening. I fixed him comfortably in a large chair with a glass close by and waited to hear what he had to say. Some forecast of it had drifted East by way of the newspapers, so that I knew roughly how high his temperature was and what he thought of the administration.

He began in the orthodox way.

"It is my belief," he said, "that it was a great mistake for us to have given the administration so few definite directions."

"Do you object," I asked, "to the way the powers you granted have been used?"

"I certainly do," he said. "It seems like ten years since last June. A lot of good American institutions have been overthrown almost casually—certainly all the things that have been done weren't thought out."

"But," I protested, "your speeches for ten years have demanded the scrapping of certain old institutions. Let's see which ones you mean. Is it the competitive system in business, the antitrust laws, and all that kind of thing?"

"You know very well," he interrupted, "that I mean this code business—you people have allowed these fellows to write their own ticket. They certainly have made the world safe for big business all right. You had no mandate from us to do that. We believe that big business is bad. We thought we were protecting the little fellow."

"Well, you can't do that just by making speeches in the Senate and by passing laws. That kind of thing is only made certain by the hard work of administration. How much have you helped in that?"

"That's not my business," he said. "A Senator helps to write laws, not to run the country."

"Sometimes, Senator, you amaze me. Were you making laws when you insisted on the appointment of a dozen lawyers from your district in the emergency administration and when you asked the Public Works Administration for a new post office for your city, and a flood-control dam on your local river out there? The only time you've been in Washington since June was when you were trying to force somebody's hand in such matters. None of us have had the slightest help in protecting any truly public interest. We've spent most of our time fighting off you fellows' claims to some private advantage."

This enraged him. "Certainly I asked for appointments. Certainly I demanded some public works money. Why not? It was the only way to get it.

"You fellows," he went on more calmly, "don't know much about politics. If you did you would know that I can't escape any more than the others on the Hill can, from this kind of thing. We have to do it to keep solid back home. Besides nothing I asked for or got was harmful in any way. It was a real benefit back home."

"I can name at least ten of you," I said, "who stayed around and helped—not by making demands about jobs and post offices, but by taking part in discussions, by acting as chairmen of committees, or by just hanging around and really criticizing mistakes as they were made. How is it that those fellows didn't have to make private demands which might cut across public plans?"

"They don't come up for reëlection in 1934," was his cynical comment.

"Some of them do," I was able to say. "But we really are arguing about something no one knows how to do anything about. I can see why you are anxious about these things. I know that your demands for jobs and for money spent in your state come from a deeper source than you like to admit when you are posing as a practical politician. You have unemployment out there, don't you—people with abilities that are not being used, even people who are hungry and cold?"

"Not now," he said. "I've seen to it that we got our share of relief funds, and of public work."

"What," I asked, "has that got to do with politics, except that these people chose you to represent them and the people of other places chose others? Why don't you confess that your heart was touched by the real suffering of real people when you went back home and that your fine Washington theories of statesmanship merely failed to stand up under the pressure? When you came storming down here last summer demanding attention for your people's needs you were merely being human."

"I suppose so," he said slowly. "I take this thing a little hard. You know how I worked over the new legislation we cooked up last spring. I think I can claim to have made some real contribution to it too. But it certainly was one thing to sit on committees and argue about the country's welfare and quite another to realize that my people—people I know and grew up with—are in distress. Who wouldn't do something drastic, even if it did upset the machinery a little? Just the same"—and here he stopped and lighted a cigarette—"that's no reason why you should try to blame our comparatively unimportant interruptions for all that has gone wrong in the program."

"I know," I said. "You aren't really to blame. I was merely giving myself the pleasure of airing a minor irritation. Of course, I'm not prepared to admit what you imply. The country really hasn't been handed over to the big fellows. This is merely that self-government of industry which all of us approved in principle—with a little of real supervision to take the place of the old competition you yourself thought was so wasteful."

"I suppose so," he said, "and I suppose things never turn out to be what you thought they would. There are always more intervening processes than are allowed for."

"It seems to me so," I replied. "It was inevitable that the whole organization of industry and the middleman trades on a new basis should involve huge efforts of organization. Just the learning of the rules of the new game is something. Then all the personnel was lacking. Everybody has had a job to learn. And policies have had to be fought out bit by bit as we went along. I don't see any reasons to be discouraged, really, as I look back over the last six months. What was lost in some fights, we gained in others—I speak of course from our common point of view."

"Are you willing to test it," he asked, "by saying over again what we fundamentally wanted?"

"Why, now," I said, "let's see. There was first higher incomes for farmers and workers; there was a more efficient, less wasteful, organization of industry so that there would be more to go around; there was less speculation and more security of occupation and income."

"Well," he demanded, "have we got any of those?"

"Not yet," I admitted. "But you don't expect results until causes go to work. The thing has been slower than you anticipated, certainly. But the thing nevertheless seems to me to be under way. We have reason to believe, in my Department, that we have put forces in motion which, if you will give them a few years, will raise farmers' incomes. The reduction of acreage has been got—"

"A few years!" he interrupted. "Good grief, man, we can't wait a few years. We haven't got that long. Do you want a revolution?"

I knew that question was coming. "Have you heard," I asked, "of public works, of civil works, of the really remarkable organization of relief? People are for the first time on this continent guaranteed a living by their government. We can't feed and clothe and shelter people forever that way, but it will certainly last until our real plans can take hold. A lot more has been done than you specifically directed, too. If you had made the rules as rigid as you now seem to think you should have made them, we should have had a lot of hungry people all this winter."

"I suppose so," he said, "and in that case the permissive powers worked out all right. But you couldn't make a very good case for them in this code business. They've allowed all these industries with codes to set prices anywhere they wanted to—and they fixed them high enough—so high that people couldn't buy. And there has been a slump these last few weeks because of it."

"I think you have a better case there," I admitted. "Still it seems to me that the Government's powers have probably been used about as far as they would stretch. It was necessary, if any kind of quick action was to be had, to proceed voluntarily. If business had had to give up too much, it would have refused to come into the new arrangement voluntarily. Codes would have had to be imposed—perhaps they would all have had to be licensed as the milk distributors have been. Anyway, I don't see how more specific directions from the Congress would have helped there. You could never have passed a law which did not contemplate a good deal of voluntarism."

"I guess," he said, "that what I am complaining about is that we allowed the executive branch to make the mistakes instead of making them ourselves. Maybe I am palpitating with the wrong emotion. We do, sometimes, you know."

"Well," I said, "there's that possibility. No one argues that perfection has been reached. On the other hand when you make your speeches this winter I hope it won't be too much out of your mind, ever, that a new deal is really on the way, that you won't be too critical because it didn't happen so quickly as you thought it might. There is, you know, a lot yet to be done if you just stick to new ground, rather than giving yourselves altogether to threshing over old straw."

"You won't get out of anything that way," he said. "We'll criticize plenty. We'll be sorry for a lot we let you do. And we'll blame you for doing what we said you could. A lot of us don't like those new things, you know. We were all in a panic last year and we took some long chances. Maybe it's a sign that things are better that we are reconsidering now. I don't suppose we'll succeed in unscrambling all the eggs; but some of us will try."

He got up and stretched himself. I motioned toward his glass. But he shook his head. "Are you sorry about that too?" I asked. There was a twinkle in his eye. But he refused to answer. Personally, I know he thinks that that was another mistake. But he is not unmindful that his state went wet by two to one. "No," he said, "I guess that'll stick. But about the rest, I don't know. Where's my hat?"

XV
SENATOR PROGRESSIVE AGAIN

SENATOR PROGRESSIVE's handling of the old brass knocker on my door is an index to his mood. The clatter he set up on his last visit warned me of a dangerous exuberance. Saying to myself that I had to deal with a man possessed of a new idea, I hastily concealed my detective story under a cushion—there's is a certain academic prestige which gives me an advantage over Senator Progressive and I am reluctant to be exposed—and opened the door to him. He was almost offensively jovial. "Meditating a plot of some sort, I suppose," I said to him.

"That only goes to show," he said, "how deep you have sunk in the official mire. It is the chief desire of a privateer coming home to port with a load of loot to escape unnoticed. All the aggressiveness which led to its acquisition evaporates. The whole crew becomes cowardly. It's the same way with officials. Everyone with an administrative office was in an attacking mood last spring—everything to gain and nothing to lose—but now when a certain line has been chosen and its machinery set up, you are all as scared as a home-coming privateer. Your hope is that no one will notice you for a long time. And, particularly, when I merely knock on your door, you can think of nothing but plots. You'll begin suppressing pretty soon—officials always do."

"Yes," I said, "but the great independent guild of newspaper publishers will prevent that. You saw the battle they put up for freedom of the press."

He snorted at this. One of his private antipathies is the press. And one of my amusements is watching him conceal it.

"Freedom! How many of them are free to support the Cope-land bill? You talk to me about freedom! No, the newspapers won't stop officials. They have been easy enough to handle in other countries. In fact, nothing will. They've even started to suppress reconsideration of any of their 'experiments.' If those were experiments I'm a billy goat. They're just as sacred now as rugged individualism was last year. And all of you fellows are nailing your flags to the mast and getting ready to go down with the ship just as officials always have. No flexibility, no open-mindedness!"

"But," I protested, "Secretary Wallace himself suggested some amendments to A.A.A. the other day. And I hear con-stant talk of stock market control, new tax legislation, new land laws—"

"All minor," he interrupted, "nothing that touches the core of the thing. And the peculiar part of it is that the whole business is inconsistent. It doesn't fit together. And you've become so theological that you'd rather try to explain con-sistency into it than to lop off one part or the other honestly so that you won't be trying to go in several directions at once."

This was a new idea to me. I knew now why the knocker had clattered so loudly. "Do you mean," I asked, "that the Department of Agriculture is going in several directions at once? I suppose you refer to that old fallacy, which is un-worthy of one with your intelligence, Senator, that a crop-reduction program is inconsistent with the efficient uses of the land which remains in produc—"

"I don't mean anything of the kind," he interrupted. "And you know it. I came out here tonight to convict you of a sin and I'm not going to be diverted by irrelevant issues which you can explain away. What I have in mind you can't ex-plain."

I saw that I was in for it; so, as gracefully as possible, I capitulated, seeking only to temper the wind by opening the cupboard toward which the senatorial eye had been wandering. The customary ritual having been concluded and the glasses filled again, I braced myself for a dressing down.

"Will you tell me," he began, "how the Securities Act and N.R.A. fit themselves into the same governmental picture? Someone seems to be making the attempt to define the progressive philosophy in two antithetical ways at once. And these two pieces of legislation will do for types. All the rest would probably fall into their categories—the Copeland bill is like the Securities Act, A.A.A. is like N.R.A. and so on—but the purposes and philosophies they represent can't possibly be reconciled."

Here he became oratorical, as legislators sometimes will. "I didn't lend my name to a movement," he declaimed, "which seemed to have a meaning to Democrats and Republicans alike, only to have it made ridiculous by these divisions. The question is, what is it to be progressive? Is it to set oneself in opposition to the plans and purposes of the lords of industry—or is it to further their ambitions for power and profits?"

The Senator seems to become another person in his oratorical moods—one which irritates me. But he had a point here, which I was anxious to have him develop. I said a little maliciously: "Maybe to be progressive is to attempt to do both. Maybe a limitation on their power and profits will further the plans and purposes of industry. I don't see any necessary inconsistency so far."

He dismissed this contemptuously. "Words," he said, "just words, idle words. Did we turn our backs on the whole anti-trust conception when we made N.R.A. a law, or did we not—"

"Well," I interrupted, "there was the so-called Borah Amendment."

He pounced on this. "Exactly what I mean," he said. "The Borah Amendment right inside the N.R.A., and the Securities Act done independently, show that we are hopelessly confused about objectives. Two ways at once—and those opposite!"

"I won't conceal from you," I said, "that something of the same sort has occurred to me. But I had hoped that the division would heal rather than grow. The principle of *caveat venditor*—as contrasted with the *caveat emptor* we are used to—is a new idea in our legislation. It's in the Securities Act as well as in the new Food and Drugs Act. I am not sure that their necessary effect is the establishment of old face-to-face relationships, as I've heard it said. In fact, I should say that the necessity for them had arisen simply because of the growth of large-scale business and the complete separation of producer from consumer. In the old days horse traders knew all about horses, or thought they did, and they were quite satisfied to take their own chances. Much the same thing was true of their investments in the small industries they knew intimately. And, of course, their food and clothes were made and bought under conditions so much simpler than they are at present that the difference is almost more conspicuous than the similarity. The consumer needs a lot more protection now than he needed then; and *caveat venditor* seems a highly desirable principle for the Government to enforce."

"What you say is true enough," the Senator admitted, "but what worries me is something a little different. The Securities Act seems to me to go much further than you suggest. It seems to imply the existence of that face-to-face meeting you spoke of. It passes the responsibility for any misrepresentation on down from issuer and underwriter to other distributing agents who can't possibly know very much about what they're selling. If it should be strictly enforced it seems to me it would break up the ordinary marketing channels for capital and require the substitution of others. Those others would be the kind we had fifty years ago and which we outgrew because they couldn't handle the volume or make the necessary connections. In other words the people who wrote that act might as well have skipped the last fifty years of our history. You'll find it can't be enforced. I don't think the same thing is true of the Copeland bill now. I understand it was changed so that the whole responsibility rests on the first issuer, so to speak, of the goods sold, or the advertiser of them. That's all right. But it seems to me in both cases that if we were to follow the theory implicit in A.A.A. and N.R.A. we should have done the whole thing in another way."

"Go on," I said. "I can see that we are getting to the point now."

"Yes," he said, "and it's a point you won't like. Well, in the case of food and drugs, the standards and protections should have been written into the codes—"

"Good Lord!" I said. "Some of us tried all summer to get the industries to do just that. And we got exactly no response at all. People are still being swindled, poisoned and chucked under the chin. Personally, I don't like that, and so long as—"

"Now, now, wait a minute," he said, "I know what happened. No real attempt, backed up by a government in complete agreement, was made, and you know it. My point is still valid. Those standards ought to be written and enforced by industries and advertisers themselves. But my main point concerns the Securities Act. What that law ought to have been addressed to was real instead of fanciful protection for the buyers of securities. The way to protect investors is to keep wildcatters out of business altogether. In fact no one ought to go into industries which are already overcapitalized. And when they are in they ought to pursue the kind of policies which would insure safe returns instead of high and speculative ones."

"I see," I said, "you feel that what was really being dealt with was the process which economists call 'capital allocation' and that the legislation ought really to have controlled that."

"Not exactly," he said. "What I feel is that this is the kind of thing which the codes ought to do—or which industry ought to be compelled to do through its codes for itself. In fact something of the kind is being done now. I noticed the other day that a lot of hosiery mills were shut down by the code authority when overproduction showed up. It wouldn't be illogical to say that so long as such a condition exists, no new business could be started or any old one expanded. And if they weren't, no investors would need protection because no securities would be sold."

"Well," I said, "you have a conception of self-government for industry which I am afraid goes further than industrialists are willing to go. Meanwhile I don't see anything improper in protecting consumers in the old-fashioned way. I admit it is old-fashioned. But I don't see industry moving very fast in the direction you suggest. Maybe it will happen. When it does these laws will become obsolete. And maybe the Securities Act goes too far in imputing responsibility. But just now I don't think so."

"But you admit inconsistency?"

"Yes, if you insist."

"That's my point. We'll have to do something about it. But right now I've got to go home. Good night."

I took him to the door. The sky dripped and the wind

blew. I closed the door and went back to my detective story. It was peaceful—and above all simple—there before the fire. What adventurousness and complexity there was in life could for the moment be kept vicarious. Sometimes Senator Progressive is a little too insistent. None of us likes to be driven too hard.

XVI

THE SENATOR AND BEAUREGARD BOONE

MY room in the Department of Agriculture has three doors. One of them, which is used by most people who come to see me, is guarded in the orthodox way; but anyone who knows how can come in by either of the other two without asking leave of anyone. On a particularly gloomy day in December both these doors opened at once. I looked up from my papers and maps somewhat casually, then with greater interest as I realized what an occasion was imminent.

One door was admitting Senator Progressive; the other Beauregard Boone; each had a newspaper in his hand. Each of them stopped just inside the door looking at the other in what I sensed was a suspicious way.

"Can it be possible," I asked, "that you two are not acquainted?"

Each acknowledged that this was true. So I duly introduced them. Beauregard Boone, of course, had known the Senator from the press gallery. He had accorded him, as I discovered later, as much credit for statesmanship as any newspaper man ever does any legislator. And the Senator, in spite of his prejudice against what he firmly believes to be a venal and ungrateful press, had nevertheless discriminated sufficient y to be aware that the correspondent of *The Metropolitan Courier* was a genuine ally in the cause he holds so close at heart.

After a few rather forced pleasantries they came and sat beside my desk.

"Are you trying to conceal those newspapers from me or from each other?" I asked.

"Did you see . . ." the Senator began.

"Yes," I said, "I'm an early riser. I saw it long ago—several hours."

Beauregard has, by mutual, even if tacit, consent appointed himself guardian of my appearance to the public. The article by another correspondent in his own paper had excited him too.

"This guy goes the whole length this time," he said. "He's been working up to it for a good while. He comes right out now and puts his finger on you as the administration radical. He says you're a Socialist, that you have designs on our American institutions—subversive ones—what I want to know is whether he's ever talked to you."

"Once," I said. "The Secretary and I had him to lunch along last April. We talked mostly about A.A.A. That was when it was in the making. He went away that time and perverted everything we said. He chose a line then and he's just sticking to it."

"And you've never seen him since?"

"No," I said. "Of course a man with his powers of divination doesn't need any more than that to go on. He reads people's minds from afar. If he really took the trouble to understand me he would be deprived of a lovely dummy. He gets a great kick out of standing me up and knocking me over. I don't see that it does much harm and it lets him work off a lot of spleen."

"What's the matter with him anyway?" the Senator demanded. "I have a personal interest in it; he puts me in the same class."

"Well," said Beauregard, "the correspondents say of him that he let Mr. Hoover's ham and eggs go to his head." The Senator looked puzzled. "Mr. Hoover used to ask him to breakfast," he explained. "You see some of these birds fall for that. And then things change. They never understand. This man can't get this New Deal and it enrages him. A lot of younger men who do get it are coming along. And they're stealing his public."

The Senator wasn't quite satisfied.

"You never were a Socialist, were you?" he asked me.

Beauregard spoke up. "He's always been the enemy of any 'ism,'" he said. "He's what you call an experimentalist— which means, I suppose, that he doesn't think it's possible to read the future in detail; so he won't tolerate any doctrine about it. Old Gloomy Gus was right about one thing though. My client believes that farmers and workers have got to get morè of what's going than they've had up to now."

"Well," said the Senator, "that's what we all believe. I myself have said so a hundred times. Why, out in my state just the other day . . ."

Beauregard interrupted rudely. "The question right now is, What'll we do about this? This guy here"—he pointed to the paper—"and some of your academic friends are by way of making you out a real danger to American institutions. That's bad. They'll get you if this keeps up."

The Senator seemed to agree, so I made the best argument I could for sheer inaction.

"In the first place," I said, "the die-hards always have to have a goat. Unfortunately, through no fault of my own, I'm it. The game is, of course, to pick us off one by one, and gradually work toward the center. I'm vulnerable because Americans don't love pedagogues and I seem to be one. Also because I really am the enemy of all these fellows represent— they exaggerate my effectiveness for their own purposes—but essentially they are right. I don't believe the institutions which gave us these years of misery can be altogether sound. I'd like to change them. Why should I hide it?"

"Yes, I know," said Beauregard, "but how?"

"Well, you see, I grew up in an American small town and I've never forgot it. No one was very rich there; but no one was very poor either. We're past Christmas now. But it wasn't really Christmas to me without snow on hemlocks, bobsleds and sleigh bells, a Christmas tree in the church by the common—all these things. They're really American to me. I can't make this Park Avenue, country-club life seem right, along with slums and bread lines. This fellow you complain of represents slums, bread lines, ballyhoo, speculation—all the elements in the last few decades that I can't make fit into my picture of American institutions. I'm for decentralization, for simplicity of life, along with a recognition of the complexity of industrial and scientific civilization. It seems to me that electricity, vacuum tubes, Diesel engines and all these other things ought to make it possible for all of us to approximate that no-riches, no-poverty kind of life in which I grew up. I'd certainly set the sleigh bells jingling again in thousands of village streets if I could. . . ."

"Your reminiscences are wasted on us," Beauregard interjected. "But, you know, that's the line you ought to develop. These guys are making you seem like the big, bad wolf."

"I wish I were to them," I said.

"I know, I know," he said, "but put the emphasis the other way. You're always negative these days. You're seeming to object to everything, holding things down, preventing these fellows from getting what they want. Just reverse it. Talk about what you want. It seems to me like what about 120,000,000 of us want. People are getting convinced that unless these birds can have their own way, the whole country will go to the dogs pronto."

"No," the Senator said, "you're wrong." He had listened to me thoughtfully. "The people really sense it. No one was

ever so discredited as these die-hards are now. The reason
they're after our friend here is that they suffer from the
illusion that if they get rid of him—and a few others of us—
they can run the Government again as they're used to doing
it. People really have an instinct that this administration is
sound. As for him, personally, it doesn't much matter. Most
of the dust up about him is irrelevant. It's connected with
the Food and Drug bill. A lot of quacks and fakers who prey
on small people and therefore have close connections with
them are spreading poison, all right, but they'll soon see
through that. He really believes that honesty is necessary in
business. So do they, really. He believes that the Government
ought to protect their livings and their standards. So do
they, except that they resent the necessity of paying for it.
But it's a good cause and it will win its own way. I believe
we ought to go on as we are, simply and straightforwardly.
If we try to fight this fire with another fire we're likely to
lose the advantages we have."

"Well," said Beauregard, "nobody likes to have bricks
thrown at him."

"But that's inevitable," I said. "They've tied me up to
some things the newspapers don't like a bit. I think they will.
I'm sure they have more to gain than to lose in the long
run. But my telling them that makes them just as mad as
it always does when anyone takes a holier-than-thou attitude.
They're telling me pretty freely to mind my own business."

He snorted. "Good grief, you do."

"I know," I said. "But that isn't the point. It serves the
purpose to call me all the names which indicate the attitudes
people detest most. Accuracy isn't desired."

"Well, anyway," he said, "it makes me sore. And I think
it's time you fixed yourself up even at the expense of a little
mendacity; if necessary, I'd sacrifice some of the program."

The Senator was horrified. "If you're going to advise him
on his relations with the public," he said, "you'd better drop
that line. No one person is as important as that. Maybe I
was wrong to say that all of us have to stick. Perhaps someone
ought to be sacrificed. Their illusions may be justified.
Maybe the whole cause would be served if they did succeed
in discrediting him. If we could go on then and seem more
respectable for having lost a discreditable colleague, it might
quiet down the opposition."

"Rats!" said Beauregard venomously. "That's an old politician's trick. And it works about as well as most of them—
just for a minute. You're always willing to sacrifice anybody
but yourselves. This guy here is my friend and I'm for him.
Cause! What's a cause? It's what comes out of someone's
head. Your cause is you. His cause is him. I like him so I'm
for his cause. But don't try the disembodied spirit on me.
If you lose him you're that much poorer however little you
may think he counts for. You'd better stick now. They'll be
at you next. Then someone is certainly going to get the
bright idea that you'd better be dropped overboard. Pretty
soon you'll all be picked off and you can decorate your pretty
causes all you like in private life where no one will pay any
attention to it."

The Senator laughed. "You're right," he said. "I'll stick.
Maybe I'd better take over more of the load myself. I might
make a speech out in . . ."

"That's it, that's it," said Beauregard. "Just what we need.
You tell 'em how he loves the little towns and the sleigh
bells. Myself, I like Broadway. But it's a good line. Well, got
to go. Don't say anything without asking me." He buttoned
his coat and pulled down his hat. "Well," he said as he
stopped by the door, grinning, "jingle, jingle, you two."

XVII

THE PLACE OF GOVERNMENT IN A NATIONAL LAND PROGRAM *

THE Federal Government will, I believe, perform two functions with respect to our land in the future. It will directly hold and administer, as public forests, parks, game preserves, grazing ranges, recreation centers and the like, all areas which cannot at the time be effectively operated under private ownership. And it will control the private use of the areas held by individuals to whatever extent is found necessary for maintaining continuous productivity. It is only by conceiving the Government in this double active and supervisory rôle that we can expect to attain a permanent system of agriculture.

A national land program as comprehensive as this has not yet been undertaken. Past developments, however, have demonstrated the ineffectiveness of a land system which depends wholly on private management. And we have already made many commitments which are inconsistent with complete laissez faire and which clearly enough foreshadow the future. It will be a different future, to which we can look forward with new hope of prosperity for agriculture and of protection for the greatest of all our resources—the land.

Our earliest governmental attitude towards the land was one which sought to get it into private ownership promptly and speedily, so that it might be settled and become productive. This attitude was in consonance with the unlimited confidence we then had in individual enterprise. We believed in

* Address delivered at the Annual Meeting of the American Farm Economics Association, Philadelphia, Dec. 29, 1933.

it for farmers as well as for business men. We expected it to produce the best results, not only for individuals but for society; and it did serve the purposes of that time. The country was settled with great speed; its resources were made use of. But the settlement was often unwise, and the exploitation was frequently wasteful.

Faced with apparently unlimited natural resources, the active and individualistic expansion was the natural movement in a pioneer economy. The public domain was looked upon as properly belonging to anyone who could find uses for it; it was also a source of public revenue, and the states at first tried to secure important income from its sale. But prices were so low that an unskilled laborer could often save enough in one year to buy an 80-acre farm; and expectations of revenue were largely disappointed. Gradually the policy shifted to one of encouraging development by outright gift, both to actual settlers and to railways. Between 1841 and 1861, three times as much public land was given away as was sold. The passage of the Homestead Act in 1862 represented the culmination of efforts to stimulate settlement. By the end of the century, most of the desirable land was in farms—including much land which should never have been put under the plow. After the homestead allotment was increased from 160 acres to 640 acres to make settlement possible in dry-farming regions, the difficulty of successful homesteading became epitomized in the western legend: "The Government bets the homesteader 640 acres of land that he can't live on it without starving to death."

The century of rapid expansion was not without its own economic difficulties. Three times—after the Napoleonic wars, after the Civil War, and in the nineties—our agricultural output exceeded the ability of foreign countries to take our surpluses; and prolonged periods of low prices occurred.

Each time, however, the growth of population in Europe, and a similar growth here among pioneer families innocent of birth control, together with a thronging immigration from Europe, created new markets and furnished a new stimulus to expansion.

But even in the midst of this, serious land difficulties began to appear in the older regions. As the railways conquered the rugged barriers of the Appalachians, cheap corn and live stock from western New York and the Ohio Valley made life more and more difficult for the small rugged holdings in the New England hills, and our first "abandoned farms" appeared. The far greater flood of produce from the prairies, and still later the cheap grain and cattle from the western plains, set levels of competition which were ruinous for eastern farmers. In some counties of the Atlantic Seaboard states, cultivated acreage has been shrinking since the Civil War, and the contraction is still under way.

These difficulties in the older regions were only incidents in the major movement of expansion, ones we preferred not to notice and which we could neglect, since westward migration was open to all. By the end of the century, the most valuable parts of the public domain, including a large part of our agricultural, forest and mineral resources, had passed into private hands. Except for emphasis on speedy settlement and full exploitation, this vast gift of resources was made by the Government to its citizens without thought of consequence.

Toward the turn of the century, doubts began to arise; some few questioners began to ask whether use of land solely in the interest of each individual holder was the only possible way to proceed. Possibly the criticisms of Karl Marx and Henry George had begun to awaken skepticism, even if not many Americans accepted their conclusions. It was then that the Government first began to study our resources and to give some thought to their possible exhaustion. The Geological Survey began to map the country; soil surveys were begun; there followed the study of soil constituents and plant needs, and surveys of farm-management methods and results.

Early in the century our doubts and our newly acquired knowledge resulted in a dramatic controversy over the "conservation of natural resources." The practical result of the discussion of those years was the understanding that private ownership did not protect posterity; and that the Government itself would have to hold and administer at least some of our basic resources if any protection at all was to be had. The Forest Service was established to administer many of the large tracts of forest still remaining in public hands; the Park Service, to develop national parks for public recreation; and the Reclamation Service, to increase the area of arable land, especially by irrigation. Meanwhile the Land Office continued to control the disposal of the remaining public domain; and the Office of Indian Affairs administered the holdings of the Indians—very largely, it might be noted, with regard to the wishes of white men who wanted to use them.

These various kinds of public action were developing, each in its own uncoördinated way, when the World War intruded itself and changed the whole course of economic development, at least for many years. Until the War, our population had been growing faster than our farm production; our agricultural exports were shrinking; and the "high cost of living" was under investigation. The War left the world with a swollen capacity to produce foodstuffs. And for fifteen years afterward we refused to face the problem of what to do about our farm production. This striking reversal came suddenly, of course, but even so our adjustment to the conditions it imposed was inexcusably delayed.

Throughout this postwar period, our land agencies largely followed the directions given them by their initial creation. The Reclamation Service continued to develop new projects without considering the failure of previous projects to pay their way, or the questionable demand for the output of the new land. The Indian Bureau continued to lease new tracts of land to settlers. The land-settlement agents of railways, states, and lumber companies continued to entice settlers into occupying new or cut-over lands and farming them, regardless of the failure of those who had tried and failed or those who were still struggling desperately to make ends meet on these lands which ought never to have been settled. The Forest Service and the Park Service continued to develop their projects and to acquire lands, but with a view to their own discursive ends and not to those of the country as a whole. Here and there, it is true, state or Federal Government agencies made careful surveys of the actual conditions among farmers in various regions, and of the success or failure of settlers under various conditions. The Division of Land Economics of the Department of Agriculture began to study the basic economic problems concerned with land, and to develop broad information on the subject. As a whole, however, there was no single Federal agency to guide settlement and to create policies.

The shock of the depression has at last awakened us to a new attitude. We no longer regard land as land alone; we regard it as one of the central and controlling elements in our whole national economy. More than that, we realize that upon the manner and character of its use may depend the welfare, not only of our descendants, but of ourselves. Widespread industrial disorganization and unemployment, together with the failure of industry to right itself through the old individualistic processes, has led by degrees to the general expectation that the Government will assume responsibility for the reëstablishment of economic activity. One part of this governmental recovery program, as we all know, is the Agricultural Adjustment Administration, with its sweeping efforts to adjust the whole of agriculture to fundamental needs.

The recovery program, therefore, brings us finally face to face with the necessity for devising a plan which shall draw together our divergent efforts and look forward as far as is possible toward permanent policy. Not only is it necessary for us to conserve our natural resources for the welfare of posterity; it is also necessary to regulate the use of land resources for the welfare of the living generations. We have depended too long on the hope that private ownership and control would operate somehow for the benefit of society as a whole. That hope has not been realized. Now we are coming to believe that our resources will best be utilized for the benefit of all if we give deliberate study to the needs of society and adjust our land uses to those needs.

What we face today is a deliberate attempt to weigh all phases of the land problem, and to map out an appropriate long-time policy, in which all uses of land and the potential need for each use are given their proper place. The job is not an easy one, and we cannot get a perfect answer at the first attempt. All alternatives seem undesirable, sometimes, when we try to penetrate the future. We have, however, to choose as best we can. But we cannot be other than tentative until the future direction of our economic growth becomes more certain. We can work out now only a first rough approximation, subject to change and modification as subsequent developments give us firmer grounds for prediction. But the mere effort of trying to sketch a plan will make us more aware of the long-time implications of particular present or prospective policies, and so help to shape the eventual developments in a systematic and really comprehensive way.

Everyone is ready to agree, I believe, that the Government should itself hold and administer those tracts which cannot be effectively operated under private ownership. As the Forest and Park Services have already demonstrated, governmental agencies can administer such areas effectively for the general welfare and still leave them available for other productive uses when they may be needed. But what of the supermarginal areas, those which are now appropriately devoted to farming?

We are now engaged in a drastic program of controlling the output of agricultural products for the emergency. This in itself means that we are trying to control the entire utilization of all our agricultural land. There are other methods already in use by which governmental agencies control the use of lands for other purposes—police regulations in towns, and zoning ordinances or laws in cities and suburbs; and even local or regional planning boards.

One way to control agricultural output is to restrict directly the use of the land; either by vetoing certain products through voluntary contracts; or by classifying and zoning and then proceeding to enforce such uses as fall into general definitions. Either of these involves maintaining more men and more land than are really needed. What is done is merely to keep a part of each field or each farm out of use. It seems to me obvious that this cannot be the characteristic feature of a permanent policy. There is no recognition in it of the basic conditions which ought to determine the use of the land. It adjusts supply to the moment's market, but it neither conserves the land nor makes provision for permanently bettering farmers' lives.

A second method of controlling the total volume of farm

products would be for the Government to limit the area available for production, by itself acquiring and devoting to other uses all the land in excess of that needed for production. It would then be unnecessary to restrict the total output on areas remaining in use, although it might still be desirable to furnish a certain amount of guidance in the selection of crops. The area of land in production would be sufficiently limited so that it could be operated at its utmost efficiency without flooding markets and destroying exchangeability. Such a system would envisage a commercial agriculture made up of the most efficient farmers operating the best of our lands, with the remaining lands being used in other ways, and the remaining farmers devoting their time to other occupations. Something of this sort seems much more reasonable than the present emergency program of blanket reductions; it may be expected that as sharp necessity is relieved, and our future needs for land become more clearly defined, the emergency efforts of the present will gradually evolve into some such program of complete control and efficient utilization.

The ways in which the land withdrawn from cultivation can be used are reasonably clear. Forests, parks, wild-life preserves, the prevention of erosion, the protection of water supplies, and the prevention of floods, all can be planned with reference to their usefulness to the present population and to the probable needs of the future. Furthermore, the use of this land for agricultural production, such as the regulated pasturage in national forests, and controlled grazing on range preserves which may later be established, can be definitely adjusted to current needs. The more difficult part of the program is to chart and develop the program of land withdrawal. It is easy to say, "Take the submarginal land out of use"; but it is more difficult to say just what we mean by submarginal land, and where it is; or to offer more attractive alternatives to the people who now live there.

Several basic problems must be answered before we can say how much of our present farm land area is truly submarginal. Three of these problems stand out as dominant:

1. How far will our future development be toward a highly nationalistic, self-contained economy, with only a minimum dependence on foreign trade; and how far will it be toward a reëstablishment of international trade?

2. How far and how fast will our population grow; and how far will population growth be offset by continuing increases in the efficiency of agricultural production?

3. Will many of our citizens continue to live at very low levels, on relatively inadequate and poorly balanced diets; or will we succeed in devising an economic organization which creates purchasing power as rapidly as it creates goods?

These broad questions would each require extensive discussion to develop adequately. I can attempt here no more than a very brief exploration of some of the background of fact which is relevant to each.

No one can say as yet whether we shall turn away from our recent economic nationalism. Certainly the world as a whole has followed this course more and more intently since the War. The expansion of agricultural production throughout the world during and immediately following the War, and the creation of many new international boundaries by the peace treaties, were a response to nationalistic sentiments; but the organization of nationalism helped to fix its patterns. The peace treaties intensified the memory of war-time privations and the rankling hatreds which had found expression on the fields of battle. As Europe restored her power to produce, and as technical improvements stimulated further increases in production in the exporting countries, the pressure of farm supplies on international markets became increasingly intense. The importing countries raised barriers to protect their farmers and to shut out competition. The exporting countries subsidized production and assisted exports. World prices fell lower and lower, while consumption diminished and production increased—exactly contrary to classical economic laws.

This system of protection brought the world to its present leaden lethargy. The current depression is a consequence of the sentiment of nationalism carried into inappropriate economic fields. It was not shared at first by the United States. But in this, no more than in the War, could we pursue a policy which ran against that of the rest of the world. We too have been caught in the universal movement toward isolation. And our emergency program for agriculture has had to reflect it. This trend may be reversed by slow, hard stages, but that reversal has not yet begun. It is true that wheat-growing nations throughout the world have agreed to coöperate with us in increasing consumption and in restricting production and exports. Recently there have been suggestions that this coöperation might even go so far as to establish definite levels of price in world markets. This agreement will at least help to hold for us a larger share in the world wheat trade than if we had reduced our wheat production while other countries continued to produce. It is even possible that world trade may be revived by a series of such agreements, covering other commodities familiar to international commerce, with definite international arrangements concerning what each country will sell to every other country, and concerning what products and services will be accepted in return. World trade might be reëstablished on such a basis. There seems to be much less possibility that restoration might take place on the old basis, with freedom of movement on an individual competitive basis, with only slight governmental intervention. But if world trade should be restored in either way, our agriculture would not need to be a self-sufficient one; we could resume our export of those agricultural products which we were best suited to produce. But if foreign trade is not restored, and remains at the low levels of recent years, we shall be forced into a sharp contraction of cultivated land. As things are now, possibly 50,000,-000 acres, or one-seventh of our entire cultivated acreage, would need to be withdrawn to balance present low demands. If all the land withdrawn were taken from the least productive regions, where yields are much less than the average, many more acres would be required to achieve the same reduction in output.

When we come to population growth we are on somewhat firmer ground. Our annual increase has been steadily diminishing; unless we change our present restrictive immigration policy very drastically, we may reach a state of stationary or even declining population within a few decades. Such a condition, with a large and increasing proportion of people in the older ages, may create profound changes in American life; but so far as food supplies are concerned fewer acres will be required to produce them. At the same time, our agricultural technologists will doubtless continue to improve seeds and breeds, as well as cultural, fertilizing and feeding practices. They have done so in the past and I see no reason for anticipating change. As a result, therefore, unless there is prolonged depression, our output per worker, per acre, and per animal, will continue to increase. If I were to hazard a guess, it would be that from this time on agricultural efficiency will increase more rapidly than will domestic population; so that if it were not for the possibility of increased exports and improved standards of living, we should need each year even less land than we now have in use, rather than more.

When we come to improved standards of living, however, we find very large potentialities of increased consumption. Our distribution of wealth has been so uneven that millions of adults and children have lived on inadequate diets—the more expensive foods, such as milk, eggs and vegetables have been denied them. Millions also have gone inadequately clothed, even while the producers of these very products have had surpluses rotting in the fields or were driving the prices they received down to levels which destroyed purchasing power and deprived many in turn of the materials we like to think of as making up an American standard. We do know that an adequate diet, properly balanced as to all the essential food elements and sufficiently ample to provide for healthy living, would require a larger area than would a more limited diet. The Bureau of Home Economics has recently published standards ranging from a "restricted emergency diet" to a "liberal diet." Preliminary calculations from these standards indicate that it would take 67 percent more acreage to supply each person with the materials for the "liberal" than with those for the "restricted" diet.

No one knows, of course, how many persons have been living on various substandard diets; neither does anyone know how long it will take us to get our economic machine to running in such a coördinated manner that every person now underprivileged is provided with the food for a liberal diet. Education will be necessary, as well as economic organization; incomes have been so low in many regions and among many classes that housewives would not know or appreciate proper food if it should be made available to them. The potentialities in this direction remain to be explored. To the extent that we can substitute increased per-capita consump-

tion of foods for the present emergency program of adjustment, we shall be relieved of the necessity for restriction
which no one likes—least of all the farmers.

The general character of the ways in which our domestic
consumption may change are already indicated by the trends
of the past decade or two. We have been increasing our per-
capita consumption of sugar, poultry, dairy products, fresh
fruits and vegetables; we have been decreasing our per-capita
consumption of heavy starchy foods like wheat and potatoes;
and we have been about maintaining our consumption of
meat. All of these changes, with the exception of the upward
trend in sugar, are in general agreement with the advice of
experts in nutrition. Comparisons among the budgets of families on different levels of income indicate also that much
more meat, especially of the smaller and leaner cuts, would
be consumed if incomes were generally raised. We shall have
to make careful and intensive studies of nutrition, of trends
in consumption, and also of different standards at different
levels of income, before we can judge even tentatively how
greatly and how rapidly our domestic consumption may
change. It is a promising and attractive field for investigation.
In comparison with the pitiful picture of the decreasing consumption of many foods during the depression years; of actual starvation and widespread malnutrition; of thousands of
persons on relief budgets both insufficient and unappetizing,
it certainly is a more inspiring prospect to turn our attention
to what and how we might consume if everyone had enough.

Lest I be misunderstood, however, I must reiterate again
that attaining such an adequate consumption of food by all
our citizens depends upon a proper functioning of our whole
economic system. We must find means to organize our activities so that each person can use his abilities in the kind of
work for which he is best suited, taking account of the need

for each kind of product; so that the production of each is in proportion to the production of other things; and so that each worker has sufficient income to purchase his fair share of all we produce. Such a proportion between production and consumption, and between production and buying power, must not be attained in a static sense, with an absence of progress, but must be maintained while continual improvement in methods of production and in quality gives each worker a constantly better standard of living and greater leisure. Such a system is the goal of all our efforts; only to the extent to which it is attained can we expect a real increase in domestic consumption.

This brings me to the fact that during the depression, over two million persons have returned to farms, reversing the population movement of many years. If our economic system had continued to break apart, more and more people would have returned to the land, preferring safety at low levels to a precarious existence with the chance of starvation or exposure in some future crisis. This back-to-the-farm movement is a temporary phenomenon of the depression; if we can reestablish industrial activity on a satisfactory basis, the normal cityward trend will reappear. The continuous increase in output per worker, both on farms and in factories, and the fact that the per-capita consumption of many farm products is not very flexible, while the demand for most industrial products seems to be almost indefinitely elastic, makes it practically inevitable that the population in commercial agriculture will continue to decrease, once a functioning industrial life is reëstablished to absorb the excess workers.

In fact, we already had too many commercial farmers before the depression. Three-fourths of our farmers already produce all that we consume domestically; the remaining quarter on small unproductive farms produce relatively little. If full use were made of what is already known of the technique of farm production, we could probably raise all the farm products we need with half our present farmers, or 12.5 percent of our total working population. These facts focus attention on the human side of the problem. There are many persons who are happier in a simple existence, living largely through their own efforts in a self-sufficient way. The peasant homes of Europe are evidence that simplicity of this sort is satisfactory. We had it once in America; and there are those who feel that we lost something valuable in our departure from it. Some of our remaining self-sufficient farmers would prefer to go on living as they are; in many cases, however, they would be glad to exchange their present unproductive farms for better-located and more fertile tracts; and to have the opportunity to do some outside work from time to time, in forestry or in a near-by small-scale industry. Our Subsistence Homesteads projects will provide some exceedingly useful experiments in this direction; the proportion of our population which likes to lead semi-independent lives, with some acres to guarantee their own subsistence, and with supplementary opportunities for income from industry, may be larger than we suspect. The cultural level of such living, too, may be raised by education in handicrafts and other home industries. As a whole, however, I am inclined to believe that such settlements will function merely as small eddies of retreat for exceptional persons; and that the greater part of our population will prefer to live and work in the more active and vigorous main stream of a highly complex civilization. To the extent that this is true, we must be prepared to absorb very large numbers of persons from farms into our general industrial and urban life.

In this brief sketch I have indicated only a few of the many questions to which we must find answers before we shall know how many cultivated acres we may require. I have indicated only by inference the vast amount of careful investigation and planning which is essential for the establishment of a policy. No one can attempt to say as yet, with any exactness, how many submarginal acres there are, or how rapidly we should attempt to take those acres out of use.

The work which has already been done on land utilization, however, is sufficient to indicate in a general way the areas from which such submarginal lands will for the most part come, even though we cannot yet say just how much will eventually need to be retired. Even in these areas there is much land which is highly productive and which can undoubtedly be continued in production; and outside these areas there are many poor tracts which might well be withdrawn. Furthermore, there are extensive unused areas in the general submarginal regions which are of much higher productive ability than other lands which are being farmed; a good part of the readjustment may involve helping families which are struggling along on very infertile tracts and who may desire to shift to better areas where they can live happier lives, though still on a self-sufficing basis. In no case, I should say, will these shifts of population need to be great in distance or severe in their strain on local affiliations and pride.

The first great region of limited productive ability is the Appalachian highland of the eastern United States, plus certain poorer portions of the adjacent Piedmont plateau and coastal plain. This region is largely in the East and Southeast. Besides the original low natural fertility of much of this land, large portions of it have been reduced in productivity by long-continued overcropping, by deforestation, or by erosion. The slowness with which purely economic pressures induce human beings to move from areas in which they have once become firmly rooted is clearly indicated by the persistence with which some of the population clings to the worst lands in this area, in spite of the availability of much better lands quite near by.

The second great area of relatively poor land is the cut-overs along the Great Lakes from Michigan to Minnesota. An enormous proportion of this land is tax-delinquent. For many years real-estate concerns have enticed new settlers into these regions, in spite of the lack of success of settlers already there. With the timber gone and with present low levels of farm prices, much of this area is hopeless from the point of view either of profitable agriculture or a decent level of self-sufficiency. Even here, however, there are better tracts which would support much higher standards of living than other land near by, on which families are now striving to exist.

The third great area extends along the western border of the Great Plains. This region is subject to great extremes in rainfall, with adequate moisture sometimes for several years in succession, followed by extreme drought for a term of years. Only by maintaining very heavy reserves, both of feed and cash, and following systems of dry farming which make the most of the moisture, can a permanent type of agriculture be maintained here. This dry-farming land came into use during the period of relatively high prices for farm products; now that the native sod has been destroyed, it is difficult to get the land back into more extensive uses. Some of it is obviously marginal at present prices of wheat; if wheat prices were to return to previous high levels much of it would again be profitable, at least if good and bad years were averaged. Here too, there is much variation in fertility and in other characteristics; even if the present and potential outlets for wheat should require that much of such land be withdrawn from cultivation for a time, there would still remain many tracts which would remain in farm use.

These three great areas, together with smaller areas which might be indicated elsewhere, constitute the regions within which the program of land classification and land withdrawal might be carried forward first and most intensively. Much more study of each area within the regions would have to be made, to determine whether it might pay to keep it in production, or to what other use it might best be devoted. The alternatives would have to be considered. Not only land and the demands for farm products would be involved, but also the cost of providing local government, and of such facilities as schools, roads, telephones, and postal services, both in the present areas and in those in which the present population might be offered an opportunity to settle. Where extensive areas were involved, provision might have to be made to offer new and better opportunities not only to the present farmers, but also to the merchants, doctors, and other business and professional people in the small towns in the region which now serve the farmers there. After the plans were made, arrangements would have to be perfected and funds provided for the purchase of such of the land as is in private ownership, or to secure long-time control through restrictive "easements" or rentals; and to offer the present population, country and town, opportunities to shift to other and more satisfactory places and ways of living.

Any such program as that just sketched would obviously have to be developed gradually over a period of time. Furthermore, it could not be based upon drastic compulsory action by the central Government; instead, it would have to be carried out with the fullest coöperation of the states and counties involved. The Federal Government might merely take the responsibility for the general scope, character, and financing of the plan, leaving most of the local decisions to the local authorities. In any event full local understanding and support would be essential, and such support would have to be developed by education and discussion, concurrently with research and planning. To succeed in America, such fundamental changes must be made with the coöperation and assistance of the persons involved; only so could the program function over a long period of time.

Some preliminary studies of the character indicated have already been made. In the eastern Kentucky mountains, for example, the resources for the support of the dense rural population are inadequate, and the resources which exist are improperly utilized. Alternate clearing and abandonment of the land has reduced the productive capacity alike for crops, grazing, and forest uses. An adequate land program for.this region would involve the transfer of part of the population to other more favored agricultural areas, and the partial employment of the remaining population in new industries. Reforestation would often be essential. Similarly, in the cut-over areas, preliminary surveys have shown that in many places the population is so sparse that the cost of maintaining schools, roads, mails and other services is beyond the community's resources. In such regions mere consolidation of the farmers on the best of the available land would markedly lower such public costs, and make the burden of taxes far more readily carried. In other areas the standards of living might be materially improved by shifting the population from the hills into adjacent valleys, where subsistence farming would support a decent standard.

Many such individual studies have been made in the past. What is needed now is to combine and coördinate them through a national policy which considers the whole program in its broadest aspects, and which provides the funds required to put the plans into definite action.

The establishment of a national land-use planning committee two years ago constituted the first step toward such definite action. Through its conferences and the many reports of its committees and subcommittees, general attention was directed to some of the problems involved and to the need for a national program. The present national administration, with its greater readiness to assume the responsibility for governmental action in fields where private initiative has not been sufficient, is proceeding to build on this foundation. Already effective steps have been taken to eliminate the conflict in objectives between the Department of the Interior and the Department of Agriculture. A Joint Land Planning Committee, representing these two Departments and the National Planning Board, has been established to coördinate all Federal actions with respect to land policy, including forests, parks, Indian reservations, public domain, reclamation, erosion, subsistence homesteads, etc.

As one of the first results of the new policy of national coördination of land programs, the President has already announced that hereafter reclamation projects will not be developed without regard to the potential need for lands. Instead, where it is found that a particular project will bring in new areas better suited to cultivation than those now in use, funds will be made available to take out of cultivation an area of submarginal land of an equal productivity. This is only a step in the direction of the proper balance between lands in farm use and area needed; but it is a step in the right direction. The funds from this commitment, when available, will provide for the first steps toward readjustment in the use of our land resources. As the recovery effort shifts from emergency devices toward more long-time planning, and as new legislation provides additional resources for land acquisition or control, we should find the long-time program taking increasingly definite shape.

The land is the common heritage of all our people. In the past, the Government has squandered it, heedlessly and wastefully. The results of this folly have long been apparent in denuded hills, eroded gullies, flooding rivers, and the pitifully poor populations of many secluded regions, and over some broad areas not so secluded. A quarter of a century ago the Government began giving some attention to conserving, for the protection of posterity, the last remaining bits of this great heritage. Private control has failed to use wisely its control of land. The postwar decade of low farm incomes, and the subsequent period of industrial collapse, now make us realize that the use which is made of the land is of immediate and vital interest to us all.

For the first time, the Government is thinking of land as a whole. For the first time, we are preparing to build a land program which will control the use of that greatest of all natural resources, not merely for the benefit of those who happen to hold title to it, but for the greater welfare of all the citizens of the country. The exact part which the Government will play, and the part which private initiative will play, still remains to be worked out. The problems to be solved are both intricate and vast. But the question is clearly before us. It is one we cannot evade. We must develop the answer to it, effectively, soundly, and workably, if our civilization is to continue on a broad and wholesome base.

XVIII
INTERNATIONAL ECONOMIC POLICY

THE recovery effort since March, 1933, has occupied so much of everyone's mind that relatively little public attention has been given to international affairs. No one in the administration, however, minimizes the importance of this phase of recovery; no one doubts the necessity of earnest efforts to reëstablish our shattered trade relations with other nations. In many ways the depression we are fighting is an international phenomenon, and working our way out of it consequently requires international action.

Any discussion of this sort inevitably works back to the War and even beyond—to the time when we were borrowers from European nations and when they sent us more goods than we sent them. It was the War which reversed this situation. We then began to loan to them and to send them more goods than they sent us. The difference was that we liked our former situation, or at least accepted it as something natural; and that Europe now withdraws from acceptance of the situation, which is understandable in countries which are debtors, but which nevertheless makes trade resumption difficult. Instead of opening her markets to our goods, she shuts them tighter and tighter, putting up tariffs, imposing quotas, impounding funds for exchange. We have been foolish in our turn, too, if our position was to be made good. For we have attempted to maintain export balances along with high tariffs, two wholly inconsistent policies. Our loans abroad enabled foreign importers to buy; but our refusal to accept goods in exchange prevented exporters there from sending us goods. This is not exchange; it is some form of enforced charity with the Americans on the contributing end.

The sentiment of agrarian nationalism has swept the whole western world in most astounding fashion in postwar years, and it is important to remember that it is a sentiment rather than a calculated economic policy. It is perhaps traceable to causes which are uncertain and obscure. So it seems to me. France, Italy and Germany have preferred to pay more than a dollar and a half a bushel for wheat rather than buy it from us at about half that price. The same is true of many other of our products, some of them industrial, but the case there is not so severe since adjustment to demand is easier. Factories can be shut down much easier than farms.

There is little that can be done about such a situation except to hope that in time it will disappear. Perhaps the causes lie in the fright which was occasioned by the success of Germany's submarine campaign, perhaps in the superior political pressures which are exercised by agrarians, perhaps in a genuine reluctance to enter on a tenuous industrial career. However this may be, our goods are refused and we refuse theirs. There is an impasse which grows worse and worse. And many parts of our recovery program have unquestioningly been adapted to the situation as though it were permanent.

This had to be so. In agriculture there seemed to be no good purpose to be served by pretending that there still existed a foreign market which was in reality disappearing. In industry the administration was determined to raise wages and shorten hours regardless of what other countries might do. It seemed impossible also to persuade other countries to enter on an economic program which would genuinely relieve unemployment or would raise prices so that the burdens of debt might be relieved. And if the United States was to do these things alone it seemed necessary to be cut off from the rest of the world and to proceed as though other nations did not exist. Of course this country was in a position to do that if it had to be done. We were as nearly self-sufficient as any nation could be in the sense that we had most of the materials of living within our borders or immediately adjacent to the south of us and quite outside the European system. If, at the London Conference, Europe had shown a disposition to enter on policies similar to ours—to engage in public works, to raise prices and relieve debtors—a genuine turn toward internationalism might have come then. But there was no such disposition. And that was the real failure at London; the responsibility did not rest, I should say, with the United States.

It is barely possible that the conference might have succeeded in this if it had been held in Washington. The exposure of the statesmen to President Roosevelt's gallantry and charm; the understanding they might have got of what it was our nation was fully determined to do; the sense of renewed hope which had come to our people out of a program of courageous action—all this might have induced them to accept American leadership and to parallel the effort being made here. But that did not happen. Their imaginations were not fired, and they preferred to follow more orthodox courses.

The result of the nations' failure to agree has been evident ever since in the deepening of mutual distrust, in the increase of restrictions on trade, in the cutting off of one from another. We are forced to go our own way alone. We had no choice, really, if we were not to proceed in the same way that Europe did; and even that way required isolation, as anyone can see who looks carefully now at the European scene. It is nonsense to say that because we were forced to follow that course for the time being we too had become determined nationalists. What it did mean was that Americans had accepted the principle of a planned national life which could widen into internationalism only when others also abandoned laissez faire and began to plan along with us. No responsible statesman in this country has ever expressed an unwillingness to coöperate with any nation with whom it was possible to coöperate. Planning can and must become international. America cannot determine when others will make that possible. That is clearly up to them. But the western world cannot be put right until it happens; and it would be foolish to impute to the present administration a policy which leaves this out of account. Certainly no president and no secretary of state were ever more internationally minded than our own in the sense that the ills of the world rest on their hearts. And the Secretary of Agriculture has repeatedly and forcefully expressed an almost religious wish that we might better the condition of all nations by wise coöperative action.

The road to recovery is long and hard, which those of us who did not know in advance are discovering now. We face innumerable economic readjustments which might be made infinitely easier if we did not have to make them without coöperation. Perhaps we shall not have to. The world wheat agreement did, after all, come out of London. That instrument was not wholly satisfactory, but it did enable all of us to make together one adjustment which urgently needed to be made. And others might conceivably follow for other commodities, and not only agricultural ones. It may even be that this way is best; for by following it those interminable and unfruitful disputes about general principles, which serve only to enrage partisans and which accomplish no results, can be escaped.

But a program of restriction, though it may be necessary

for adjustment to changed conditions, cannot, even if it is world-wide, go to the root of the matter. These adjustments are needed; but something more is also needed. And this is an international program which will increase some kinds of trade as well as restrict some other kinds. For the United States the lesson which must be learned is that imports must be expanded. If it could come home to every workman, every farmer and every business man that there would be an increased number of jobs at higher pay, an increase in the market for farm products at higher prices, and an increase in the volume of trade at profitable levels, if our imports were enlarged, we should be in a better position to proceed with means to enlargement. But many Americans emphatically do not believe that. They still think it possible to sell abroad without buying from there; and how that paradox can be driven out of American minds no one seems to know. It is perhaps so stubborn a belief that we shall have to proceed in some such way as we proceeded in the other matter of the wheat agreement. It would, at least, be worth trying. The administration was fairly committed, by President Roosevelt's campaign speeches, to bargaining agreements. As these are worked out into a real system, the practical problems which are faced one by one may clear away the general difficulties. We may find foreign trade enlarged without ever having undergone a systematic revision of the tariff. The difficulties and dangers are obvious. We cannot bargain unless we have something to trade. Every country will demand the opening of our markets to some kinds of foreign goods. To this there will be interested opposition. There is real question whether the incurring of these vehement oppositions one by one is not more dangerous than it would be to incur all possible ones at the same time, falling back on the general defense that trade must be increased.

It will be interesting to see how all this works out in the coming months. It seems unlikely that we shall stay where we are in the matter. It would make the agricultural adjustment program vastly easier if some of our goods could move to foreign markets. And great efforts will be made to move them. It will not be possible to do so, however, unless we discover some way for payment to be made. This will inevitably involve the acceptance of imports; and a decision as to what imports these will be, will become a more and more pressing problem. There are other industries than agriculture which would benefit from exports; none, of course, which involve so great a percentage of our production, or in which surpluses have become so burdensome, but still many that could expand immediately under the stimulus. We shall come more and more clearly to see that this expansion and the consequent employment and profits, depend on the acceptance of imports which cannot come in unless and until we reduce certain tariffs either generally or for a given period. This close connection of our own expansion with the acceptance of imports will be a powerful lever for revision, and it seems to me almost certain to come.

There is good reason for feeling also that some new devices will be used for guiding the channels of this trade. We shall want it used, probably, as directly as possible for expansion purposes; and this might not happen if the old mechanisms of foreign exchange were trusted to. There will therefore be many suggestions for ways of accomplishing this and for the substitution of new devices for old ones. The most obvious of these is that export and import corporations be set up which would guide and handle the *new* trade which was bargained for. Many people have suggested this device and it might commend itself, suitably worked out, to the executive committee on commercial policy and to the President.

Whatever devices are used and whatever discussions take place, they must ultimately center upon the position which Secretary Wallace has urged so forcibly. We must guide our internal policy by what it is possible to do in the international field. But we cannot create the kind of foreign policy which will jeopardize our program for recovery. The expansion of foreign trade must, if we can accomplish it, be made effective. But it must take place in commodities and by means which do not threaten other measures which are equally important. It is a nice problem; it calls for a kind of thinking and negotiation which is utterly different from the laissez-faire procedures we are used to. But an administration which found the resources to create a program for domestic recovery ought to be able to find others for international coöperation to any extent that other nations make possible.

XIX

WIND, WATER AND SOIL

THERE would appear to be nothing more substantial and permanent than the soil. People from the city have been led to believe that, however anything else might change, there will always remain the brown earth of the countryside. It has been regarded as a great world mother to whom, even after periods of blackest revolution or the worship of false gods, men might return and derive new strength.

In a state of primitive culture, this might be quite true; for to all practical purposes, the slow destruction of this earth's surface by vast, geological changes, would have no significance to the human race. Left alone, this earth of ours would have flung itself ceaselessly through space, rain would have fallen, been caught by the broad leaves of trees or speared by the narrow blades of grass. Gradually it would have percolated to some stream, running thus away to the sea; then it would return again as rain. So the circle, endlessly repeated, would have been closed. The highest mountain would very gradually wear down to a rolling plain—barring some great cataclysm which might once more squeeze together the earth's surface and reform its mountains. This, geologists might be willing to say, would have been the normal development of our planet, with changes so slow and so imperceptible that we should never realize their existence.

But the earth and climate were not left to their own devices. Men conceived the desire to cultivate plants, and to warm themselves and fashion the instruments they invented from the wood of trees. Hillsides were stripped of their forests to supply these needs; the soil was turned and exposed to wind and rain. Nature's cover was stripped off the earth, and great areas of bare soil invited the elements. Through man's own efforts, therefore, the greatest of our resources was made impermanent. We have now to think of its conservation.

Even the ancients realized that water flowing down a hillside could move tons of soil, and they formed elaborate benchlike steps out of the hillsides to check the run-off. Today it is possible to drive for hours through the hilly lands of Spain, Southern France, Italy, Sicily and Greece, without ever losing sight of the sharply indented slopes of hills covered with vineyards and orchards of oranges, lemons, almonds, and olives. In our own country the vastness of the still unspoiled virgin lands which stretched out, apparently limitlessly, from our western frontier, for a long time made unnecessary resort to such drastic measures for preservation. By the middle of the last century we had begun to use terraces in some parts of the southeastern states; but it was not until the beginning of this century that the entire problem began to get careful study.

Erosion is of two principal sorts—wind and water. Today, throughout an area of many hundred square miles where the States of Colorado, Oklahoma, New Mexico, and Texas meet, there has been a long drought which has so dried the top soil that for more than a year the wind has been carrying it away in spite of the efforts of the 50,000 farmers of the district. There is misery in that country for men and stock. This is an example of wind erosion's destructive force. No one would go into this area now in search of traditional rural stability and peace. All that has been lost.

But erosion by water is of more compelling general concern. It happens over wider areas and is practically continuous there. Water can carry soil away in two fashions: it can wash it off the top of rolling, flat lands in thin layers of mud or it can dramatically carry it in concentrated form through V-shaped hollows which may soon develop into good-sized troughs and eventually into miniature valleys or gullies. One is called "sheet washing," the other "gullying." Both are caused by the same force; that is, both happen because soil which has been laid bare by men cannot absorb all the rain which falls, and so must "run off." In this running it carries with it particles of the earth over which it passes. The overwhelming effects of this process are caused by the fact that even if the slope is increased only four times, the velocity of the water is about doubled and the power of the water to carry away soil is increased some thirty-two times.

The cumulative results of water erosion are stupendous. 1,500,000,000 tons of soil are carried away by erosion each year; and of this 83,000,000 tons have been conservatively estimated to be the minimum amount of plant food material which is lost. This represents a drain of such elements as potash, phosphoric acid, nitrogen, lime, and magnesia, which is twenty-one times greater than that annually removed by the crops themselves. Its commercial value would be over $2,000,000,000, of which evidence shows that at least $200,-000,000 can be charged up as a direct tangible loss to the farmers of the nation. Such a loss would be a staggering blow to any industry! A further result, not so directly connected with the farming problem, but still of the utmost importance, is the contribution which erosion makes to the spectacular floods which periodically terrorize the countryside and to the subsequent silting up of river channels and engineering works.

From a purely economic standpoint, the problem is equally acute, for the cost of terracing an area 15 inches high, 20 feet wide, and 1,000 feet long in light soils on moderate slopes has been estimated to range from $1.50 to $15.00 an acre, depending upon the number and depth of the gullies. This, however, is figured on the usual costs for labor, team, and tractor power. Frequently, during off seasons, the farmer might be able to construct terraces with a homemade V-drag for practically nothing.

On the credit side of the ledger, the actual gains accruing to the farmer seem considerable. Credit institutions making loans on agricultural land have become aware of erosion's dangers. A representative of the Federal Land Bank at Houston, Texas, said recently that he had analyzed 200 fore-closed farms and found 70 percent to be definitely "badly eroded" and that "in numerous instances within a few years securities upon which we have made loans have gone to utter destruction and have been abandoned because of erosion." Three nationally known insurance companies have com-menced control work on properties whose mortgages they hold, in order that their investment may not literally be washed away.

Both sheet washing and gullying, then, can and are being controlled. We possess adequate technical knowledge to deal with the engineering side of the problem. Gullying is more spectacular than sheet washing and is treated in more spec-tacular fashion. The usual method employed to check the process in advanced stages is the construction of numerous small wooden, stone or earthen dams along the gully's bed. These retard the water, allow the silt to be deposited, and thus gradually build up the floor of the gully until, com-bined with plowing over the edges of the ditch, the whole gully disappears. In its place there remains only a gently sloping hollow upon which crops can once more be grown or along which such plants as black locust and Lespedezas may be planted. This is the sort of work which has to be done under the supervision of competent engineers and which is now being efficiently handled in many localities by Civilian Conservation workers.

Sheet erosion, however, is not so easy to deal with. For ages it has been partly controlled through bench terraces, which make the side of a hill look like an amphitheater. Comparatively recently, this type has been displaced by the broad ridge terrace which is formed by plowing the land into earthen ridges thrown across the hillside, which are either given a slight grade to carry off the water at a low velocity or maintained level, so that it will be held in long, narrow pools until it evaporates. One of the reasons for adopting this type of terrace is that it can be cultivated with our modern agricultural machinery.

Unlike gully work, such erosion control probably has to be carried on by the farmers themselves; for it involves the planning of his entire farm. Each year, the Department of Agriculture has been given a few hundred thousand dollars to aid individual farmers in laying out their terraces and to disseminate information regarding the necessity for, and the economy of, erosion work.

In accordance with the President's belief that more can be accomplished through group coöperation than through individual relations with the Government, a new approach to the entire program is contemplated. It must be abundantly evident that the maintenance of our soil is a national problem. Five million dollars has been given by the Public Works Administration to help safeguard this rich heritage.

It is planned to enlist the farmers' support and to organize, among farmers who are willing to contribute their labor and machinery, some twelve "erosion control districts" in this present year, with others to follow as they can be organized. These districts are to include from 100,000 to

200,000 acres each and care will be taken that they represent good farming land on which a little labor might permanently save the soil but where erosion is a real problem. They are not to be areas definitely submarginal, which should be taken out of cultivation altogether.

In order to comply with the provisions of the Public Works Act, 70 percent of the funds expended on such projects must be contributed by other agencies than the Federal Government. In this case, it has been thought that the farmers, organized in these large districts, might give their 70 percent in labor and machinery, while the Government's 30 percent might be contributed by the Soil Erosion Service in the form of supervision and technical assistance.

Each district would have an agricultural engineer, a soil expert, and an agronomist in charge; for, although terracing might in some districts be the chief method of erosion control, it is also contemplated that strip cropping and seeding to permanent pastures, with possibly some tree planting and gully control work, will be carried out.

To this enterprise, three bureaus of the Department of Agriculture would contribute—Agricultural Engineering, Chemistry and Soils, and Plant Industry. Their efforts will be closely watched, for through the choosing and administering of these ten or twelve areas, we clearly commit ourselves to an experiment in planned land utilization. In order not to waste the public money, it must be utilized in the most effective manner, and, in order to do this, the right areas must be chosen, as well as the right types of control, and the right seeding program; in short, for each area the most practical system of control must be devised and put into operation.

It will be an interesting and instructive experiment in the control of land uses, but its very existence will depend upon the support it receives from farmers. The Government in this case, as in that of such other recent activities as the cotton and wheat reduction programs, has not tried to dictate, but rather to coördinate and assist. The farmers of the country must contribute 70 percent of the labor necessary to carry out the erosion projects in the ten or twelve areas; only if they will guarantee to do that, can the Government carry out its plans. This, then, is another appeal to our democratic institutions.

XX

WINE, WOMEN AND THE NEW DEAL *

I FIND that there is a fairly general attitude that the men who are engaged in administering the policies of the New Deal are a pretty grim lot, that we are painfully serious and so ferociously in earnest that we take no vacation from the eternal verities. Exception is always made, in this generalization, for the cheerful good temper of the President, but the rest of us are usually portrayed as cadaverous fanatics or haggard heroes wrestling with stupendous problems in a spirit of humorless ferocity.

Our problems are, of course, very large and must be dealt with seriously, but it would be treason to the entire spirit of the New Deal to lose sight of the fact that its objective, as stated by President Roosevelt himself, is to make possible a more abundant life for the American people. A more abundant life implies a happier and perhaps a less hectic type of existence for the average man and woman; it implies the enjoyment of the good things of life in security and contentment, and the cultivation, through such enjoyment, of the good things of the spirit—reflection, philosophy, conversation and leisure.

Instead of people arguing that we are too grim, we might justifiably contend that the Old Order has made people too grim, that the presence of physical abundance in an increasing variety hitherto associated only with the tropics, should not imply an increasing struggle for existence among the heirs and assigns of this abundance. We see that our task is

* Address delivered before the Women's Democratic Club, Washington, D. C., Feb. 5, 1934.

fundamentally the spiritual task of calling a halt on the in-
temperate national tradition of going places and doing things
and labeling the result pleasure. Our political dedication to
the pursuit of happiness, as one of the fundamental rights of
humanity, has been too rigidly interpreted as a species of
buffalo hunt or a riding to hounds, in which we either exterminated our quarry or risked breaking our own necks.

Happiness is a shy creature and can be pursued in other
ways than by organizing a posse or imposing a cover charge
on those who would capture it. It must be approached delicately or, better still, encouraged to approach its pursuer, or
else it takes flight and then, if captured by swift and resolute
pursuit, is swiftly slain. You may hang the trophy on your
wall, but it is apt to stay there, and not again to afford you
pleasure.

One of the oldest and quietest roads to contentment lies
through that traditional trinity of wine, woman and song. If
either bathtub gin or three weeks' whisky is substituted for
the first element in this combination, the result is best charac-
terized by the associations we have with the word "jazz." We
all know what this led to in the pre-war saloon era and we
all know that the excesses of the bootleg decade produced the
revulsion of national feeling which has brought back legal-
ized alcoholic beverages. While youth and high spirits must
be served, there is no sense in converting them into a moral
servitude which dictates that drunkenness is the chief end of
drinking or confuses intoxication with happiness. We have a
chance, now that the repeal of the Eighteenth Amendment is
an accomplished fact, to clamp down on these lusty juvenalia
and to substitute a tradition of greater maturity.

This is the tradition of wine, used as a mild social
stimulant, together with good food, good talk and good company and, let me add, good song. "Sweet Adeline" may serve

to blow off steam, but that is all it does, and it is, to my mind, an unfortunate survival of the old saloon tradition which implied that men desired to escape from the company of their womenfolk and raise the roof in one another's company. I am frank to admit that I am partial to the European tradition of open-air cafés and beer gardens, where decent men and women can drink quietly in the open air under the eyes of their neighbors and where the two sexes can exert on each other the discipline of each other's presence. Covert drinking is akin to segregated drinking and segregated drinking is akin to secret drinking and secret drinking is the mark of the drunkard. I prefer that anything so natural as the result of the process of fermentation should be treated naturally and not, through moralistic regulations, converted into a clandestine and hence artificially exciting form of sinful self-indulgence.

The women of this country have a great opportunity to establish and maintain a civilized attitude toward wine, now that we have all seen what comes of not cultivating such a civilized attitude. It is within their power to shape and direct their own social attitude and that of their men toward this good thing in life. If they follow the old line, they can drive their men back to the barroom and the short stiff drinks which go with the barroom. If they follow a new and more civilized line, they can accompany their men to the cafés and beer gardens and consume at leisure the long, slow drinks which are appropriate to pleasant conversations and mature social relationships.

You may wonder why I, as an official in the Department of Agriculture, should concern myself with the drinking habits of the American people, when there already exist other governmental and police agencies for dealing with these problems. The answer is very simple. Wine and beer are made from agricultural produce and the consumption of American wine and beer cannot only serve the broader purposes of the New Deal in making for a calmer and happier type of existence, but will help the American farmer to find a better market for his produce.

The repeal of prohibition found the American wine industry totally unprepared to meet an enlarged demand. Twelve years of home-brewing, of grape bricks and grape concentrates, of bootlegged "red ink" and occasional bottles of smuggled foreign vintages, with a small continuing output of sacramental and invalid types of wine, had almost completely destroyed the old American vintages. The new stuff is coming on the market but it is, as yet, far too young, and the new companies and new producers have yet to make their reputations.

I think that the best lead which American women can follow is that which has been given by Mrs. Roosevelt herself: to serve wine in their own homes, to favor American wines as much as possible, to choose them with discrimination, and to assimilate their use to the habit of food. The best way in which this can be done is to try out sparingly all the varieties of American wine which are coming on the market, and to judge them with reference to flavor, bouquet and price, rather than with reference to their ability to produce the recognizable symptoms of intoxication in the shortest possible time. For the alcoholic content of a wine is a matter of balance and its social importance should be measured by its power of gentle stimulation in the realm of social relaxation. The price of good wine must be measured by the demand for good wine rather than by the producers' desire to obtain a fat profit. Excellent table wines should be sold at between fifty and seventy-five cents a bottle, at the present level of prices, and should yield a fair profit at that price. Rare and delicate vintages will always cost more. So I urge those of you who buy wine, to try American wines, without reference to the misleading labels which indicate that the produce of California is burgundy or the produce of northern New York is champagne. Those wines which are not good or not worth the money should not be purchased again, and you can help if you will inform your wine merchant of the fact that such-and-such a brand is terrible or that this-or-that vintage is good for ordinary table use but is far too dear at $1.50 a bottle. In that way you can carry your preferences and sense of values back to the wine industry and thereby stimulate and direct the improvement of American vintages.

I mentioned a little while ago the importance of not paying attention to labels which define our native American wines as burgundy, champagne and the like. This is because it is both stupid and unnecessary for our wines to sail under false colors. Our California vineyards are stocked with Mediterranean vines and have been, in the main, cultivated by European immigrants; but the California wines are not only quite good enough to stand on their own merits, but are, in many cases, superior to the European product. The little canyons of the San Francisco Bay region are especially adapted to the production of delicate dry wines, while the great irrigated stretches of the Sacramento and the San Joaquin Valleys can produce excellent table wines in volumes which may rapidly outdistance the valleys of the Rhone, the Rhine and the Loire.

Nor should you forget that the eastern and southern wine produced from the native American wild-grape stocks, which our horticulturists have tamed and crossbred for generations, is another distinctive American product. The eastern grape belt stretches from the Finger Lake district in northern New York, to southern New Jersey, crosses northern Ohio and reaches into central Missouri. The dry gallized wine produced in this region is admirably adapted for table purposes. Then, again, there is the southern scuppernong grape belt, extending along the southern coastal plain from Virginia to Texas. The Florida orchardists are producing admirable cordials from their citrus fruits, and the old rum industry of the Virgin Islands, which once made Santa Cruz rum famous throughout the world, is being reëstablished, for the benefit of those who like liqueurs.

To return to my point, however, I should like to see the names of San Joaquin, Sacramento, Napa, Sonoma, Chautauqua, Niagara, Seneca, Keuka, Erie, Finger Lake, Roanoke, Scuppernong, and others of our own localities mean exactly as much—and perhaps more—on the world's wine lists, as Burgundy, Bordeaux, Rhine wine, Chianti, Tokay, Oporto, and the other glorious names of viticulture. And I should like to see the great American commercial subdivisions supplemented by the widest possible variety of small local vintages, that wine of the country which can be obtained in almost any European province and which rarely if ever reaches the metropolitan markets.

This is particularly because the cultivation of good wines is an art, a handicraft which has proved hitherto invulnerable to the advance of the machine age. We are seeking a more diversified agriculture and are endeavoring to solve some of our industrial problems by the decentralization of industry into rural regions and the establishment of industrial workers on small subsistence homesteads, where they can supplement their receipts from the industrial pay roll by the production of their own foodstuffs. This means that the average farmer and the average industrial worker will have greater leisure and greater incentive to experiment with new forms of agricultural production. Since soil adapted to the production of high-quality grapes and high-quality wines is found in small pockets—I do not overlook the fact that the supposed output in the last forty years of the few acreages of the Veuve Cliquot would have filled a large lake—good wine implies careful and skillful cultivation of a kind which is foreign to the methods of mass production. We have seen how the Appalachian mountaineers for the last hundred and fifty years have developed and maintained a high degree of individual skill in the production of potable whisky, and have resisted and frustrated every effort of the public authorities to suppress their traditional handicraft.

I foresee the possibility of supplementing this tradition of handicraft hard liquor with a new and a better tradition of handicraft wines. I foresee a plethora of small local vintages, some good, some mediocre, some perfectly dreadful, out of which will arise in future some great names and great traditions of American wine. I foresee the day when the average American home will be able to enjoy good beer and good wine produced in the neighborhood at moderate prices, leaving to the huge commercial vintners and brewers the task of supplying the metropolitan centers and serving our export markets. And better still, I foresee that, with this change in the drinking habits of our people, may come a change of temper and of temperament, a less furious striving for happiness at the bottom of the whisky barrel. I foresee fewer deaths from heart failure, fewer nervous breakdowns, far fewer of the myriad ailments brought about by overwork and overworry. In their place, I anticipate a calmer and more leisurely type of civilization, in which there will be time for friendly conversation, philosophical speculation, gaiety and substantial happiness.

For today we have in our possession all the elements which are necessary to that more abundant life which is the real objective of all of us. We have foods and factories, we have a highly efficient system of communication and transport, we have, above all, a patient, hard-working and self-respecting people, who are distinguished for their social good will and for their political self-control. All we need is to find the way to the enjoyment of that heritage which lies at our hands.

It is here that the women of America can make their most vital contribution. They have it in their power to define our moral objectives and to lead us into channels of good taste and good judgment. We can find a sufficient salvation here at home; it is not necessary to blame Europe or Asia for our failure to solve our own problems. The New Deal has, therefore, adopted a policy which its critics and some of its friends describe as economic nationalism, but the fundamental purpose of which is to solve our own problems in terms of our own traditions and our own resources. Such a policy in purely masculine hands has too often in the past led straight to international greed, imperialism and armed conflict. It is for the women to see that the same canons of deportment which permit a member of society to conduct his own business without destroying his neighbor shall permeate our national attitude toward other countries. Too often we regard the welfare of another as our loss and his discomfiture as our gain, in world affairs.

The more civilized attitude is to recognize that we are all members of one another's group and that the good of one may be the good of all, unless it is achieved at the direct expense of another.

Historically, wine has been, I think, a genuinely civilizing influence in that portion of the world which stems from Europe. Historically again, women have been the custodians and the transmitters of culture. Song, also, has been the spontaneous expression of civilized happiness. In thinking together of wine, of women, and of song, we can lay the foundation for a deep and enduring social attitude of mutual forbearance and friendly toleration. Without such an attitude, I am convinced, it will not be easy, if indeed it is possible, for the American people to enter upon the more abundant life which is rightfully theirs.

XXI
WHEN CORPORATIONS SAVE *

THE habit among business corporations of building up surplus reserves is one of those practices which seem at first to be purely individual but which turn out, on examination, to have serious social consequences. The corporate surplus is a carryover from a simpler and more individualistic age. To lay by something for a rainy day has always seemed a sensible proceeding. It was the only way in which the crises of sickness, unemployment or old age could be met. The only alternatives were the poorhouse or charity, both of which were so abhorrent to Americans that the impulse to do whatever seemed necessary to prevent such a catastrophe came to have a powerful hold on people's minds.

The managers of corporations are the same individuals who have grown up believing that any good citizen had, as a matter of duty, to spend sparingly, to live within a known income, and to build up a nest egg which would be available in case of need. It was a logical inference that good corporate management required the same policy. Duty to stockholders involved the creation of a fund which could be drawn on when earnings failed. The corporation which did this possessed a certain guarantee against the future; it was more provident and stable. The growth of knowledge concerning the business cycle, in the last ten years, has intensified this desire. It became common knowledge that every so often depression would spread its blight throughout the business world and that earnings would then dry up; the business

* Notes made in Feb., 1934.

which possessed a great reserve could nevertheless go on meeting its obligations.

It is nevertheless true that what seems like the only sane and sensible course for any corporation to pursue is anything but that if all corporations try to do it. This is one of those instances in which the following of a sensible course defeats the very purpose which it is intended to meet. For when everyone saves, no one buys enough to keep things going. When every corporation turns its earnings into surpluses, a good deal of the purchasing power of the community is made sterile.

There are a limited number of ways of saving. A corporation has only a few choices in its handling of a surplus fund: (1) It may keep its funds in a bank; (2) it may purchase government securities; (3) it may buy the securities of other corporations; (4) it may loan funds in the money market; or (5) it may enlarge and perfect its own plant. The curious thing about any of these choices is that none of them causes the full flow of the funds into the hands of ultimate consumers. If a corporation keeps its money in a bank, the bank loans it to others for productive uses; if it purchases government securities, the Government uses the funds it borrows in this way for purposes which require ultimate taxation for repayment—the use is productive but consumers' purchasing power is not enlarged; if it buys the securities of other corporations, it permits some other industry to enlarge its productive facilities; if it uses its funds in the money market, it forms a basis for speculation which inflates values but does not make them any more real.

If, instead of using its earnings to enlarge its surplus, the corporation used them to increase its pay roll or to reduce its prices to consumers it would be enlarging the demand for its own products along with those of others, because it would be placing purchasing power in the hands of those who actually use it. This would be better insurance, really, against an anticipated rainy day than following any of the courses open to it in the management of surplus. Even if it paid these funds out in dividends the effect would be better than that of saving, for at least part of them would be spent for goods instead of being added to an already overdeveloped productive equipment.

It is as a result of following the course of saving that industries find themselves periodically with a failing market. When too much is saved and finds its way into factories, warehouses, transport facilities and the like, our productive equipment tends to outgrow any demand there may be for the product. One of the favorite devices resorted to in this situation is an enlargement of high-pressure salesmanship and advertising in an attempt to create markets forcibly. But if physical purchasing power is actually deficient the only result this can have is to take business away from someone else, destroying the momentary equilibrium—the whole cannot be enlarged.

Good business policy clearly requires that demand should be built up and conserved as carefully as productive equipment is. The one is useless without the other. This cannot be done by sterilizing earned funds in surplus accounts or in forcing attention on particular goods. It can be done only by enlarging and protecting the stream of purchasing power. The great difficulty in accomplishing this is that it is to the interest of all businesses to do this but not to the interest of any one of them. Consequently no one of them can be expected to do it alone or without some guarantee that others will join in the movement. One of the important results which may ultimately come out of the Recovery Act is just this: the provision of a mechanism by which the interest of each business may clearly and adequately be identified with the interests of all.

This would not be a greater extension of coöperative activities than would seem appropriate to our present views. Industries which have come to trust code authorities with the allocation of production—and some have actually done that—may move on rather quickly to the consideration of further coöperative devices. So far, most activity has been of a negative, repressive sort, the reduction of production schedules, the maintenance or increase of prices and so on; but there soon will come a time—once all business has fitted itself into the structure of the codes—when more positive measures will have to be taken. They will be taken because only in that way can consumption be increased and existing capacity used with advantage, to say nothing of the expansion which everyone hopes for. Then, too, industry will soon have to think of ways to reduce prices rather than to raise them; and it can do this only by cutting costs. The most fruitful field for this will be, in the immediate future, in the neighborhood of the central offices, rather than the factories. When this becomes apparent, the handling of surpluses will certainly come in for closer scrutiny.

There is every reason, therefore, for calling attention to a situation which is as undesirable socially as it is individually, and for suggesting that through a mere extension of the activities undertaken in the codes and otherwise under the Recovery Act, all that is needful to be done may be accomplished. If something like this had been done years ago such a law as the Securities Act, to which there has been so much recent objection, would be less necessary. One of the greatest sources of security to investors would be the maintenance of some central controlling body which managed capital allocation and at the same time centralized a sufficient reserve to guarantee minimum payments on authorized capital issues. The greatest of present wastes would be prevented in this way by taking care that investment was made only in enterprises which had a clear prospective market for the goods it was expected to produce, and which would not reduce the value of old enterprises by new competition. Both the old and the new investor would be protected in this way.

There is sufficient authority under N.R.A. for industries to do this for themselves without governmental compulsion. To be sure there is still another achievement to be made in the structure of the codes which cannot very well go forward until practically all our industries are organized in this way. This is, of course, the organization into a coherent body of the code authorities themselves. But this is so obvious a necessity that it may follow very quickly, once all the codes are completed even in a preliminary way. The necessity lies in just such possible gains in efficiency as I have been calling attention to here. There are many ways—of which this is only one—in which conflicts among industries, as contrasted with those among businesses within any industry, need to be resolved by fitting into a larger scheme. They cannot be settled until sufficient organization has been attained so that the larger purposes of industry will seem as important to its leaders as smaller, more immediate purposes seem at present.

We seem to be on our way to that kind of organization now. When we have it the enlightened intelligence which used to be attributed to business men will have a chance to function again in the fields where it is, in a modern sense, significant. There can then be a government of industry. There are many critics of present arrangements. The codes for this industry or that are said to be imperfect. They allow certain interests to prevail over others; they do not give adequate protection to consumers' interests; they are perfected without regard to one industry's relation to another. This criticism might all be true and yet the *structure* of the codes, as contrasted with any one of them is so important that it must seem worth while, to anyone with a genuinely long-time vision, to sacrifice anything for the larger gains which are at stake in the process of codification.

We are pressing forward, sometimes in what seem devious ways, but forward nevertheless, toward a new régime for industry. There will be new freedoms in it as well as new compulsions—freedom from fear of the rainy days of depression, freedom from the necessity of gaining something at others' expense, freedom from the kind of competitive slavery businesses have had to endure. The compulsions involved may seem onerous to executives who have been used to the present rules of management. But even now there are signs that resentment is overborne by obvious advantage. The educational process of code-making is giving us a new race of business men. They are likely to transform the industrial system, I think, more quickly than most people now suspect.

XXII

THE RETURN TO DEMOCRACY *

IT is an honor to have the opportunity of speaking face to face with those responsible for the editorial opinions of the American press, for I realize that the President's program can be attained only in the presence of full comment of interpretation and of criticism from the newspapers and magazines of this country. It is human, I suppose, to prefer praise to blame and to desire sympathy rather than hostility to the great national movement of free social coöperation which we are now in; but I realize that the science of human nature which we describe as politics becomes cheap and tawdry chicanery if its practitioners are debarred, even by the unorganized coercion of mass emotions, from the right to oppose and criticize. And since there is no major point of the President's policy where it is necessary to shrink from criticism or to conceal the facts, I desire to congratulate you on the recent evidences in your respective publications of an awakened public interest in and discussion of our public affairs. I only wish that the more analytical phase of this interest and critical discussion had begun earlier, at the time when the main features of the New Deal were being hammered out in Congress and throughout the administration. At that time there was almost too easy an acceptance of any and every measure which was proposed. Today, my only regret is that you did not earlier realize that coöperation with the efforts for national recovery did not imply the absence of interpretation and criticism.

* Address delivered before the American Society of Newspaper Editors, April 21, 1934.

Because discussion is now wider and more disposed to be critical, this seems to be an appropriate time and place to restate some of the fundamentals of that Americanism to which we are born and which we all desire to cherish. This is appropriate, from my point of view, not because my own motives have lately been questioned by those who consider themselves and the country to have been injured by the President's program, but because it has been made to appear that what is being done by this administration is somehow alien to our traditions and institutions.

It is my belief that the core of the American tradition is to be found in a kind of defiance to fate. We will not do what we do not want to do and coercion cannot make us. We can be fooled, but not for long. We have a precious inventiveness which gets us out of holes. We have a saving irreverence of authority. These basic traits determine the structure of our laws and of our Government. No one, with the slightest sense of history, would try to fit such a people into a regimented scheme, would try to think for them instead of getting them to think for themselves. Indeed, anyone who has known them by living their lives, by really being one of them in body and spirit, would know in his heart, with no need for consideration, that law, government, and social organization for such a people must be instruments through which their characteristic actions, resistances, imaginations could find appropriate expression. Law, government and social organization will inevitably fail if they are not this. In this respect I unhesitatingly avow myself a thorough conservative I do not believe that people can be compelled to do for long anything that is alien to their national character, and I do not believe that there are any safe compulsions which may be used on human nature.

This is not always easily remembered by those who are not

part of us, or those who have lived so long away that they have forgotten our intolerance of restrictive means. It was forgotten by those who thought that prohibition might succeed. This will do for illustration in the field of government and law. But most conspicuously it has been forgotten by some industrialists. If you look for regimentation in American life you will find your best illustrations in industry. We never tolerated prohibition and we finally got it out of our Constitution. We have more difficulty and more confusion in getting rid of regimentation in industry. When there are thousands of people working together in a business enterprise, and those people are Americans, things will not run smoothly unless that enterprise bases its operations on free and full consent throughout the organization, rather than on economic coercion or arbitrary management.

It seems to me ironic that measures which are taken to assure the democratic process throughout our industry and our agriculture should be said to be regimentation. There is a distinction to be made between *people* and *things* which is overlooked in this. A part of the conspicuous victory over nature on this continent has been the power which has been exhibited in subduing natural materials and forces to a will for well-being. Nature has been reduced to order, to regimentation. This is a process which should have freed men as it enslaved nature. This is what it was done for. If that does not result from it, the thing was not worth doing. But until lately it was not happening. As the industrial system developed, men found themselves more and more the slaves of machines, of systems, of corporate and financial devices. Naturally, being Americans, they eventually revolted and asked for a New Deal. It is my conception of the New Deal that it shall ensure the subjugation of things, and restore to men the freedoms they have earned, together with all the advantages which ought to accrue from our victories over nature. Those who are shouting "regimentation" now do not recognize the inevitability of this process; they are those who have greatly benefited from the subjection of man to things. The beneficiaries of private industrial regimentation cannot prevail, of course, for it is not in the nature of Americans to permit it. But it offers an excellent illustration of the confusion of thought into which we fall in trying to sort out those purposes and plans which we shall ultimately want from those which we shall ultimately reject.

There will be plenty of time to ponder and discuss the policies which have been written into law and put into operation during this administration. Those who do not like them will object with customary argument; those who do will make the customary defenses. But ultimately the measures will stand on their own ground and be judged as parts of a continuing American tradition. They cannot be judged by the men who, for the moment, happen to be administering them. If these men misconceive their mandates, or if they are inefficient or arrogant, they will disappear and others will take their places. But the social movement by which new accommodations to the requirements of industrial life have been made cannot be undone. The abuses which they sought to correct are too imminent still; and the process itself was too democratic. If there was any failure of the democratic process it lay in refusal before 1933 to realize the fundamental causes of the present crisis and to frame remedies which might succeed because they did go to causes rather than to symptoms. We fooled ourselves for a while; but millions of eyes have been opened now that will not close again until the right things have been done.

Social change in America cannot go on any faster than the people who are affected want it to go on. That is one of the assurances against any danger that it may go too fast in this country. Those who are favored under present arrangements have too ready a remedy against excessive speed. Also, it must be remembered that for the present we suffer from years of blocking. Changes can come slowly if progress is not altogether stopped. But when it is stopped, an accumulation of desirable policies is ready to be let loose and much more rapid changes result. The resistance mechanisms are almost too perfect. They brought about complete collapse in 1929 and prevented any change for some three years. Now that some of the necessary measures have at last been taken and some recovery has been assured, the forces of reaction are again in full cry. No one could be found a year ago who wanted to stop everything. Now there are a noisy few who want to go back to 1929. And they would pillory as enemies of what they call the American system those who still do not want to interrupt the orderly movement of democratic change or to go back where we were when that movement had been successfully inhibited. The sovereignty of the American people is the real source of this administration's power; there is not a man among you who does not recognize this, though there are some who appear to resent it. I for one do not wish to supplant this sovereignty with another kind whose theory is that for some groups and interests there should be immunity from political control. That way lies economic oligarchy. It involves the creation of autocratic institutions which are alien to the American spirit. We were drifting toward them in the postwar years. Our present return to democracy constitutes, as I believe, their final repudiation in this nation.

Time will tell which in these times is the better American —he who believes that the racketeering, the financial juggling, the exploitation of workers and consumers must be ended once for all, and that the continuity of industry must be definitely assured by whatever political means can be found; or he who believes it more important that some few insiders should be allowed to manipulate materials, natural forces and social institutions for their own good at the expense of all the rest. Which of these alternatives is really the regimentation about which so much has recently been heard? Which is closest to the democratic process?

The Agricultural Adjustment Administration has been spoken of as one of the regimenting agencies. I should like for the moment to examine this idea.

The best comment on it is furnished, I think, by pointing out that it does no more than make its machinery available to coöperators. Its lifeblood is furnished by the County Production Control Associations. It is true that quotas are established at Washington, with a wide view of national and international conditions. But with the great cash crops—cotton, wheat, tobacco, corn and hogs—no single farmer, not even any regional group of them, is in a position to take this sufficiently wide view. Every unit of these crops is dependent on a world-wide market and that market is extraordinarily sensitive to increases and decreases in production and to the existence of surpluses. Only nation-wide action is sufficient to make the necessary adjustments; and the farmers seem satisfied to have the Federal Government, which represents all of them, function in these common matters.

But the threads which run backward and forward between the county associations and the administration in Washington are sensitive to local wishes. Quota-making has been carried out with fairness to everyone. The calculations are complicated, but they have been carried out in a way so disinterested and with such dependable results that complaints have been infrequent; and once the quota is made, everything else is left to the association, with such assistance as may be demanded from extension agents who are jointly responsible to the county, the state and the Federal Government.

It is a democratic process revised to meet the necessities of a world economic system. It is not laissez faire, but neither is it anything else for which a doctrinal name is appropriate. Curiously enough, this stubborn unwillingness of such practical devices as these to accommodate themselves to literary terms infuriates many people. "Why don't you come out," they say, "and admit that this is Socialism or Fascism or Communism—or something." I sympathize with this impulse because it is a highly academic one, and, as you know, I am a professor. But I can't agree that national policies ought to be shaped with reference to any dogma just so that detractors can conveniently attach a label to them and find a library full of ready-made criticisms. I have been interested in the kind of argument which has been made against present policies in default of easy labeling. Of course, some of the less discriminating have not hesitated to use labels, even though these might be obviously inappropriate.

Some of the less discriminating also do not hesitate to resort to rather willful misrepresentations. I suppose I should be annoyed when someone publicly and repeatedly distorts an expression of skepticism regarding planning into an advocacy of wholesale regimentation; or when an individual becomes so cleverly selective as to make an entire chapter in Secretary Wallace's pamphlet, *America Must Choose*—which opposes nationalism and its accompanying restraints—appear to be an argument in favor of those restraints. Such things are annoying, but after all they are exceptional. Probably we shall never be wholly rid of them, and I doubt that they amount to much in the end. I may be old-fashioned, but I still think there is much to be said for intellectual honesty.

Seven years ago I visited Russia for two months. That visit has often been considered sufficient proof of my adherence to communism, as though communism could be caught by contagion, like mumps or measles. I suppose there does not exist in the whole country today a more convinced believer in the democratic process than I am. But I happen to be really interested in its survival and eager to adapt it to the modern world so that it can survive. For this, something more than windy eulogies to liberty is necessary. Democracy has been living a precarious life among our business institutions; its enemies in this country were in a fair way to have it strangled and laid quietly aside, until the New Deal came along. For they did not realize that real democracy cannot be destroyed without provoking a revolt on the part of its practitioners. Farmers were being starved off their land; workers were denied access to idle factories. You know all these recent chapters of our history. And you know as well as I do that a kind of specious and purely formal political process was being used as a stalking-horse for privilege and threatening oligarchy. I have never lent myself to this supreme chicanery and I am not likely to do so so long as I keep any realistic sense at all.

It is perhaps necessary to create a philosophy to fit the Rooseveltian method. The time has not yet come when that can be done with any assurance. It has sometimes been called experimental—that too has been used as a word of opprobrium; but perhaps for all that it may describe something desirable. Certainly if we are to accommodate our institutions to the flexible requirements of a world economy, large-scale industry and the rapid development of science, we cannot expect to do it successfully by filling in the outlines of some rigid doctrinal system invented before these new forces appeared. And if we did that we could not hope to make essentially American the changes which must come, fitting them to our genius and our institutions. No, I am afraid that those who desire to thwart the national will for enlarging the boundaries of democracy will have to go on as best they can without the benefit of labels. This will try their ingenuity a bit, but I am sure they will prove equal to the challenge.

In any such process of social experimentation a good deal depends on who does the experimenting and what it is done for. The objections to the process which have been made most vociferously up to now have come from industrialists and financiers. This is, of course, because for the first time they have been made the subjects of it. Hitherto they have been used to experimenting with the rest of us without other penalties than financial ones. When they built a factory, installed a new machine, introduced a novel process, arranged a new wage scale, paid bonuses to executives, threw a group of corporations together in a holding company—they were experimenting. Some of the experiments turned out well, some badly. It was, and still is, important that such experimentation should take place. It has given us our high level of living; it will help us to keep it. But it is equally important that when the holding company becomes a factor of importance, when prices are manipulated by a monopoly, or when new machines or processes displace workers, public bodies should also make their accommodations to these new devices in our social life. No doctrine is needed for this purpose; in fact a doctrine would be a handicap. What is needed is to try new devices from the public side, to adopt them if they succeed or reject them if they fail. But I do not see how there can be objection to a method which was forced on the Government by the effects which were felt from the same method used elsewhere.

The real objection is not to the method. It is to its

success. For the first time controls of sufficient timeliness and flexibility have been found to be really effective. Critics say that the Government ought not to experiment because it destroys business certainty. But the same argument works both ways. Industrial experimentation has made men's livings insecure. It came to the point where even a good farmer cultivating fertile soil efficiently could not succeed, where very few workers were employable after forty, where unemployment was growing yearly even in prosperity. The price we paid for free experimentation in industry was too high to be tolerable. And now it is being said again that the Government must end all this foolishness, settle down to the old certain ways and leave the field of experimentation to business again. If this argument prevails I am willing to prophesy that the results will be just as intolerable as they were before. And that much the same thing that happened in 1929 and after will happen again.

The two essential features, then, of the Rooseveltian method are the modernized democratic processes which it fosters and the experimental nature of its approach to and its handling of problems. It can work if democracy is workable and if experiments can really be carried on. It ought to be obvious that a certain atmosphere is important to these processes—not one which is friendly to what is done, necessarily, but one which is not so unfriendly as to confuse all the issues and to misrepresent all the results.

A servile press which represented the will of a political dictatorship could destroy business prosperity. A servile press which represented the will of a financial oligarchy could prevent both democracy and experimentation from succeeding. Perhaps a free press should do the same thing if its editors believe that democracy and experimentation should be destroyed, but it ought not to do so by choking off real freedom of speech for one group with which it disagrees and according it to another group in which it is interested. Freedom of speech means freedom for every opinion and every group, whether or not there is consent or agreement. It means holding open the channels to the public mind, not using them as valves which will admit only opinions which are approved. It means a fair and objective representation of the facts, regardless of bias in favor of any dogma, tradition of authority. I do not presume to suggest that American newspapers have ever in the past been used to promote a private interest or to obstruct a public one, but I do plead with you, as exponents of freedom of speech, to ask yourselves whether democracy and experimentation are not the only practical means for overcoming the present evils with which the country is beset.

I say this because the modern world is full of forces which have proved themselves inimical to democracy and to that freedom of speech which lies at the root of democracy and because those forces are growing more and not less powerful with the passage of time.

I also say this because of the peculiar dependence of these democratic processes on your good will. Believe me, everyone realizes this. If you have felt some apprehension that the New Deal menaced your freedom, it must have been something born in your own minds. There are enemies of that freedom abroad; but they are not members of the Government. Indeed they are not people at all. They are ideas. Does the press enjoy the same freedom under other systems which it enjoys under ours? Those who would create conditions which require violent correctives are your real enemies. No matter what those conditions are, whether war, or social upheavals at home, or even the rise of one of those militant nationalist movements with which the world has had too much experience lately—those are the real threats to that freedom which we regard as precious. Over 350,000,000 people who thought that they were free fifteen years ago are now living under dictatorships of one kind or another. Those who can look out upon the world as you do cannot fail to appreciate that a great part of it is already in the grip of nationalist movements which have extinguished democracy and written warped definitions of freedom. There is the real enemy—not at Washington.

The democratic process of the experimental method will never threaten the real freedom of the press. That would be a contradiction in terms, for neither can succeed without the fullest and freest discussion of every proposal. There is no other way in which the necessary foundation of public consent can be built. The New Deal is not something which can establish itself in the mind of a dictator or a small governing group. That was the fatal theory of the system from which we are turning away. Its base has to be as broad as the economy which has to be brought under control and as deep as the minds and the hearts of the people whom it affects.

If you will probe the objections to it you will discover, I believe, that they mostly come not from those who by their works have earned the right to speak for underprivileged men and women. They come, on the contrary, from those who represent the exploiters and the privileged, whose interest is not the country's interest but only that of a very few. We in this nation believe in a concert of interests and not in a group dictatorship. But that seems to have been forgotten of late years. Those of us who desire to return to the true tradition of our people, who really hold that there ought to be equal opportunity, and who think that any American is too good to starve, are taunted with the empty shibboleths of an era which was destroyed by those who now go back to it for words. No, the objection is not that the nation is entering on a dictatorship; it is that ways are being found to end one and to make the Government responsive again to the people's will.

The press—the free press—has therefore everything to gain from such changes as are taking place. And the American system has everything to gain from the guarding of that freedom with jealous care.

Freedom is one thing; wisdom in its use is another. The avenues to public attention have become extremely complex along with other things in this complicated world of ours. The newspaper is still the most important of these; and its position with respect to its independence and the character of its service is a matter in which everyone has an interest. As to that I think it only just to say in this company that there are among newspaper men with whom I have had dealings here in Washington some of the finest spirits I have ever known. From the point of view of an official they are often too enterprising. It is literally true that they sometimes know more about things I am supposed to be familiar with than I do. I have often told them that most of what I know about what is going on here in Washington I read in the papers; and that is literally true too. The public is admirably served in this respect in spite of great difficulties. Your newspaper representatives at Washington have had to deal intelligently with highly complicated economic problems one after another, as the various phases of the great wheel of recovery have come uppermost. They are doing it extraordinarily well.

This is mere acknowledgment of faithfulness to an old tradition of the press. For myself I ask nothing more than that this tradition may be preserved and strengthened, that it too may find its accommodation to changing times. Newspapers are not what they were when circulations were a few hundred at most, when types were set by hand, and when one man wrote most of his paper. The press then was an extension of editors' personalities. I sometimes wonder what it is an extension of now. It has succumbed to mass production, as every product of manufacture has to do; and there is group ownership which has arisen to complicate our old theory of personality. And the recent reëmergence of the signed column and the growing emphasis on the signed news story indicate to my mind that the press is responding to the demand for real journalism—the free publication of the facts and the free expression of one man's opinions for what they are worth. And even with respect to our so-called anonymous journalism—that which helps to fill your columns every day— it is still true, and this I think is the saving grace, that every line in every paper is still the product of some writer's mind. No machine has yet been invented which can think or write for us. And I have noticed that attempts to mechanize and control these creative processes have a way of meeting stubborn resistances which defeat them in the end. Men can be caught up in great organizations for a time. But there are still intangible loyalties in their minds which they must serve in spite of everything. The creative spirit functions best in the interest of conscience.

There is no man in these times who is not aware of the crisis we are in the midst of. And especially no newspaper man. This battle for a New Deal is not yet over; indeed I suspect it has just begun. You realize, you must realize, that only a beginning has been made. At the most optimistic estimate we shall end the year we are in with millions of unemployed. There will be millions, even, who will not have had a steady job for three years or perhaps more. And this in spite of all our work and ingenuity. How do you suppose these men and their families feel about the academic question whether it is recovery we want, or whether it is reform? My friends, these two words have no separate meaning. Either it is a New Deal or it is the Old Deal. The Old Deal brought this insecurity into the midst of their homes; if we returned to what we had before it would still be there, and we should have outraged them baselessly. We have set our faces not toward theories or labels, but toward the necessary actions. The facts are stubborn and ugly. We are driven by them to find a better way of life than we have had. For myself I propose to go on laboring for it; and I hope to go on working with you gentlemen for a cause which, fundamentally, I believe we share.

XXIII
ON LIFE AS A LONG-TIME ENTERPRISE *

FOR this visit to Dartmouth, I am indebted to a young man whose memory is dear to all of you.

Late in winter, the invitation came to me from Robert Michelet. It was relayed to me by his father, who is a Washington attorney, reaching me through close friends in the Department. The suggestion was that I might talk about the New Deal's meaning to the college men of this country. The idea appealed to me. The Roosevelt administration's activities should be especially significant to the young men and women. The future belongs to them.

The invitation also had a particular appeal, coming from Robert Michelet. In his twenty-two years, he had attained remarkable success. Head of your student council, outstanding in athletics, Phi Beta Kappa and Rhodes scholar, he seemed to combine in himself the mental and physical power of American youth.

I think I had a right to feel proud that such a young man should have a personal interest in his Government. His wish for more information seemed a good omen. I thought I should tell him, and all of you here, about the Government's activities. But now Robert Michelet is dead. So this talk is partly a memorial.

There is no man among us who does not have moments when he questions the future, both as it affects himself and as it affects others. These are the quiet, the introspective interludes which all our ingenuity cannot entirely banish from

---

* Address delivered at Dartmouth College, April 26, 1934.

experience. They come oftener, perhaps, to our generation than they have to any other. So much is done for us in a physical way that our business is more limited than it was for our fathers and our grandfathers. We make strenuous attempts to fill in the gaps. We invent sports and spend vast sums in their promotion; we devise amusements and give ourselves to them with an avidity which in itself is revealing. We desire to escape, but we are often unsuccessful. And to each of us soon or late, often or seldom, there come times when we must look out on the world with nothing between the mind and reality and with no alternative but to face fate and consider its consequence.

One of my favorite philosophers made a deep record on my mind with a passage in one of his now-forgotten books: "Life," he said, "is a long-time enterprise." Of course it may not be. He was as well aware as you or I that chance may cut it short. And there have been men, philosophers, who have counseled humanity to act as though each day were to be the last. I have never forgotten the experience I had as a young boy one summer day, driving along a lazy country road with horse and buggy. We came around a bend and I saw in staring letters on a boulder: "Prepare to meet thy God!" There used to be a mendicant few in this country who went about painting scriptural quotations on roadside objects, and this was the work of one of them. It was their belief, and it has been the belief of many sects, that since this world is only preparatory to the next, this particular passage of time ought to be used in avoiding any chance of being unfavorably noticed by a jealous deity's recorders. The trouble with this as a social doctrine is that it centers attention on the individual's relationship to the world in such a way that the world is accepted, even neglected, in favor of a life to come. Now no man could be important enough in the eyes of the God of this concept to spend a lifetime studying the avoidance of disrespectful activity. But there is a psychological appeal in this attitude to which all of us are exposed, and it has been used to good effect by those who would like to keep the world as it is for one reason or another. Besides, it exaggerates the importance of the individual. It says that I, myself, am the center of my necessary regard. I must attend to my own salvation. It is, you see, the antithesis of saying that each of us is his brother's keeper.

I did not comprehend all this, of course, as I went along the road on that summer day. But, as I remember, it was a long and lonely drive and I went a certain way. I think young people are more afraid of death than older people are. Perhaps it is a kind provision of nature that, as we ripen toward harvest, we should incline toward its consummation. And the very old cross the threshold into the unknown with what seems to their grandchildren incredible fortitude. It is probably not so much that as merely being gathered home, and no doubt they have been made ready for it. To the young there is sheer terror in the thought that tonight or tomorrow the great adventure may have to be entered on. And the idea is rejected with an energy which betrays the unnatural element it contains. To you, to each of you, life has got to be a long-time enterprise. To regard it as such, in those interludes when you face the abstractions which invade life everywhere, is to go as far as it is in your natures to go in preparing to meet your God. I was frightened on the day when I was first brought up against the ultimate dictum. It was an experience which sunk deep; it was hard to think it out of my system. I know, from what I went through, that it ought not to be printed, in that fashion, on young minds. Nature has set plenty of lessons by the roadside; and none of us is so blind that he cannot come gradually, without shock,

to their understanding. Life is, indeed, a long-time enterprise, and it is right, irrespective of the chance there is that
it may not come to completion, that it should be undertaken
in that way without the hindrance of intrusive horror. If
something happens, that is tragedy; but in the racial experience tragedy is accepted unwillingly. This is also right; our
purpose is, and always has been, set toward its circumvention.
Why otherwise do we fight disease, poverty and the other
causes which contribute to it? One who serves has taken no
contract of performance. He has undertaken the job in that
spirit, but if he should be cut off, his contract is there completed. He did not prepare to meet his God this side of his
appointed years; but there is where he was required to fasten
his regard. We sometimes, for fertility, plow under a field of
growing grain. It was not in the nature of that grain to do
otherwise than move toward the ripeness of its seed. It is not
required of us that we should do other than move, with
assurance of rightness, toward the consummation of life in
appropriately timed death.

There is therefore set for us a long-time enterprise. But, as
it is regarded, we come to see also that it is an enterprise
which we do not undertake either alone, or without regard
to the past. You and your fellows in your generation, as I
and my fellows in mine, stand on an accumulation of experience. You are not asked to go forward from where Adam
did, or from where those ancestors of yours did, who had no
fire, no levers and no wheels. The enterprise you are in is
the more serious and the more demanding because of this.
Physically and mentally it is doubtful if your equipment is
much better than man's ever was. You, perhaps, have a right
to be a little resentful because you are asked to use it more
vigorously, even to make it perform tasks for which you may
think it unsuited. You can be resentful, if you like, but there

is no one on whom your displeasure can have effect. They are gone. And you are inexorably alone with your task.

The generation which went before you was alone with its task too. It was so resentful that it failed in certain respects. It did some things well; it changed the world considerably. But it made one momentous error. It missed the appropriate moment of history for accepting the consequence of its own creations. The Western World approached uncomfortably close to disaster a few years ago; and it is now struggling desperately to find the means for reconstruction. This is at once your burden and your opportunity. We, who are older, were not wholly persuaded either that life is a long-time enterprise, or that we stood intermingled, one life with another, with the duty of shaping future experience. We prepared daily to meet our God—only our God was what we loosely call money. Each of us regarded his own salvation as an individual matter. We tried to get all the evidences of salvation we could gather together and inclined toward measuring our success in life by their sheer quantity.

Everything else was incidental to this grand passion. We did perfect numerous devices for accumulation. The men we hired to help us were ineffective in turning out the goods we coveted and so we invented machines, perfected factories, devised new financial and commercial processes, and even made something like an exact science of management. But we were intent on a purpose which, although we did not understand it so, was suicidal.

It is not to be supposed that a generation which made so colossal a failure of social management, will succeed much better in reconstruction. It is true that governmental affairs are now intrusted to others who always had misgivings concerning the old acquisitive ideas. But where there is everything to be learned about so complicated a business, and where new attitudes are not shared by a powerful minority, it is doubtful whether the gains will be very rapid or very complete. It is not true that we shall be able to offer your generation of university men a wholly new deal when you emerge as graduates. You will confront the same old system with some few changes. It will depend on the same motives; it will operate almost as inefficiently and with too much of the same injustice. There will have been some protestants, there will even have been some challenging of complacency. Perhaps these will have been of enough importance to furnish the opportunity you need for greater improvement in your time. You cannot count on much more than this. But this is what makes it so important that you should examine, with critical freshness, your contemporary relationship to the world. While you are here, and before you are asked to assume the responsibilities of leadership, you ought to use this time for examination and for decision. If you will really regard your lives as long-time enterprises and ask yourselves not what you must do today or tomorrow but what you would like to look back upon a half century from now, you will come nearer, much nearer, your desire than we are able to do who have to spend most of our time and energy defending our objectives.

There are some superb tools ready to your hands. I have perhaps made too much of the disabilities of human nature. After all these are mostly matters of choice, of reaction to immediate environment. We have at least discredited the worst qualities of the environment you will share with us. It will not be orthodox to respond in the old way. And so you will have gained a certain freedom. With this freedom and with the tools we shall give you there is nothing you might not do. You will have a knowledge of things and forces which is the product of thousands of years of scientific accomplishment. There will even be much of the physical equipment around you which represents these years of effort. Factories, communication systems, devices and processes for making things efficiently—these will be at hand. With them you can, in your generation, see the consummation of many racial longings which have hitherto been unattainable but for which men have never ceased to struggle. You can free this whole land of undesired labor; you can supply every individual in it with all those material things which are necessary to a good life; you can bring ease, freedom and security to every individual, and such assurance of happiness as is furnished by access to wealth.

I do not prophesy that you will accomplish any of this. I merely point out the obvious opportunity. Perhaps the desirability of these achievements will not seem so great to you as it does to us who have had to walk with fear and misery all our lives. Perhaps you will determine on other purposes. And yet it is impossible for me, modest as I feel about pointing out duties to others, to believe that you also will not see these as the first objectives to be gained. Mankind has waited for them so long, and with such infinite patience in the midst of suffering, generation after generation, undergoing the living torture of slavery to things and forces, that I cannot believe you will turn aside to further purposes until these are established beyond the possibility of jeopardy. And I regard it as established that the possibility exists, and with challenging obviousness.

Obvious as the challenge is, however, I know in my heart that there is the gravest danger that you will not choose. Perhaps not enough has yet been done to clear the way, to make such a choice an inescapable one. Those who have gone before you have found escape easy enough and perhaps you too will find it easier than I think. For you will be caught up in a system which will require of you, inexorably, service to quite other institutions. You will have to make a living, to provide for a future which includes that of those you love and for whom you feel an individual responsibility. It will still be hard for you to set other achievements above those of money-getting, even though you may be aware that other activities are more worth while. There will be the temptation not to modify institutions which exist, even though you have convincing knowledge of abuses so grave as to dictate drastic change. You should, of course; even the institutions of what we call the New Deal may soon outlive their usefulness, and their survival should depend upon your independent judgment of their value rather than upon a tradition of existence.

Being caught up in the system in all ways which befall men as they go about the ordinary business of life, it will be nearly as easy for you as it has been for your predecessors to spend your waking hours in collecting things and amusing yourselves; and only sometimes in the interludes of business or sport, or when you are wakeful in the night, turning over in your minds the questions I have forecast as challenging ones. Even in your university life it is difficult. So much of the educational apparatus is designed to turn your minds backward to other times; and so much else devotes itself to the accumulation of the knowledge necessary to the individual who would compete successfully, under the going rules, with his fellows; very little time or care is left for considering the future or for speculations concerning better criteria of living.

Sometimes it seems almost as though we had designed the whole of modern life so that important decisions might have no consideration. If you will allow yourselves to be kept comfortable and secure; if you will believe that you are a favored few whose superior abilities and whose equipment, gained in these seductive surroundings, will insure good lives for yourselves; if you are not made aware that grievous injustices are chargeable to your irresponsibility; if it fails to come home to you that a man's work in this world awaits his own judgment in the time of his departure—you will do no more and no less than most of your elders expect of you, and you will have passed through life but not have lived it.

To have lived—in the definition you will sometime formulate for yourselves—you must have participated livingly in the decisions of your time which matter. You must have done even more than that—you must have set your race forward in some positive way by a contribution which only you could possibly have made. You will become dust soon enough; the line of your descendants will disappear with astonishing enough completeness; your chance of survival in the eyes and mouths of men, or in their written records, will be slim enough. And perhaps you are of those who can use this temporalness for excuse, saying: "It does not matter then. No one will know in a hundred years, or a thousand. I may as well make sure of comfort here." Or, perhaps, if you are a believer in immortality of some sort: "I had better make my peace with the rules for getting into heaven, and after that be careful not to be offensive."

To the inclination toward these attitudes I would object merely that, in your judgment, when you are old and living largely on a diet of recollection, these will not seem sufficient. You will say then that you could have lived differently and better. You will have become mellow, benevolent, and unafraid, rather than active, self-regardful and cautious. You will say that you have not done what you should have done; that the world is not better for your having been in it; that in living for selfish certainties and an assured supply of things, you sacrificed the chance that the race to which you belong might once for all come into the promise which was set in its mind from its first appearance on this earth. You will hate yourselves and die unregretted and full of remonstrance.

If I had the power I should not scruple now to disturb you young men mightily. Too much depends on your participation in the real work there is to be done. I have not the necessary mental affiliations to threaten you with some sort of catastrophe if you fail to waken. It seems perfectly clear to me that you can go through existence serenely and comfortably, making money, playing games, marrying and begetting. There might be disaster close to you and for many other people; you would probably escape it. You would not like yourselves very well in age; but you might, almost until the last, find distraction in senile amusements which would usually stifle any uncomfortable recollections. It would not be easy; but it might be done. No, there is no legitimate threat I know of. But there is the tremendous challenge of opportunity which, once it has been seen by men, has never yet failed to stir their blood. There is something deep in us which responds to the growing challenge of the tyranny of things and calls out efforts which no other reward could possibly evoke.

The incentive, I suppose, which has changed the world most, is exactly this. And I have no desire to appeal to any other, believing any other to be superfluous. I simply say to you that when our generation has done what it could, the world will be in your hands as it has never been in young men's hands before, to make of it what you will. I simply point out that we have come within a very short way indeed from economic abundance and security; and that it is within your power to carry your people, your fellow countrymen, into the future which has been so long and patiently awaited. If you will not do it with this simple motive and with the clear opportunity I know you have there is no further resort for appeal. But I have some faith that this will prove enough.

Man is distinguished among the animals by his ability to learn from the experience of others. Few of us realize the extent of our dependence on previous learning. It is communicated to us in such casual and subtle ways that its entry into our own systems of action is frequently unnoticed. We accept many of the fundamental forces of civilization, and act with them, without inquiring into their origins. Only a few have any knowledge of chemistry, of physics or any of the other branches of learning; but we ride in motor cars, listen to the radio and do numerous other things, which depend on qualities and forces utterly mysterious to all but the highly trained expert. This is never a source of worry. We depend, with a kind of sublime faith, on the perpetuation of expertness by the attractions it holds out to singularly gifted minds. The upshot is that we delegate to a certain few in each generation the tasks of learning from others' experience and accept, by a kind of tacit arrangement, the contrast of doing a few things knowingly and most things on faith.

There have been numerous suggestions that the fields of government and economics ought to be likewise specialized. There has been more resistance here. Abdication has seemed more dangerous, the sciences less exact, and men have felt that the basic decisions ought not to be by other than general consent. This, I think, is sound. And yet there is a problem here which becomes more clear with respect to all social decisions as time goes on. We did not allow people to vote for the acceptance of the vacuum tube or the internal combustion engine; we have not consulted public opinion concerning the reconstruction of railway equipment which will follow the streamline train. Yet these things affect the common life as widely and as deeply as any legislative change could possibly do.

Evidently there is need for definition of the fields within which expertness may be trusted and of those within which a more democratic procedure is necessary. We have developed rather carelessly, in our generation, a policy of autocratic decision about matters which have momentous social effects; and perhaps we may have kept democratic some decisions in which a degree of expertness would be desirable. I think it would be impossible for me to point out to you a more pressing task, among those which lie before you, than this determination of the sphere within which freedom should be given to the expert. You will have a good deal of experience to learn from. Some of our departures from tradition have done great harm because they were not discussed and thoroughly understood beforehand. Each great technical and industrial change has had effects for which society was totally unprepared. An intelligent approach to them would have required adjustment in all the institutions and situations they affected. But our autocratic theory in one field and our democratic theory in the other have prevented this.

You are well aware, of course, that the New Deal involves some of these decisions. You are well aware, also, I suppose, that the balance of weight tends to fall on the side of democracy. This is not, I think, merely because those who have administrative responsibility are prejudiced in favor of democracy; it is at least partly because of a belief that in the long run the democratic method works best. Many of our past troubles seem to us to have resulted from ill-considered change in certain places without regard to the effects they might have in other places. It seems absurd to modern minds used to our customary procedures to think of popular referenda regarding the use of certain scientific devices, certain new processes and the like. But the moment we admit their wide effects and the right of the individual to have a say concerning their intrusion into his life, the question of how they shall be chosen becomes a pressing one. But then there arises the question of conformance. Consent is never quite complete; but social devices usually will not work without complete coöperation. What shall be done with the recalcitrant minority? Administrators in Washington have faced these problems with a good deal of reluctance. They have been inclined to interpret the classic majority as meaning 90 percent rather than 51. That is to say, they have stayed well within the limits of the democratic definition.

Even so there have been bitter complaints of "regimentation" and of "compulsion." So that a kind of dilemma has arisen. Shall the few regiment the many into noncoöperation; or shall the many require the few to conform? I have been speaking of learning from experience. You will be able to learn a great deal from the experiences now being undergone in which you have not participated. Perhaps, as a result, your generation will be able to work out new forms and procedures for democracy which will combine the use of expertness with popular decision concerning the desirability of the processes which are recommended.

I cite this question of democracy for illustrative purposes. It is not more important, perhaps, than many others. But it does serve to show the kind of challenge which is certain to face you. The issues will not always appear clear; they will be complex, confused; they will arise, as they are arising now, on matters which at first seem to be remote, of specific or local interest only. But if they are settled without reference to a view, an attitude, a philosophical conception of life, they will not do more than postpone the issue; and they cannot possibly contribute to the gaining of the better life I hope you may succeed in establishing. I am not suggesting that each of you ought to be a philosopher nor that you should meet practical problems with hampering preconception; but rather that you should always ask concerning them: How does this contribute to those aims which Americans hold in common? This may seem to you an indefinite criterion. If you will use some of your free hours now to explore the American character, the development of our traditions, our background of thinking, it will seem less so.

Besides, you will need to experiment and you will learn from that. One of the methods which the New Deal has borrowed from science, in its attack on our present ills, is just this experimental approach. You ought to find it easier to use in public affairs because of the pioneering which is being done now.

Armed with a personal conviction of rightness in regarding life as a genuine long-time enterprise, with an apprehension of the problems you must meet, with an awareness of the American way of meeting situations, your lives ought to be lived through in one of the most interesting periods of all history. Your generation ought to come to its reward of recollection feeling that something unique has been accomplished and that the world is really better for your having lived. I commend you to your future with the confidence of one who has spent most of his mature life working with young men and who has sensed something of the need there is in these years for the strength and intelligence which resides in you.

XXIV

ECONOMIC FREEDOM AND THE FARMERS *

AMONG the lessons of depression and recovery, one which
stands out clearly is the demonstration of the interdependence of banking and agriculture.

Early in the twenties, the postwar decline in farm prices
manifested itself in failures of many banks in the farming
regions. When, at times between 1920 and 1932, appearances
seemed to indicate a lack of relationship between the economic status of agriculture and that of banking, such appearances were merely temporary and superficial.

The income of agriculture fell from $12,000,000,000 in
1929 to $5,000,000,000 in 1932. Such disappearance of farm
buying power had the same immediate effects upon outlying
banks as if a large part of the people themselves had van-
ished. The shrinkage in farm income curtailed farmers' demand for goods, aggravating industrial unemployment and
accelerating decline in consumer buying power. Farm prices
fell faster and further than other prices, reaching the lowest
recorded levels. This decline carried down the value of lands
and chattels which were security for farm credits. The heavy
rate of bank suspensions in rural regions became a wave of
failures in 1930 and 1931. These difficulties, together with
the many other forces of depression, gradually spread to the
financial centers, tightening credit there. This happened in
spite of all the Government's efforts, prior to 1933, to sustain the banks with loans.

Finally, little more than a year ago—on March 3, 1933—

* Address delivered before the New York State Bankers Association, Buffalo, April 28, 1934.

the banking system of this country was in a state of collapse.

That situation has now been surmounted. Under the leadership of President Roosevelt, the beginnings of economic recovery have been safely achieved. It is important to observe that the interdependence of banking and agriculture has continued to be a factor in recovery, just as it was in depression.

The first objective of the Roosevelt administration in March, 1933, was the reopening of the banks, so that the nation's business could go on. The second objective was the initiation of measures to rehabilitate agriculture, and these were followed promptly by plans to stimulate employment. Thus improvement in the purchasing power of farmers and urban populations was recognized as the base of the financial structure. The administration founded its recovery program upon the proposition that the sound functions of banking are inseparable from the prosperity of the people.

Since March, 1933, the validity of that premise has been established. Reopened under governmental supervision to assure their soundness, the banks have been strengthened by the improving conditions in agriculture, and by increased consumer purchasing power.

It is because of your undoubted appreciation of the interdependence of banking and agriculture, because much of the strength of banking and in fact of all industry, traces directly to farm purchasing power, and also because I know of your interest in the long-time aspects of these things, that I am happy to address you here today on the progress of American farmers under the Agricultural Adjustment Act.

This Act, one of the corner stones in the recovery legislation passed by Congress last spring, seeks to restore to basic farm commodities a purchasing power on a parity with their purchasing power in the five years before the World War.

In this period, from 1909 to 1914, production was fairly balanced with demand, and prices to farmers and consumers were reasonably satisfactory. As we look back upon it, this period of relative stability seems by comparison with what has happened since, like agriculture's "golden age." It was not that farmers were then rolling in wealth. Money was not too plentiful with them, and their homes still lacked many of the comforts and conveniences already common in city homes. But, in general, they were free from the gnawing fear of losing their farms, they received a reasonable share of manufactured products in exchange for the things they produced, and for some, at least, life had a fine rural flavor.

All this was upset by the World War. Demand for American farm products increased, as the European nations concentrated on waging their battles at the front. Then the United States entered the War, and the demand was intensified. All prices rose. For a brief period of a year or two, prices of farm products, except where an arbitrary limit was established by the Government as in the case of wheat, rose faster than other prices.

With the slogan, "Food Will Win the War," the farmers were called upon to do everything possible to increase their production. The result was that some 45,000,000 acres of grassland and forest land were put under the plow.

Agriculture's period of prosperity, as it turned out, was short. General deflation came in 1921. All prices tumbled. The decline in prices of farm products was more extreme than the fall in the general price level. Although farm land values, except in rare instances, never had been capitalized, on the basis of the extreme price levels of 1919, they collapsed and farm land became almost unsalable. Farm mortgages, contracted when prices were high, became frozen assets, causing the demise of thousands of rural banks, many of which had been mushroom growths of inflation, without permanent farm purchasing power to sustain them. Millions of farm people migrated to the cities and obtained work in factories and offices.

The situation was made worse by three other developments. Just as farm prices fell, the railroads were permitted to increase their freight rates. This, while it gave certain competitive advantages to the farmers of the eastern states, had a strongly adverse effect on the farmers of the West and South. Higher freight cost hit the farmers going and coming. It meant lower prices at the farm for the things they sold and higher prices at the farm for the things they bought.

A second development was the motorization of America. With automobiles, trucks, and tractors coming into almost universal use, the number of horses was greatly reduced. Horses eat hay and grain; automobiles and tractors do not. Therefore, an outlet for the product from approximately 35,000,000 acres of crop land was gone.

Third, the United States emerged from the War as a creditor rather than a debtor nation. Before the War we had paid the interest on our debt abroad principally with exports of farm products. After the War we kept on exporting our farm and other products, but we made no conscious adjustment for the change in our status to that of a creditor nation. As a result, sales of our farm products were limited. Europe was able to buy our products only with money we advanced in loans.

The combined effect of all these factors was to plunge agriculture, beginning with 1921, into a long period of tribulation. It was obvious that surplus was the heart of the problem, since there was a greater supply of farm products than could be sold at prices which could enable the farmer to keep on buying the things he needed. But there was much diversity in the remedies suggested. Coöperative marketing was attempted by the farmers on a large scale, but this by itself was inadequate. The tariff on farm products was increased, but this was only a futile gesture, since the most important farm products, including wheat and cotton, were sold on a world market. Farmers were urged to diversify. This was a gain to many farmers individually, but it also had the effect of shifting the trouble from one region to another. Farmers were urged to practice more intensive methods of production. They did this also, with great savings which were shared by consumers, but with the further result of increasing production beyond market demand and depressing prices still more.

During this period of the twenties, proposals for surplus control received the most attention. The McNary-Haugen plan of "making the tariff effective on farm products" by means of the equalization fee, received wide support and actually passed Congress twice, but was vetoed each time by President Coolidge. There was also the export debenture plan, which received wide support but was not enacted into law.

Finally, at the beginning of the Hoover administration, in 1929, the Agricultural Marketing Act, establishing the Federal Farm Board, was passed. This attempted to meet the surplus problem by stabilization operations—holding farm products off the market so as to maintain prices at a satisfactory level. In a period of rising prices, the plan might have operated with greater success than it did achieve. But as it turned out, prices fell and it was impossible to market the supplies held by the Government except at great loss. Meantime, the very presence of those huge supplies overhanging the market tended to keep prices down.

The effect of the general business depression, which began

late in 1929 and continued with increasing severity for nearly four years, was calamitous for the farmers of the United States. For a decade they had failed to maintain their share of the national income. With prices of the things they sold remaining low and their fixed charges of debts and taxes remaining high, they strained every nerve to grow as many units of their crops as possible. In this way, if they worked hard enough and were lucky, they could just barely meet their fixed charges and retain their farms. This meant the robbing of the fertility of their soil. In effect, they were mining their soil and giving away its fertility to the people—both here and abroad—who bought their products.

As deflation continued and prices fell lower and lower, the farmers had less and less money to spend for manufactured products. A constantly increasing number were unable to meet interest payments and taxes; mortgage foreclosures became more frequent. Farm strikes were frequent. Finally, in the winter of 1932-33, the farmers, thoroughly angry, here and there began taking matters into their own hands. You all remember the mortgage foreclosure riots, which in a few instances resulted in near-lynchings.

This decline in farmers' buying power had unfortunate effects, which I have already outlined, upon the banking system. First the small outlying banks began to go. Then, as the farm depression deepened, the effects upon banks spread in continually widening circles. The loss of farmers' buying power was just one among the forces which undermined the financial structure, but it was unquestionably an important factor.

It was evident that more fundamental measures than any tried thus far would have to be invoked by the Roosevelt administration in behalf of agriculture. From the point of view of the farmer himself, and correctives available to him, the heart of the problem was still overproduction, as it had been for twelve years.

Looking back over the period I have been describing, it seems as if the logic of events led inevitably up to the Agricultural Adjustment Act. Every Secretary of Agriculture since the War had pointed to the necessity of doing something about the surplus. Secretary Henry C. Wallace, in his report of 1924, issued after his death, declared that "overproduction . . . brought about the collapse in farm prices."

Secretary William M. Jardine recognized the surplus as the central difficulty. In 1925 he wrote:

It is well known that small surpluses exercise a depressing effect on prices altogether disproportionate to their amount. . . . It is to the interest of the entire community that agriculture should not be periodically depressed by overproduction and low prices.

In 1926 he said:

As to the surplus problem, there are two general avenues of approach to its solution. One is through a better adjustment of production to market requirements.

And in 1927 he declared:

While farmers themselves are reducing their costs of production through increased efficiency, public agencies should coöperate with them in effecting a better adjustment of production to demand.

But it remained for the operations of the Federal Farm Board to reveal the full extent of the surplus problem. Secretary Arthur M. Hyde, in his 1930 report, wrote:

One aspect of the farm problem overshadows all others. Production . . . is out of balance with the market, and surpluses pile up continuously. . . . Our difficulty is not a sudden emergency, but a cumulative overproduction. . . . I want to emphasize the need for equitable, intelligent, systematic, and collective action [notice that word "collective"] to bring supply into better relationship with demand. . . . The answer to overproduction is less production.

Again in 1931 Secretary Hyde wrote:

American agriculture must adjust itself to a declining export trade. As things stand, this need will persist, no matter how favorably matters develop in Europe, because our production is over-expanded in relation to Europe's wants. . . . This is a policy of constructive adjustment to a radically changing market situation.

As a matter of fact, during the years when agriculture was in such difficulties, industry, though it had no mathematical limitation upon satisfied wants such as is defined in the case of food products by the capacity of the human stomach, still had effectively contracted production. Figures compiled by the Federal Reserve Board show that the index of production for iron and steel fell from 130 in 1929 to 31 in 1932; for bituminous coal, from 102 to 59; for anthracite coal, from 91 to 62; for automobiles, from 135 to 35; for boots and shoes, from 110 to 95; and for textiles, from 115 to 83. The combined index for these products fell from 119 to 63.

Meantime, what about agriculture? The combined index for cotton, grain, meat animals, dairy products and poultry products declined only 5 percent, from 109 in 1929 to 104 in 1932, with stocks of wheat, cotton, tobacco, and lard accumulating year by year.

Agriculture, in effect, was exchanging an average unit of its production for little more than half of the normal amount of manufactured products. This relationship was expressed in corresponding price ratios. By February, 1933, the exchange value of farm products for industrial goods had fallen to 50 percent of the prewar average. Their exchange value for taxes and credit was even less.

When President Roosevelt took office, March 4, 1933, it was evident that something more than persuasion was needed to curb the agricultural overproduction. This method had been tried by the Federal Farm Board and had signally failed. No farmer could afford to reduce his production without assurance that enough of his fellows would do likewise to permit all of them to gain by so doing.

The Agricultural Adjustment Act, which became effective May 12, 1933, was the answer to the demand from all sides for action to cope with the twin problems of farm surpluses and farm debts.

It was recognized that part of the reason for the low prices of farm products—particularly live stock, dairy products and perishable fruits and vegetables—was the lack of buying power among city people. The general recovery program aimed to correct this situation by spreading purchasing power among both groups.

Right here it seems appropriate to say a word about the seeming paradox of the simultaneous existence of surpluses on the farms and bread lines in the cities. In so far as the people in the cities were actually underfed, this was inexcusable. In the United States, with its rich productivity, every person should have enough to eat, of the right kind of food to maintain health. It was the responsibility of the people at large, acting through the Government, to see that no person should starve. This responsibility, I may say, has, since March 4, 1933, been assumed directly by the Federal Emergency Relief Administration and the Federal Surplus Relief Corporation, and indirectly by the other recovery agencies which have created employment and distributed purchasing power in various ways.

But it certainly was *not* the responsibility of the farmers, who themselves were in sore straits, to feed the destitute.

And those who now are saying that it is wrong for the Government to aid the farmer in restricting his production overlook one very important fact—that even though every hungry person in the United States should be well fed, there would still remain a surplus. This is because of the disappearance of over-sea markets. Our normal wheat production, for example, has been more than 800,000,000 bushels a year in the past, while our normal domestic human consumption is around 500,000,000 bushels. With the amount needed for seed and feed added, the total domestic consumption is around 600,000,000 bushels. This would leave a normal exportable surplus, assuming no adjustment in production were made, of more than 200,000,000 bushels. During the last few years, the world's markets have refused to take this amount of our wheat. If the rest of the world will not take our wheat, what are we to do with it? I know of no law which will compel people to eat 20 percent or 40 percent more bread than they are accustomed to. Why should agriculture go on producing for a market which does not now exist and which may not again exist for years to come?

Some persons are urging that the way out of the depression is to produce, not to restrict. It is true that there is no absolute surplus of manufactured products, and that the only reason our factories cannot run full blast is the maldistribution of purchasing power. Otherwise, why should we have had only one-fourth as much steel and three-fourths as much textiles in 1932 as in 1929? Surely, if we had been organized to use the abundance which nature has provided, we would have been able to use the same amount of steel and textiles in 1932 as in 1929—and perhaps much more.

But let us not be confused in our thinking. We can arrange to have abundance where abundance is needed and can be consumed. We need not waste our energies producing that which is not needed and which must inevitably pile up in warehouses, as nearly 400,000,000 bushels of American wheat piled up in 1932 and 1933.

It is important to note the extent to which farmers are regaining their lost purchasing power. You as bankers are interested in this because you are interested in having bank loans repaid. You are interested in the condition of life insurance companies, which have huge amounts invested in farm mortgages. You are interested in the railroads' condition, which depends in great part on the volume of their shipments, including shipments of manufactured goods to the farming regions. You are interested in the continuous operation of city factories, which cannot run full time when farmers are unable to buy.

I have not time for a detailed account of what has been done by the Agricultural Adjustment Administration. You may find this in the four-hundred-page report, *Agricultural Adjustment,* recently issued by Mr. Chester C. Davis, Administrator. It will suffice to say that the assistance offered by the Adjustment Administration has been accepted by more than 1,000,000 cotton farmers, more than 500,000 wheat farmers, nearly 300,000 tobacco growers, and 1,200,000 corn and hog producers. Unable by their own individual efforts to bring production into line with demand, they have eagerly coöperated with the Government to accomplish this. As a consequence of the cotton reduction program of 1933, and other recovery measures, including especially devaluation of the dollar, the potential gross income of the cotton growers from the 1933 crop, including rental payments and profits on options, is $857,000,000, as compared with $425,-000,000, the farm value of the 1932 crop. Gross income from grains, including wheat benefit payments, was close to $700,-000,000 in 1933, compared with less than $325,000,000 in

1932. Striking gains have been made also in the income of tobacco farmers. The estimated total value of the 1933 flue-cured tobacco crop is $115,000,000, compared with $44,-000,000 for the 1932 crop. Growers of other kinds of tobacco are profiting also. Corn-hog farmers will soon begin to receive the first installment on their benefit payments, to be made by the Government in consideration of their reduction in corn acreage and hog supplies. The program calls for a maximum total of $350,000,000 in these payments. Government loans on corn also have added to the corn growers' income. Growers of rice, walnuts, fruits and a number of other minor crops have been placed in a materially improved position through marketing agreements. As to dairy products, we have not been able to accomplish all that we would like. Problems of this industry are the most complex of any branch of agriculture. Conflicting local interests have made it difficult to get general agreement within the industry on any adequate national program.

And now I should like to invite attention to a corollary effort of the Government in behalf of agriculture. This is the work of the Farm Credit Administration, under the outstanding leadership of Henry Morgenthau and his successor as governor, William I. Myers. While this operation has not been of a spectacular kind, and hence is not so much heralded in headlines, it has had a vital part in the assistance to agriculture.

Without such governmental operation, the collapse of farm buying power would have resulted in a wave of foreclosures far exceeding all previous experience. The depressions of 1873, 1893 and 1921, no less than that of the present, have shown that farmers suffer acutely from the fact that their long-term risks are subject to the contractions of a short-time credit system. Hence the Government's farm loans with gradual amortization, afford them real and needed protection. If the threatened foreclosures had been permitted, the land would have gone out of the hands of farmers and into the involuntary ownership of banks and insurance and investment companies. This would have happened before the effects of the adjustment program could have been felt sufficiently to save the situation. What could the banks and insurance companies have done with the land holdings which, though not wanted, they would suddenly have acquired? Probably there would have been an immense increase in corporation farming, with farmers regimented into the ranks of farm labor.

Against such a development, the Government employed the measures and resources of the Farm Credit Administration. Thus far it has placed $1,100,000,000 in the farming districts in refinancing mortgages and providing other forms of agricultural credit. This whole operation unquestionably has supplemented and strengthened the entire credit structure of the nation. Just as the efforts of the Farm Credit Administration have saved the day for agriculture until the adjustment program could get under way, so the adjustment program, increasing farm incomes, will insure the soundness of the Farm Credit operations.

The combined effect of the credit and adjustment programs and the Government's other recovery measures now is widely felt. The increased income of the farm areas where the adjustment program is operating, particularly in the West and the South, has already quickened every phase of the economic life in those regions. Surveys made by the Agricultural Adjustment Administration have revealed that one of the first concerns of the farmers is to pay their debts and taxes. Bankers are receiving payments on loans they had long ago written off. In the buying of goods, the farmers are using their money judiciously. Much of it is going for needed articles, such as shoes and clothing, household utensils, furniture, sets of harness, paint, roofing, fencing, farm implements and, in some cases, automobiles. Since most of these articles are manufactured in the northern and eastern states, factories in these sections have derived a substantial amount of business, which in turn has made possible corresponding increases in employment. The state of New York, including the farmers of New York, have without doubt been aided materially by the increase in factory pay rolls caused by the farm revival in other sections.

The nearly 3,000,000 farmers voluntarily participating in the adjustment plans sponsored by the Government are not complaining about "regimentation." This cry is coming rather from those who, during the years when farmers by the thousand were losing their homes, congratulated them on their rugged individualism, and now that they have succeeded in retaining their homes, commiserate them on losing their traditional American ways. If you do not believe me, go and talk with farmers in the wheat, corn-hog, tobacco and cotton regions of the West and the South. To them the Agricultural Adjustment Act, far from being the yoke of a despot, is a recognition of their right to economic freedom. The operations under the Act are not perfect, and grounds exist here and there for individual dissatisfaction. But you will find that to millions of farmers the Act stands as an economic bill of rights. For half a century they have fought for the principle of equality which it contains, and they will not sit idly by while a few selfish interests, accustomed to exploiting the farmers' disunity, attempt to tear it down.

Now that we are developing programs for most of the basic commodities originally named in the Act, and also for many minor ones, the question naturally arises: What of the future?

Secretary Wallace has pointed out in his booklet, *America Must Choose,* that our course depends a great deal on what we do about our foreign trade. If we can reopen the export markets for our products, our adjustments of production will not have to be nearly so drastic as otherwise. But Europe cannot buy from us unless she can also sell to us. The old policy of financing exports by foreign loans could never be anything but temporary and is out of the question now. Reciprocal agreements which will assist other countries in finding markets here must be made. That is why the work of the Export-Import Bank, headed by George N. Peek, is so important. That is why the bill now before Congress giving the President power to adjust our tariffs is imperatively needed.

But the rest of the world, in order to absorb enough of our farm products to make restriction of our output unnecessary, would have to sell us approximately $1,000,000,000 more of goods a year than at present. A change of such magnitude could only be made gradually and with great care. It could not be completed in the near future. Some restriction of output, therefore, will have to be continued if our agriculture is not to suffer a new collapse.

The situation may be remedied somewhat by gradual government acquisition of marginal farm lands. Through the Federal Surplus Relief Corporation $25,000,000 has already been made available for the purpose. But the program of taking land out of production by this means also must necessarily be extremely slow. Lands to be purchased must be selected with care, and new opportunities must be created for the people living on these lands.

Another possible development is the replacement of the present system of piecemeal adjustments, commodity by commodity, with a comprehensive plan involving all production on the farms affected. Instead of separate contracts for wheat, cotton, tobacco, corn and hogs, and so on, a composite contract may be worked out. This would have to be adjusted to fit the needs of the individual farm and the wishes of the individual farmer. In this way temporarily adjusted production would give way to more lasting coördination in production.

Whatever system is worked out should be based on the principle of voluntary coöperation, just as the present system is. The county production control associations which have been formed to operate the adjustment program constitute the greatest demonstration on record of the functioning of a responsible democracy. They show how the persons directly concerned can carry out, through a system of decentralized control in the 3,000 counties of the 48 states, plans developed with the needs and desires of the whole nation kept in view.

Underlying and interwoven with this whole adjustment program is the necessity for returning 50,000,000 acres from cultivated crops to grass or pasture or roughage—in other words, a return from more intensive to less intensive use of the soil. This will be the reverse of the process which took place at the time of the War. It is part of the program of land utilization and conservation now being developed.

The necessity for this land utilization program, like the measures for control of production, was foreseen by Secretary Hyde. Addressing the National Conference on Land Utilization which he had called at Chicago in November, 1931, he said:

Our Federal and State land policies have . . . encouraged the rapid transfer of public lands to private ownership with little regard given to the uses to which the land was best adapted or to the demand for its products. The economic and social difficulties in agriculture, which are so widely recognized at present, are in considerable degree traceable to the effects of these policies. . . . It is recommended that land development enterprises be licensed and regulated. . . . We are not thinking of agriculture nowadays as a local problem. We must see this as a national problem, and as a whole.

He further recommended the removal from private ownership of "lands that cannot be utilized profitably by private individuals or concerns without serious wastage of the soil through erosion or other causes."

In his report for the same year, he pleaded for immediate action and made eight recommendations, including these:

Encourage farmers operating poor land to find better opportunities in agriculture or other occupations. . . . Promote compact communities. . . . Create conditions that will make possible the use for which land is best adapted. . . . Discourage the over-expansion of agriculture.

One of the biggest differences between the agricultural and land policies of this administration and those of previous administrations is the difference between talk and action. There is the widest distinction between the perception of a need, and the painstaking creation and operation of machinery to meet that need. The Secretaries of Agriculture in the Coolidge and Hoover administrations perceived that the surplus was the heart of the farm problem. They vehemently urged that production be reduced to a balance with demand and that submarginal lands be taken out of cultivation. They talked a great deal about the necessity for action. And now, so to speak, President Roosevelt and Secretary Wallace have followed their advice and in this administration we finally have action itself.

I think it is fair to say that intelligent use of the land is the first criterion of any civilization. The fertility of the soil is the ultimate source of wealth. When that is gone, the civilization built upon it soon decays. Already, as a result of the twelve-year agricultural depression, the soil fertility in whole regions is sadly depleted. Painstaking work will be needed to conserve what is left and to build up the land to its former fertile state. The chief difference between the fertility of the great plains of the Mississippi Valley and the desolation caused by erosion in the river valleys in the interior of China, is a difference in time of cultivation. Our methods have been as negligent and as destructive of fertility as theirs. By coördinating activities of the Department of the Interior, the Federal Emergency Relief Administration and the Department of Agriculture, it will be possible to use our lands more effectively. For the first time in our history we are now undertaking the control of erosion on entire watersheds. We want to create better opportunities for those who now are barely able to eke out an existence on poor soil. We made a start in this direction in New York State under Governor Roosevelt.

It is true that some have sought to condemn all these efforts by the mere use of such words as "collectivism" and "regimentation."

But the Agricultural Adjustment Administration's plans, and the kindred programs of the Government, are too fundamental and too pressing to be dismissed in that way. All are based on the time-tried principles of American democracy, upon the self-government and self-discipline of county and local associations, and upon voluntary coöperation on a grand scale.

Of one thing I am sure: the American people had enough, previous to March 4, 1933, of the kind of thing that regimented thousands of farmers off their farms like the Acadians of "Evangeline"; the kind of thing that regimented 12,000,000 men into the ranks of the unemployed, closed every bank and brought our democracy to one of its darkest hours. That was surely an economy of chaos. What we are building now is an economy of order and, provided selfish interests do not thwart our efforts, we shall build an economy of abundance.

The thrifty American farmer can be freed of the future tyranny of a grudging and impoverished soil by preventing its erosion and preserving its native fertility; he can employ the democracy of his local associations, and the help of his Government, to win freedom from the weight of uncontrolled surplus production which beats down his prices and destroys his income. The farmer can strengthen his hold on economic freedom by use of the Government's long-time credit facilities, removing the threat of loss of his home. In time, as submarginal areas go into forests and parks, he can be freed of the hopelessness of trying to wring a living from lands which are unfitted for the plow.

These aims mean the conservation and not the wasteful exploitation of our resources and our man power. They contemplate care and thought about the grave agricultural problems of the day, with devices to meet them, not mere passive reliance in the name of rugged individualism upon the sheer forces of economic compulsion. The interdependence of banking and agriculture is, after all, just one example of the enlightened self-interest which lies in coöperation among great economic groups. The welfare of business and financial interests is directly dependent upon large consumer purchasing power of agricultural and urban populations. The opportunity for coöperation to bring it about should not be permitted to go by default, but should be employed to build a civilization which is worthy of Americans.

XXV

THE SOCIAL RESPONSIBILITY OF TECHNICAL WORKERS *

WHOEVER chose this topic, "The Social Responsibility of Technical Workers," has rather blithely, I think, proceeded on an assumption which technical workers usually reject. Most spokesmen for science, at least, are quite vehement in their contention that the research worker has no social responsibility. He is, they say in effect, a being apart from the world, permitted to remain so because of the fruitful results to society of an extraordinary intellectual curiosity applied successfully only in isolation. Save the isolation, they argue, and you save all.

The case for isolation was most persuasively argued a few months ago by Mr. A. V. Hill, in the Huxley Memorial Lecture before the British Royal Society. "If scientific people are to be accorded the privilege of immunity and tolerance by civilized societies," Mr. Hill said, "they must observe the rules." Then he quoted the rules, as summarized by Robert Hooke 270 years ago after the passing of the Second Charter of the Royal Society. This summary began as follows:

The business and design of the Royal Society is—To improve the knowledge of natural things, and all useful Arts, Manufactures, Mechanick practices, Engynes and Inventions by Experiments— (not meddling with Divinity, Metaphysics, Moralls, Politicks, Grammar, Rhetorick or Logick).

Those were the rules for the research worker of 270 years ago. And he has, since then, done more to upset them, turn

* Address delivered before organizations of Government employees, Washington, D. C., May 1, 1934.

them inside out, and force the acceptance of new rules for the rest of us, than any other kind of individual. I need only remind you how the physicist, without any conscious attempt to meddle, of course, has played hob in the domain of meta-physics; how the research worker on electricity and the gas engine, say, has turned some of our moral, economic, and political traditions into very faint shadows of their pristine selves. Even logic has not escaped the influence of the scientific method, nor rhetoric the consequences of the machine age. He may not have been aware that he was meddling, this early researcher, but how mistaken he was!

Mr. Hill quotes approvingly something Newton is reported to have said shortly before his death:

I know not what I may appear to the world, but to myself I seem to have been only like a boy playing on the seashore and diverting myself in now and then finding a smoother pebble or a prettier shell than ordinary, whilst the great ocean of truth lay all undiscovered before me.

Even discounting for modesty, there is surely no preoccupation with social responsibility here, nothing but complete and perfect observance of the rules of isolation. And so Mr. Hill sums up for the defense:

Not meddling with morals or politics: such, I would urge, is the normal condition of tolerance and immunity for scientific pursuits in a civilized state. I speak not with contempt of these— indeed the scorn with which some superior people talk of such necessities of social existence as morals and politics seems to me intolerably childish and stupid. The best intellects and characters, not the worst, are wanted for the moral teachers and political governors of mankind; but science should remain aloof and detached, not from any sense of superiority, not from any indifference to the common welfare, but as a condition of complete intellectual honesty. Emotion, entirely necessary in ordinary life, is utterly out of place in making scientific decisions. If science loses its intellectual honesty and its political independence, if—under Communism or Fascism—it becomes tied to emotion, to propaganda, to advertisement, to particular social or economic theories, it will cease altogether to have its general appeal, and its political immunity will be lost. If science is to continue to make progress, if it is to lead to the advancement and not to the destruction of human institutions, it must insist on keeping its traditional position of independence, it must refuse to meddle with, or to be dominated by, divinity, morals, politics, or rhetoric.

I think I have quoted enough of Mr. Hill's paper to refresh your minds with the traditional attitude of most scientists towards social responsibility. You will find other examples of it in almost any contemporary collection of the after-dinner statements of prominent scientists. The spirit which animates this defense of scientific isolation—the desire for complete and uninterrupted intellectual freedom and intellectual honesty—is surely beyond criticism, but the assumption that any intrusion on scientific isolation, any acceptance of social responsibility by scientists and research workers, means the end of intellectual honesty, does not necessarily follow.

The scientist who abhors meddling with society is altogether too naïve. During the last two or three centuries science has been the chief meddler, no matter how unwittingly. From the scientist's splendid isolation has come a new civilization, much of it magnificent, much of it quite the reverse. The conventional speech in defense of science against those who would reduce appropriations for research, for instance, is to stress the benefactions of science and to ignore the rest. Yet society knows, even if a few prominent scientists do not, that some of the results of science have not been beneficent. The charge that society, in these instances, has perverted or misused the product of research, does not obliterate the unfortunate result at all, nor does it improve the attitude of society toward science.

The problem would be difficult enough if the consequences of science extended only to our material culture—to machines, say, and roads, and houses, and material standards of living. The impact of these material changes on our traditional institutions would be serious enough, but the fact is that the consequences of science have gone beyond this point to affect our institutions themselves, our modes of interest and activity, our very habits of thought. As Mr. John Dewey has said,

We have broken with the intellectual traditions of the past and the mass of men have not had the nature of the change interpreted to them, although science set the terms on which men associate together. They transform life in ways that have created social problems of such vastness and complexity that the human mind stands bewildered. The intellect is at present subdued by the results of its own intellectual victories.

What, then, is the way out? If science is convicted of being our greatest meddler, the sentence of the police court, no doubt, would be imprisonment until it promised to stop meddling. No intelligent person would agree to such a sentence, of course. We don't want to go back to the Middle Ages, no matter how complex our problems seem to be. Nor would America wish to put science under the restraints which exist in certain parts of Europe today. To most of us that is unthinkable.

No, the unwitting, unpredictable meddling of science with society will continue—for we believe that we have more to gain than to lose by it—provided we are willing, quite realistically, to distinguish between a social gain and a social loss, and to act to preserve the one and to prevent the other.

Taking the long view, Mr. John Dewey suggests that

the wounds made by applications of science can be healed only by a further extension of applications of knowledge and intelligence; like the purpose of all modern healing the application must be preventive as well as curative. This is the supreme obligation of intellectual activity at the present time.

I suppose that means a vigorous, long-continued pressure for the use of scientific methods in fields where ordinarily it has never been permitted. I suppose it means the rejection of prejudice, of dogma, and of emotionalism in economics and politics, to name only two likely fields. Finally, it means a dependence on the slow, unsensational process of education.

I have, quite naturally, considerable sympathy with that point of view. It is not excessively hopeful, however, for those who expect some improvement in things a few years this side of the millennium. It is slow, and it therefore may be poorly equipped to run at the pace which science demands; for if society accommodates itself to science only about one-tenth as fast as science imposes the necessity for further accommodations—well, that disparity cannot, in all probability, go on forever. There may be some safe relationship between the speed of science and the speed of society which we ought to discover and strive for.

Meanwhile, is it too much to ask that scientists abandon their fiction of isolation and join the rest of us in contemplating the consequences of their handiwork? And I am wondering whether they might not, after a little such contemplation, be moved to demand that society so utilize their researches as to establish social gains rather than losses. They can demand that of society, it seems to me, without impairing intellectual freedom or honesty.

The difficulty is, of course, that certain powerful and selfish interests may not like such demands. And they will neatly revive the appeal to scientific isolation, and invite the scientists to return to their ivory towers and stay there, on pain, perhaps, of a reduction in appropriations. This is a danger, I admit, but if science cowers before it, what becomes of its intellectual integrity and freedom?

This fear of those who hold the purse strings may be one reason for the reluctance of many scientists to assume any social responsibility, but I cannot believe it is the controlling one. A much greater obstacle, it has been my observation, is the rather surprising fact that many scientific men still hold that there is a region of beliefs, social, economic, and political, which is reserved for sheer acceptance and where unbiased inquiry should not intrude. Not many express it that baldly, but their implicit acquiescence amounts to the same thing. They seem not to appreciate that science has done things to men's institutions, traditions, and beliefs, as well as to an industrial order. Science operates, they imply, in conveniently isolated, water-tight compartments, and it operates only from 9 to 4:30; what happens after hours or outside the compartment doesn't count. And in effect they deny the possibility of applying the scientific method, the impartial spirit of inquiry and experimentation, to any but the physical sciences.

It is not surprising, therefore, that the economic and political views of many of our most prominent men of science are as dogmatic, orthodox, and unrealistic as their views on the atom are undogmatic, unorthodox, and continually experimental. Especially do they seem to consider economics a series of statements of absolute, unchangeable laws, derived deductively, and, as one economic historian phrased it, therefore closer to medieval scholasticism than any other intellectual activity in the modern world.

Because they are uncritical about economics, they class the gold standard with the laws of thermodynamics, and they put the theory of free competition in the same category with Archimedes' principle. And while they accept these laws and principles in the physical sciences only after scientific demonstration and proof, and are always willing to admit the possibility of their modification through further experimentation and proof, nevertheless they seem reluctant to expose many of our so-called economic laws to comparable tests. Not only scientists, of course, are guilty of this dogmatism; business men and even many economists have a similar inclination. Consider, for example, the way in which we cling to the doctrine of laissez faire in a world radically different—thanks, largely, to science—from that world for which the doctrine was first formulated. Only lately, in popular discussion, at least, has there arisen the suspicion that there might possibly be some difference between laissez faire in theory and laissez faire in practice—a difference between the way in which men behave, that is, and the way in which believers in a traditional doctrine assume that they behave. Incidentally, I have often wondered whether many business men really believe the dogma of laissez faire as firmly as many professors of economics seem to; and I have come to the melancholy conclusion that if they do, it must be because they dislike to let theory interfere with practice, just as so many professors dislike to let practice interfere with theory.

Those people who have so extravagantly praised the beauties of laissez faire have always done so on the assumption of highly flexible prices and a degree of freedom of competition. Yet for at least forty years the practices of business have been making increasingly heavy inroads on that assumption. In 1929 we did not have a system of free competition and flexible prices. What we had was the spotted reality of competition and control—with the control intrusted to irresponsible trustees.

In farming, there was no control at all, responsible or irresponsible, there were highly flexible prices and there were millions of individuals competing in both production and price. If prices—all prices, all charges, that is—throughout our economy since the War had been as flexible as those in the farm area, it is possible that the depression would have been of minor consequence. But prices of some of the most important goods and services were not flexible. The theory bogged down in practice. An important part of our economy had prices which were not responsive—as theoretically they should have been—to changes in supply or demand. At the furthest extreme were railroad and public utility rates, steel rails, and many other goods and services whose prices were fixed over very considerable periods of time. In such areas, the whole impact of changes in demand is taken in the form of changes in production without any changes in price.

Between these two extremes of rigidity and flexibility lies most of industry. In this intermediate area prices are fixed for shorter periods of time, but are periodically revised over longer periods of time. In varying degrees, therefore, changes in demand are met by changes in production, and more slowly and over a longer time only, by changes in price.

Offhand I can think of no important product whose price and production movements have behaved as the basic concept of laissez faire says they ought to. Illustrations of the discrepancy between fact and theory, on the other hand, are embarrassingly plentiful.

This discrepancy between a fundamental theory of laissez faire, and the actual practice of it, is exceedingly important. The legislation of the New Deal recognizes it, and in administering the legislation it is evidently proposed to keep on recognizing it. There are implications here, of course, for much of our thinking about economics and about other phases of modern society as well. But in essence the thing to insist upon is that we distinguish between "It is" and "I wish," that, to use the phrase of Mr. Justice Holmes, we "wash with cynical acid" the assumptions on which our theories rest.

I have gone at some length into this distinction between the theory and the practice of laissez faire because it demonstrates so clearly, or so it seems to me, the necessity for what Mr. John Dewey spoke of as "a further extension of applications of knowledge and intelligence," for a very real use of the scientific spirit. The important thing is not this particular interpretation of our economy and our price system; the important thing is the subjection of all our economic and social dogmas to some systematic analysis in the spirit of science. Whether our own generation, with its heavy burden of shibboleths and prejudices from the past, can carry the impartiality of science into such controversial fields as economics and politics, is of course anybody's guess; but that at some time or other it must be done, seems beyond question.

I would not leave you with the impression that there are no difficulties in this conquest of economics by scientific method. At times they seem insuperable. Perhaps it may be useful at this point to discuss this problem in the light of the evolution of economics. In the first place it seems evident that economics is evolving toward matter-of-factness and away from abstruseness. This is partly because facts with their new measuring devices become plainer, and partly because of distrust in the generalizations of the economists of America today who either proceed from facts not now to be observed or are guided by too grim a determination to defend existing institutions and privileges. Release from rules-of-thumb procedure and from the prestige of traditional thought, makes a vast difference in any discipline, economics no less than others.

To the physical scientists, I suppose the possibility of a science of economics seems especially remote because the field of economics is cluttered up with variables. There is no "pure" social science in the sense that there is a "pure" mathematics, or chemistry, or physics. The economist, of course, cannot work in a social vacuum, even when he does his best to isolate his problem from human entanglements and variables. He still cannot claim too great a detachment from them; the motives and aspirations of men are too frequently brought to bear in his field. He still deals with human initiations and human consequences; it will not do to pretend that people are atoms or that social groups are stars.

Economics is one of those social studies about which its devotees used to think they knew a great deal more than they now think they know. Partly this is because the economic world once followed simpler patterns and could be understood more clearly. Partly it is because of changes of another sort in our philosophical inheritance. The period of Adam Smith, for example, was one in which the science of physics and chemistry made a great impression on all kinds of people. Here was the type of exact knowledge which students in all fields hoped to approximate. At the foundation of these sciences lay a beautiful clarity and precision of mathematical demonstration worked out in fields of facts which were beyond the power of man to change. It was no accident that true science began with astronomy and proceeded to physics and chemistry, touching what we know as social science last of all and perhaps in no real sense even yet.

This mathematical clarity and precision was not without its effect upon the economists of those days (the natural scientists of those days incidentally were more certain of their laws than they have since become). The economist living in this atmosphere of scientific study endeavored to follow suit in his own field. There developed then the major phase of the economics of the nineteenth century, which resulted in the simple laying down of so-called laws from which practical application in ordinary economic activity could be deducted. There were successfully developed the law of population growth, the law of wages and rent, of diminishing utility, and others which purported to serve in economics the same function that the basic laws of natural science served in their own fields.

So long as this phase of economics lasted, no great progress in the science could occur. Just as it seemed that everything which possibly could be known about physics and chemistry would soon be uncovered, so it really seemed to many nineteenth-century economists that all possible knowledge concerning economic affairs was in process of unfolding itself from the premises the great economists had enunciated. If this view had continued to prevail and if economics had really been deducible from a few simple theorems governing the fixation of prices, the apportionment of wealth, and the means of production, life for the modern economist would be much simplified. He would need only to refine his deductions, to expand the truth inherent in his laws, and to devise a public policy based on their teaching. As a matter of fact, let it be said at once, many economists do take a view of their science almost as restricted as this and much of their public policy has been based on exactly these assumptions.

The conception of the scientific procedure has changed. It is plain that the activities involved in making livings are ones which human beings carry out and that the establishment of uniformity, or the forecasts of results when human behavior is involved, is something less predictable than was once supposed. For here the scientist deals with elements which behave according to their own laws and wishes, not with those which behave in fixed fashions without choices for themselves.

The classical examples of scientific advances in the natural sciences all depended on the verification of hypothesis, hypothesis tried over and over again for direct and certain proof; but this can be done only when the scientist can arrange and manipulate his materials in a way which anyone by following his technique can repeat for himself. Obviously no one is able to do this with social materials.

Perhaps as much actual work of an intensive sort by eminently capable persons has been expended on such social problems as the business cycle as on almost any single problem in the history of natural science, and yet the best workers in this field all agree that no means of prediction has been arrived at or even approached. The longer work goes on, the more complex the problem seems; and, so far at least, the greatest single result of intensified effort has been to bring more and more difficulties to light.

These then are among the difficulties which beset the science of economics. It has a large number of able devotees who desire to work with their social materials in scientific fashion. Yet the results so far achieved seem to the layman pitiably small. Poverty, even accompanied by downright hunger, still torments vast numbers of people in the world. Very little has been done toward softening the tragic practical paradox of progress and poverty. For periodically there is the spectacle of factories idle and food going to waste on farms, while food, shelter, and clothing in adequate amounts are lacking to many millions. Now food, clothing, and shelter are simple and elementary needs for many folk, and an economics which has not yet shown a way to provide them has, at least from the layman's point of view, not achieved very much for all its efforts and devotion; and this is more especially true when they exist in great quantities but are denied to those whose need is greatest. This is somewhat like the failure of medical men to prevent that lowliest of human ills, the common cold. Perhaps the problems are somewhat alike; research into the causes of both has led only to the revelation of difficulties piled on difficulties, until it seems that the solution of either must wait until a thousand contributory causes have been explored and many victories less dramatic than the central one have been won.

The early example of natural science was a bad one for economics, or perhaps the method was misunderstood. At any rate the economists hurried on to elaborate their "laws," forgetting that the laws of physics and chemistry which they admired had been arrived at by rather rigorous testing. What the economist produced was mostly of the nature of opinion. Yet the economists did offer their conclusions to be applied by statesmen, the conclusions were accepted as an intellectual orthodoxy, and they fitted most conveniently the aspirations of a century of business men who were "on the make."

To question this sort of intellectual and business heritage has never been popular. The opposition was not only determined but orthodox, fortified as it was by a century of acceptance. It was able to stifle dissent, prevent experiment, indoctrinate youth. And we are only now winning a little freedom here and there.

But if anyone thinks that this pressure of prevention can be kept up indefinitely, he is very much mistaken. The penalties of orthodoxy are upon us now. The disparity between our social and mechanical institutions seems suddenly to be coming home to millions of minds. The economists are no longer so intrigued by their assumptions, having been made humble by facts; the mood of the world has changed and, especially among business men, faint glimmers of uncertainty begin to appear.

Nevertheless, let me emphasize, the task of replacing a foundation of outworn assumption with a foundation of ascertainable fact is not going to be accomplished overnight. It will be a long, slow process, and it will have to rely, in a democracy, largely upon education. The economist can, of course, upon the basis of what facts there are, make his suggestions. More than a thousand of us, for instance, violated our instincts of professionalism in 1930 by petitioning against the passage of the Smoot-Hawley tariff bill. But President Hoover apparently thought Senator Smoot was more nearly right than the economists, and he had the say. We might now get some consolation from saying, "I told you so," but that is extremely academic comfort.

Perhaps, however, the consequence of that episode is another indication that the sources of opposition to experimental control of economic forces are drying up. In a generation or two—not next week or next year, please note—it may be difficult to discover even a public official who has not had to learn that hypothesis and testing are necessary to policy-making, and who has not had to drop so many orthodoxies by the wayside in order to get along that he will understand their maleficent rôle in social life. And this will come, it seems to me, because the increasing complexity of our economic system will not permit the absurdity of selfish, short-sighted muddling. This system of ours becomes more vulnerable to shock as its higher nerve centers assume more complete control. Just as a war now inevitably involves the whole world in some degree, so also does a tariff, a bank rate, a price for wheat, a strike, a reduced factory output. The waves of disturbance run through our private enterprises like a tropical hurricane through the palms. And we all of us finally ask for common limitation and protection. I cannot imagine that the power to make these limitations and to confer these protections can long rest in any hands but those of the sovereign people, and it is likely that this power can only be sustained on a foundation, not of traditional economic assumption, proved to be false, but on a foundation of fact.*

I hope I have given you some measure of the difficulty and the necessity "of further applications of knowledge and intelligence" in economics. Some economists, as I have indicated, are still reluctant to accept this challenge, and a majority of business men and workers in the natural sciences, I suspect, are even more reluctant to do so. Yet the social implications of natural science suggest that the scientific method has somehow to gain universal acceptance in the social sciences, if our civilization—and science itself—is really to flourish. From the technical worker in other fields, therefore, the economist invites not only moral support but active coöperation. The man of science today has no choice but to come down from his ivory tower to contemplate the universe he has so greatly modified; and while he is among us, I hope he will be willing to discuss ways and means of helping society convert the product of physical science into enduring social gains.

* Cf. The essay "Economics" by the present author in *Roads to Knowledge*, edited by W. A. Neilson, 1932.

XXVI
AMERICA TAKES HOLD OF ITS DESTINY *

THE twentieth century found the American people psychologically and financially unprepared to utilize the wealth which the technological revolution of the last thirty years has made possible. For the first time in human history, it was possible to foresee a period during which a nation need not live from hand to mouth, but could, instead, count upon a steady increase in the supply of physical wealth accompanied by a steady decrease in the amount of human effort required to produce that wealth. A surplus of economic goods and services had been brought into existence and remained to be dealt with by the methods and ideas which were appropriate to the eons of scarcity.

As it became apparent that a more abundant life was within the reach of all our people, if we could only display the social inventiveness necessary to deal with this new abundance in such form as to convert anxious unemployment into secure leisure, we were shaken by a profound moral crisis. On the one side stood the sincere group of wishful beneficiaries of the Old Order, who—in the words of a gifted Englishman—sat "waiting for the twentieth century to blow over." On the other side stood the mass of our people, who were increasingly bewildered by the failure of the old principles of our society to assure the distribution of those goods which were there for all to see and which were rotting away for want of buyers. The result of this crisis and conflict was the New Deal.

A new deal was absolutely inevitable. People will submit

* From an article, somewhat modified, in *Today*, April 28, 1934.

to grave privations and will even starve peaceably, if they realize that actual dearth exists, but no man and no race will starve in the presence of abundance. The possibility of revolution, either peaceful or violent, against any system which denies the visible means of life to those who have produced those means, will always be with us. Therefore, the only choice before the American people, after four years of patient privation, was whether their revolution should follow the course of violence and destruction or should express itself in orderly, legal channels. The answer was given in November, 1932, when the American people gave to President Roosevelt a peaceful mandate to attempt to devise a better means of distributing the national income than had previously existed.

The objective of this administration is accordingly a simple one: it is to give our citizens the opportunity for a richer life. But simple and easily stated as this objective is, the methods it imposes are difficult and complex. This because riches do not appear in answer to wishes; they result only from careful thought, arduous work and rigorous choosing. These processes are going forward now through the various agencies which have seemed appropriate to the task. The activities involved are carried on in so many different fields, they seem so different and sometimes so contradictory, that it is valuable from time to time to remind ourselves what the central intention is, how everything which is being done fits into the service of that intention, and to look forward, even if only a little way, toward what is coming.

In order to understand, it seems to me necessary to keep far up in the foreground always the idea that the possibilities of the future are always greater than were those of any time in the past. As we multiply inventions and add to our store of processes, as the different sciences are enriched by the accretions of scholarship, we move forward with a changing and growing equipment. The possibilities of every new year are therefore greater rather than less. That is why, in my opinion, it is a fundamental error to assume that we have now reached the end of the "swing to the left" and that we ought to forego any further important policy changes. The real economic revolution is just beginning and social policy will have to move rapidly to keep pace with it.

I have very little patience, therefore, with those who say that we have come to the end of a period of progress, that we must now retrench and economize, hoarding our gains against a poverty-stricken future. One of our troubles has been that we have hoarded and economized too much, rather than devoting ourselves to organizing and expanding our resources and capabilities. We do not seem to realize that it is our own abundance which compels us to make radical changes, first in our ideas and then in the institutions based on our ideas. This is as true of government as of individuals. As individuals we are apt to ride in airplanes with horse-and-buggy ideas in our heads. And our Government has done the same thing. It has attempted to function in a world which has long since outgrown it. All the prejudices and shibboleths which survive in people's heads seem to crystallize in government—perhaps because, very rightly, we think of it as somehow sacred. But it will not stay sacred long if it is set apart from change in a changing world. It will simply become atrophied and obsolete and will either be ignored or contemptuously brushed aside by those in the community who have important affairs afoot which they desire shall not be interfered with.

Something like this has been happening to our Government. I think it fair to say that until last March it was fast becoming ineffectual in its relationships with industry. It in-

sisted on an interpretation of industrial life which belonged
to an era which had disappeared. It broke up trusts as a sufficient answer to the pressing problem of control; and when
it discovered that the more they were broken up, the more
they remained as they had been, it fell into a kind of trance.
It was unwilling to give up competitive theory; it could
therefore think of nothing to do except to restore competition; and when competition refused to be restored, industry
continued to exist in a kind of purgatory—half the heaven of
freedom and half the hell of ineffectual public disapproval.

The various recovery acts proceeded from a theory which
was in the sharpest possible contrast to all this. This theory
recognized the changes which had occurred in industrial
society and it sought to secure the benefits of industry as it
actually existed for the public good. It said, "Industry has
developed out of the face-to-face stage; huge factories exist;
central-office organizations control many even of these organizations, great as they are in themselves; financial controls are
superimposed on this; scientific management has come to
stay—therefore, the Government must legalize all these heretofore horrid developments so that it may shape them into
social instruments."

In effect, this was the theoretical basis of the recovery program. The Sherman Act and the Clayton Act were not repealed; but in so far as the codes could become effective,
their operation was suspended. The codes have now become
operative over most of industry; and it can be said that we
have turned our backs on competition and have chosen control. This transformation, very nearly complete as it is, provides, as I believe, an instrument suitable to the purpose of
enriching American life as it is our ambition to do. With it
we can, for the first time, proceed to the management of purchasing power. And when purchasing power is provided, the

potentialities of our vast producing equipment can be released. It is toward this that we have been working. It would be folly to assume that, having created the means toward our chosen end, we should forego the end for which these means were created. To suggest, therefore, that it is time to call a halt on the application of social control to the physical distribution of American abundance, is on a par with that old legislative spirit which decreed that no man should drive an automobile on a public highway unless he were preceded by another man afoot, carrying a red flag to warn pedestrians to keep out of the way. The New Deal is conceived in no such spirit of obscurantism. It is a beginning, not an end.

This new legislation is best described in some such terms as this—as a charter for experiment and research, for invention and learning. The new institutions have not sprung full grown from these legislative acts—the Agricultural Adjustment Act, the National Recovery Act and the rest—any more than the original Government of the United States sprang full grown from the Constitutional Convention. They mark a turning point just as that Convention did. We had to learn about democratic government in practice, we had to grow into it by trying various devices and by learning to live together within a new framework. And the same thing is true of this better planned society we are entering upon now. In both cases we expressed a determination to go forward in a general direction and within an agreed framework of rules, but without specific commitment to policies concerning problems which could not yet be foreseen. In entering on such an untrod path it is unwise to lay down too specifically the structure of new things; it is always better merely to register a change of heart and mind and then begin to work out, patiently and carefully, the requirements of the conversion.

No one could have foreseen at first in what the processes of code and agreement-making would result. Even now no one can foresee the final structure of industry which may result. Whatever it may be, it will be worked out by the essentially voluntary and democratic processes now going on. But we can begin, at least, to look forward to the time when the preliminary structure will be complete. Every industry will then have set up a kind of government of its own, within which those aims which it holds in common can be pressed for and those discords and controversies which exist can be compromised and mediated. It was necessary to pass through this rather protracted period of conflict and discussion before these industrial groups could be made ready for planning. Up to now much of the energy of business men has been dissipated in the overpraised conflicts of competition. Each was trying to beat the other fellow—to reach success by standing on the exhausted bodies of fallen competitors. And the success for which all this striving took place was usually defined as the right to exploit consumers by selling them goods of doubtful quality at prices which lowered the general standard of living.

This competition is being outlawed. Code-making, if it had done nothing else, would have been worth while for the revelation it has given our industrialists of the essential futility of much of their activity. We are fast approaching the time, therefore, when each industry will be able to devote its best energy to the fundamental purpose of industry—which is to produce goods rather than competition. And already this has gone far enough so that some of the problems which will be involved in the next stage of progress are beginning to be disclosed.

At the first stage it has seemed to many business men—and this is why they consented to be drawn in at all—that if they and their immediate rivals could mitigate their differences, and if they could combine even in informal ways, the obstacles to price-fixing might be removed; and since every business man has always lived under the immediate and intense pressure of prices, this seemed wholly good.

Some of us have foreseen the difficulties which would arise at this stage, and these have given us a key to the next major development of public policy, so we have pressed continually for a double check to be applied when the time should come —both for the protection of the consumer—a check on quality and a check on prices. But this protection of the consumer was not conceived merely in the consumer's interest. It was rather in the interest of a continuous and permanent economic organization that it was desired to oppose the consumer's interest to that of the producer, or, more accurately, the principle of value to the principle of profit, in the interest of a sustained and adequate purchasing power which could absorb the products of industry and agriculture.

Industry cannot permanently base itself on public deception. It cannot even keep running unless it provides, through decent wage policies and rigorously lowered prices, for continuing customers. And this is the next problem which has to be faced—the one which will be most prominent in public discussion during the months to come. We have now ended the stealthy robbery of a rigid monetary standard; we must proceed to end the robbery of consumer deception.

The industrialist who went into code and agreement-making with the idea that he had found an excellent device for exploiting the public is apt to be disillusioned pretty rapidly. He had, of course, a line of defense to fall back on—but one which will not stand exposure any better than will shoddy goods or extortionate prices. This was the principle of limiting production. This is not a new idea, either, any more than was the easy exploitation of consumers. For, it was said by industrialists, we will fix prices where we want them to be—where they will yield good fat profits—and then we will make only as many goods as the public will take at that price. The difficulty with this principle heretofore has been the danger that someone who could do the job as cheaply or perhaps cheaper would come into the market and undersell the price-fixer. One reason why the codes looked good to business men was the chance they saw of outlawing this competition. If the fellow who was willing to sell better or cheaper goods could be kept out, their own poorer or more expensive goods would have all the market there was.

It is undeniable, I think, that some of the codes have already been used in this way and that we are worse rather than better off in a permanent sense because of them. But grave difficulties have arisen. Industries do not sell only to gullible individual consumers; they sell to one another. And buyers, in this case, know the game as well as sellers do. So that even before the completion of the code structure there was a sharp challenge to the policy of limitation. There is already great resistance from industrial consumers. Indeed, there is a kind of game now going on, which must be amusing to some sardonic bystanders, in which industries try to prevent others from doing what they themselves are making the most determined efforts to do. It is part of the nature of this process that all of these chiselers must discover that only by subordination of their particular ambitions to those of all can they continue to exist in passable peace. The thing will iron itself out in the processes now going on.

This reconciliation of differences, however quickly it may come, or whatever contractual relationships it may establish among industries, is not, however, sufficient. For there always remains the essentially defenseless ultimate consumer. The

Government may turn out to be his only refuge; and if this is so, the Government will have to assume more and more responsibility for pushing his case.

There are two broad ways in which industrial policy may be shaped from this point on to secure this objective. Industry may be required to define the quality of the goods it offers and to sell them at prices which are suitably low, so that when the transactions of a year, for instance, are totaled up it will be found that our energies and our producing plant have been used to the utmost and that the goods and services they yield have gone to consumers without increase of debt; or industry may be allowed to proceed with the policy of establishing high prices and maintaining them by limitation, and of selling goods whose qualities are mysterious to most consumers; and much of the resulting profits may be taken in taxes and returned to consumers as free goods by the Government—in the form of facilities for health and recreation, insurance against old age, sickness and unemployment, or in other ways. We shall have to accept one or the other of these policies because unless we do we shall sacrifice most of those objectives which we associate with what has been called the New Deal. The choice which lies before us is, therefore, a choice between a socially wise economic policy and the application of socialistic taxation. I prefer the former method.

One, certainly, of the distinguishing characteristics of the present is the power of our industrial machine to produce goods. This power has astonished and frightened us. We have not known what to do about it. It required that we should either chain it up and prevent its free functioning or that we should reorganize our machinery of distribution so that consumers could take possession of the vast flow of goods.

If we are to accept fairly and squarely the consequences of what we have done in the way of invention, the perfecting of new processes, scientific management, transport and communication, these arrangements must be made, consisting in freer access to the goods which are made. To enter on a policy of limitation is really to deny the best work of the last fifty years. If we are to do this it would be more consistent to go back to where we were, to scrap machines and processes, to exile, execute or imprison our inventors and engineers, to depend once more on handwork, to use less power, and generally to stop the flow of goods at the source. Otherwise we shall have to resort permanently, as we are doing now in emergency cases, to limitation of hours, making unnecessary work, and letting our magnificent plant stand idle. This would not be progress, as we understand it; it would be an admission that we have created a Frankenstein which we are unable to master.

It is my belief that we shall prove unwilling to accept limitation in this sense as a permanent policy. This does not mean that we may not plan; it does not mean that we may not choose to use our resources in one way rather than another, limiting in some instances and expanding in others, so that all may run smoothly together as a considered and coordinated whole. That industry shall choose to proceed in this fashion is extremely important; and this is why it is so necessary that all industry shall begin to function as soon as possible under the codes.

Furthermore, we shall not know to what lengths the Government will have to go until it is seen whether industry is capable, under the new dispensation, of arranging itself so that the full resources of our productive capacities can be used. For the first time it is being provided with an adequate organization for accepting its obligations. It remains to be seen whether these responsibilities will in fact be met. If they are not, and if the objectives of the New Deal are to be achieved, there will be a greater governmental task to be done than is foreseen at present.

It is, as I conceive it, better that industry shall try for itself to find the road to continuity; it is better also that such price and wage policies shall be adopted as will insure the full and free flow of goods into the hands of consumers. Only in this way can the rising demand for governmental intervention be stifled. I think this way is better because I feel that if the Government should be forced to intervene seriously, it would be compelled to adopt the less efficient policy of rigorous regulation, of extreme taxation, and of widespread provision of free social goods.

This would be bound to interfere with efficiency. Many of the controls would necessarily be negative. And a great deal of otherwise unnecessary machinery would have to be set up. All this would be expensive and repressive. But if industry, working as it now has the chance to do in coöperation with the Government, will adopt policies of low prices, high wages, and a planned use of its capacity, foregoing speculative profits in some periods as well as speculative deficits in succeeding ones, all the objectives will have been accomplished. This would, in fact, be a new kind of government.

I think it is perfectly obvious that we can have nothing new in the Government which does not correspond to a new need on the part of our people and of their economic institutions. The New Deal is a very definite attempt to evolve a new governmental-economic relationship in response to the needs and opportunities created by the past methods of operating our economy. To inhibit further growth of these new methods is, therefore, impossible and to attempt to deny their application is the ultimate folly of fossilized ways of thought. Using the traditional methods of a free people, we are going forward toward a realm of coöperative plenty the like of which the world has never seen. It will be no anti-septic utopia and no socialistic paradise, but a changing system in which free American human beings can live their changing lives.

I have tried to make it clear that the objectives and the instruments being used in the reconstruction which is now going on are novel only in the sense that they are devices which have not hitherto been used.

I have also stressed their experimental nature. That seems to me their most important characteristic, and that is something which is American if anything is—at least there was a time when Yankee ingenuity was a byword of praise. I have been too closely associated with all that has taken place to be anything like an impartial witness; nevertheless, I cannot help feeling that the nation has taken hold of its destiny again in ways which show that we have not lost our courage and resourcefulness. It was simply stifled for a while. There is no reason to think that year by year we shall not learn to better ourselves with the full use of energies and instruments which we have at our disposal. If this be Socialism, make the most of it!

XXVII
CONSUMERS AND THE NEW DEAL *

IT seems to me appropriate that the Consumers' League should ask itself at the present crisis in American life, what are its duties and its opportunities. I am sure that no previous administration ever took its responsibility to consumers so seriously; yet I think it fair to say that this sense of duty has been largely frustrated. What might have been done if there had been a strong, organized consumers' movement no one can say; but it is clear that up to now the lack of support for this point of view has made it possible to make only a very little progress, and this of an uncertain and feeble sort.

At the beginning, in the organization of N.R.A. and A.A.A. it was conceived that consumers and producers had equal and conflicting interests and that the resolution of the conflicts and the reform of industrial processes required substantially equal representation. But for governmental machinery of this sort really to work something more than organization is needed. There must be behind the organization a pressure of interest for which representation is only the outward manifestation. From the very first the consumer organizations have been spear heads without shafts. There is little but praise to be said for their work. They have consistently been wiser, I think, in their conception of problems, and their proposals for solution, than the representatives of other interests, perhaps because the interest they represent is a wider one, one closer to the needs of the whole pople. Yet the drive behind their proposals has seldom been sufficient to

* Address delivered before the Consumers' League of Ohio, Cleveland, May 11, 1934.

gain acceptance. It might have been if there had been more consumers' leagues; and this is why I am prepared to urge upon you new efforts of organization, a greater militancy in operation. Only in this way can the hands of those in the Government who are really your representatives be sufficiently strengthened to be effective.

Historically your organizations have endeavored to use their power in support of the trade-union movement and of numerous attempts by various groups to raise the living standards of working people. An instance of this last is the effort to reform labor conditions by organizing refusal to purchase sweated goods. This has been worthy both in its inception and in its development. But there has been, I think, but slight realization of the need there is at present for focusing your power and interest behind the formal consumer representatives in the new Government. Only on rare occasions have consumers' leagues taken the lead in other consumer movements than those I have mentioned. Perhaps the time has come for a broadening of the movement. A slowly growing consumer interest has now a point of focus within the Government; you ought to make the most of it.

Those of us who have been interested at all in economic ideas will remember the arguments of the great exponent of laissez faire, Adam Smith, that the essential protection for consumers is to be found in competition among business firms. Later theorists stressed that vague thing known as "utility," which in simple terms is nothing more than the consumer's satisfaction in the use of goods. These theorists also insisted that the greatest utility for the community at large is secured under a system of competitive production. Whatever the weakness of the psychology on which these ideas are based, the fact remains that most of our theorizing has rested on such assumptions.

It should be noted that the protection of the consumer is assumed to come from conflicts among productive units. The individual consumer, by making his choices in a free market, is assumed to have a final control in the economic system. It is further assumed that he needs no protection other than his own good judgment. There is a degree of truth in these conclusions when the premises are as stated. They may have been true in the past, but economic theorists are apt to assume as fact at one time what was the fact at an earlier one. In an economic system organized as is ours, such an assumption is unreal and can only lead us far astray. Such competition as exists tends to take on an entirely different character from that which is postulated in this theory. Most of our production comes at present from big businesses rather than small ones. Great corporations, coördinated and related through holding companies and other intercorporate devices, are the characteristic units of our time. So far has this development gone that students of this combination movement tell us that in America today over 54 percent of all the assets of non-financial companies are controlled by 200 corporations. In the field of manufacturing alone 200 corporations control nearly 60 percent of the instruments of production. But this statement minimizes rather than exaggerates the degree of control, for these great combinations exert tremendous influence over the units with which they do business. They control prices and trade practices, the types of goods which are manufactured and the methods by which these goods are presented to the consuming public. To a very great extent the consumer buys on the basis of information or misinformation which is supplied to him through these various outlets. The consumer has few disinterested sources of independent judgment.

Thus far have we departed from the theoretical picture of

our economy as painted by some economists. In place of many small competing businesses, we have great corporate business firms; in place of independent individual consumer judgments discriminating between the various services offered by these companies, we have mass standardized judgments shaped by the press, the radio, the movies. The great mass of consumers, the 30,000,000 families who spend 60 percent of the national income over retail counters, all too often do not know what they are buying. Their purchases are characteristically made on the basis of "intangible and glowing generalities."

In spite of our achievements in making large quantities of goods, the present economy from the consumer's point of view has failed to give consumers many of the things they really want. For example, in the field of housing, the choices which the consumer has are slight. As a city dweller, he must make the choice between living in an apartment where he is cramped and hampered and living in a suburb where, if he has a little more space, he has no opportunity to use it because of the inordinate amount of time necessary to travel to and from work. I have often wondered if the average American's love for an automobile is not the direct reflection of the average terrible housing conditions which he is practically forced to accept. An automobile, at least, gets him away from home. And many have no automobiles with which to escape.

So bad have housing conditions become that it has been essential for state after state and city after city to pass laws and ordinances prescribing minimum standards. Likewise the demand for minimum health protection has necessitated municipal ordinances and public health services. The Federal Government, in addition to its many other services, has administered the food and drug laws formulated fundamentally for consumer protection.

If we are to be realistic, however, in dealing with this problem we must recognize that a certain amount of this consumer protection has been secured only because producer groups have given their backing to these laws. For instance, the bona-fide medical authorities have consistently opposed the sale of patent medicines and quack cures. Likewise in many instances real-estate interests of one type have opposed real-estate interests whose investments depend on the perpetuation of present housing conditions. That is, the competition between producer groups still provides a meager, accidental protection of consumer interests. In speaking thus I am not contradicting my previous statements that competition no longer operates as the great protector of consumer interests. I am simply saying that competition cannot be relied upon as an adequate protection for consumers. If it does so at all, it is by accident rather than by design.

Again, if we are to be realistic we must recognize that few consumers exist purely as consumers. In most cases consumers are also producers. Those sections of our economic life in which the consumer point of view is dominant rarely hold the balance of power either political or economic. The largest group which thinks primarily in terms of consumption rather than production consists of the housewives of the nation. By and large, their main job is spending the family income. But even they have been more interested in seeing that the pay envelope of the family wage earner is large than in seeing that the funds which are in the pay envelope are used most effectively. The family's point of view is still dominated by the fact that the wage earners of the family are producers; that the family income comes from producer activities. Of course, housewives are also producers, but they are not producers for a market. They produce for the immediate use of the family. There is no intervening market place.

This great group upon whom a consumer movement should naturally rest have their point of view so dominated by the wage-earning activities of the family that they are torn between two loyalties in which the seemingly most important dominates.

It is this fundamental situation which throws the burden of consumer protection, at present, upon the Government. But the Government cannot do more than is wanted of it; and the powerful producer groups are always alert to protect their own interests.

Hitherto, efforts to assist the producers have formed the usual basis of public policies in dealing with economic legislation of either a permanent or an emergency character. But recognition that reduced money incomes and unequal distribution of wealth, rather than lack of useful goods, are in large part the roots of our present difficulties, has pushed the importance of supporting and broadening consumer purchasing power into the foreground of the recovery efforts.

One objective of the present national administration is conceived to be facilitation of exchange of goods among various producer and consumer groups. This is assisted by a number of emergency measures, including public works, the emergency works program, the conservation corps camps, credit measures, and agricultural plans—all designed to stimulate revival of consumer purchasing power. If the distributors of these goods were to take advantage of farm and other recovery plans so as to increase their spreads by as much as or more than the assistance given producers and consumers, they would tend to defeat the whole administration program.

The establishment in both the National Recovery Administration and the Agricultural Adjustment Administration of agencies concerned with consumer aspects of the recovery program can be regarded as part of an attempt to prevent such frustration. This is only a beginning, but it does provide the channel through which whatever consumer pressure there is can be brought to bear.

The necessity of considering the needs of consumers and using their ability to satisfy such needs as criteria for judging the present national program appears nowhere more strikingly than in the efforts to rehabilitate our agriculture; the agricultural program has from the first recognized the necessity of protecting consumers, not simply as a matter of justice to the general public, but as an aid to farm relief itself.

Before the War, American farmers were relatively as well off as our industrial workers. The war demand led to greatly expanded farm production, but after the War the markets for this increased output fell away drastically. This caused a severe disparity between prices of farm products and prices of other products, and reduced farm incomes greatly. Even at the crest of the business cycle in 1929 farm products could be exchanged for only 91 percent as much of other products on the average as they could have been exchanged for in the period before the War. During the depression the disparity grew. By February, 1933, the exchange value of farm products for industrial goods had fallen to 50 percent of the pre-war average. Their exchange value for taxes and credits was even less. The disparity was present in the price of every farm product. It was most severe in the export commodities, such as cotton, wheat, hog products, and tobacco, where the disappearance or the severe contraction of export demand had built up great excess stocks of commodities.

The immediate cause of this disparity was the pressure of surpluses of farm products on the markets. But what is a surplus? The term "surplus" is used loosely and there are various conceptions of its meaning. Plainly, a mere seasonal surplus differs from an exportable surplus. For example, the United States always has cotton for export, whether the crop is large or small. This is an exportable surplus, whereas the extra amount produced in favorable crop years is a seasonal surplus. Considered from another point of view, a surplus is a quantity so abundant as to depress prices below a figure which will adequately reward the producer, whether or not it is below normal, or whether or not any portion is exported.

Many persons have wondered why the Government should be concerned with reducing the production of farm products when there are people who must depend on public relief for food and clothing; and who are reduced to a bare minimum of both. To some extent it is true that the disposal of agricultural surpluses is closely related to the consumer purchasing power, and the prices of many farm products are directly dependent on factory pay rolls. But, paradoxically enough, the very existence of a glut of farm products has been one of the important causes of the lack of consumer purchasing power.

The pressure of abnormal supplies on the market tends to upset the delicate balance of price and income relationships. When too much cotton and wheat and port are forced into trade channels, prices received by farmers dwindle to levels so low that they themselves cannot buy the goods which city workers manufacture. The result is that factories close down and employees are thrown out of work. They in turn are unable to buy the products of other city workers, who also lose their jobs. When the other factors tending to slow up business activity appear, there follows the whole vicious downward spiral with unemployment, falling prices, bank failures, business bankruptcies, hunger, and suffering. Millions of people, unable to support themselves, are compelled to depend on public support. The Nation's economic machine, gorged with an excess of farm and other products, breaks down just as surely as a human stomach gets acute indigestion if too much food is forced into it or if the food is of the wrong sort.

Something like the foregoing is what has happened in the last few years. For a variety of reasons—among them the failure of many of our foreign markets—the exchange relationship between the supply of and the demand for farm products was deranged. Consider wheat, for instance. If every person in the United States had all the wheat he could possibly eat, there would still have been a surplus as long as production continued at the same rate as in the last few years. With no one to buy this surplus and with foreign markets sharply limited, the supplies of wheat piled up in elevators and storehouses, and the carryover attained huge and unprecedented totals. Prices fell to the lowest levels in history. Consumers, who could or would eat only a certain amount of wheat, had but a slight advantage from this surplus. Millers and bakers obtained their wheat at a much lower figure than before, but since flour is only a minor part of the cost of bread, the retail price was but little affected. Against this small temporary benefit felt by consumers was the serious injury done to them ultimately through the maladjustment of the whole price structure and the dislocation of exchange relationships between farmers and city workers.

And when prosperity returns, the amount of wheat which people eat is not likely to be greater and may even be less than it has been during the depression. This is because when people's purchasing power increases, they eat more of other food products which are part of a balanced diet or which they turn to when their incomes are greater. It is not difficult to follow the reasoning that surpluses of farm products have actually contributed to the dependence upon relief; at any rate it is because of the series of maladjustments initiated by the overproduction of farm products that the Government has undertaken to assist in the control of their production. This adjusted production on the one hand and restored buying power at home and abroad on the other, stood out as absolutely indispensable to agricultural recovery. The recovery program for agriculture was based upon these twin requirements.

Congress provided the means for dealing with adjusted production in the Agricultural Adjustment Act. Its stated purpose was to promote the prosperity of the farmer by returning to him a fair share of the national income and to foster national recovery by making the farmer as good a customer for nonagricultural industries and services as he was before the World War.

The Act states that it is the policy of Congress to approach parity for the farmer at as rapid a rate as is feasible in view of the current consumptive demand in domestic and foreign markets. In other words, consumer needs are to be the gauge of the rate at which inequalities in purchasing power are to be corrected. That is, the whole Agricultural Adjustment program must be regulated by the consumer demand for agricultural commodities. It is evident that the Act implicitly requires close study of and decisions based upon the actual or potential effect on consumers of every aspect of the program.

It was obvious that no power could raise and maintain prices of many important agricultural commodities whose carryover stocks were several times normal, until the surpluses had been reduced or eliminated. Furthermore, suddenly pushing up the price of certain commodities, which have been long depressed, before making adequate provision for control of production, would bring in new production from less profitable fields and result in new surpluses which would make it difficult or impossible to maintain the desired level of prices and would thus defeat the purpose of the Act.

It was also recognized that a precipitous scaling up of prices would in some instances disrupt consumer-producer relations and would actually reduce consumption to an extent that would do more harm than good to agricultural producers. A reasonable relationship must be maintained between prices and effective demand. Raising prices too rapidly would reduce the purchasing power of consumers and impede national recovery.

The Agricultural Adjustment Act provides for an attack on the problem of the surplus, recognizing this to be the most important problem standing in the way of farm recovery. Ordinarily the producers would attend to the matter themselves, but circumstances prevent that. Often there is no escape from the farm, except into the ranks of the unemployed; and low prices compel competing producers to maintain the volume of their output. Farm production in the United States has not changed much since 1924, although the demand has fallen greatly. The only remedy is concerted action under central guidance, a course provided for in the law by several methods, which include the leasing of land, the payment of cash compensation in return for output reductions, the cotton option plan, and marketing agreements to regulate production, distribution, and prices. The Act also makes provision for processing taxes, a means of raising revenue to help accomplish adjustment of production through benefit payments to coöperating producers, and, of course, the benefit payments are themselves a direct contribution to the incomes of the coöperating farmers.

Along with the crop reduction program the Act authorizes efforts to obtain for farmers a larger share of the consumer's dollar. Part of the consumer's dollar now goes to support wasteful and unnecessary competition, duplication of selling expense, a needless multiplicity of services to consumers, dubious credit arrangements, and various unethical practices. Eliminating these wastes should mean better conditions for honest and efficient business, as well as better prices for producers.

Thus the law provides the conditions for an agricultural industry in which the forces of production are so managed as not to outdistance the demand, and to increase the demand by redistributing purchasing power so that consumers can come more readily into the market. It is a colossal job requiring a finesse of judgment and a technique of administration which we are only beginning to master. Mistakes will be made. But it is not likely that they could be more serious than the distortions produced by the system from which we are departing.

The mandate of consumer protection contained in the Act is second only to that of raising the incomes of farmers. In conformity with this mandate the Consumers' Counsel was created last summer as an integral part of the Agricultural Adjustment Administration. The activities of the Consumers' Counsel have consisted mainly of research in connection with consumer problems arising under the Act, investigation and publicity with respect to food prices to consumers, and critical examination of marketing agreements and codes. But the representatives of consumers have assisted at every stage in the formulation of policy. They have done what they could to protect this interest; and what they could do has been a great deal. They have been handicapped by a lack of public support and understanding, but they have always fought a good fight. Many a dubious proposal has been stopped by this critical analysis and a number of positive achievements have been gained. A long fight against the processing tax on cotton was emasculated by their showing that great price increases in that commodity could not be caused by a tax of 4.2 cents per pound on the weight of cotton in the manufactured commodity. Incidentally this particular controversy helped keep down the price of cotton goods.

Again, repeated press releases on bread prices prepared by the Consumers' Counsel apparently have had a deterrent effect on unjustifiable increases in bread prices. These press releases were started in July and were based upon the proposition that the processing tax on wheat, amounting to approximately half a cent per pound loaf of bread, did not justify any of the much more substantial increases in the price of bread which then threatened. The Secretary of Agriculture initiated the campaign of publicity, warning bakers of the injustice of pyramiding a tax or using it as a basis for profiteering.

By these frequent comments on bread prices, coupled with the issuance of periodic tables of these prices in forty-nine cities throughout the country, there was developed a definite attitude of inquiry concerning bread on the part of consumers. This, in turn, led to a more general attitude of caution on the part of the bakers, a majority of whom appeared eager to conduct their business so as to refute the charges that they were gouging the public.

In connection with these price differences there arose the intimately correlated question of bread standards. There appeared to be considerable shifting of bread weights and formulas in an effort to avoid the implication of undue price-raising. The Consumers' Counsel repeatedly pointed out the difficulty of ascertaining the justice of bread prices because of this lack of standards, and urged the baking industry to arrive at a uniform set of standards to be submitted to the Government for approval.

This problem of bread standards is typical of the problem of standards relating to a multitude of other food products. It is one of the most serious problems that has occupied the attention of the Consumers' Counsel, and which it is helping to solve in conjunction with other agencies of the Government.

In the analysis by the Consumers' Counsel of proposed marketing agreements and codes, serious attention has been directed to provisions relating to standards of quality, advertising, and labeling. It has consistently been maintained that it is not enough merely to protect consumers from goods that are worthless or injurious or falsely labeled and packaged. Most of the industries seeking codes or marketing agreements have been unwilling to go beyond the requirements of existing legislation on this subject. But consumers should know which among the great number of goods that meet the requirements of the present Food and Drugs Act are of superior or inferior quality. Business enterprises and governmental agencies commonly purchase goods on the basis of standards of specifications. It would be of great social importance if other consumers could purchase similarly. Accordingly, the Consumers' Counsel has urged that wherever possible agreements and codes should include provisions requiring the adoption of existing standards or the development of standards relating to package fill, identity, and quality of the product, and requiring that labels properly identify the product and the manufacturer and indicate the quality standards of the product. In some few there has been a gain in this respect.

But many manufacturers and distributors have bitterly opposed such establishment or extension of standards. Various reasons have been offered in support of this opposition. Sometimes it is maintained that the product is not one to which definite standards are applicable; sometimes it is held that regulations on this subject should come through new legislation and that the industries concerned should not have regulations imposed upon them in advance of such legislation. However worthy of serious consideration such reasons may be, there is always an inference that the decisive reason for opposition is that the extension of standards would tend to break quasi monopolies founded upon private brands and advertising. None of the objectors, however, has been so candid as to admit that standardization would cut into profits attributable to consumers' ignorance.

It should be noted that in a few instances proponents of an agreement of code have asked for and supported provisions for standards. Instances of this are offered by the milk agreements and by various fruit and vegetable agreements, wherein it is evident that the success of price or market-supply control demands recognition of an adherence to grade standards. In other cases (as for example, in the codes for the peanut-butter and fruit-preserving industries) provisions fixing minimum quality or package standards have been proposed because of a desire to eliminate competition arising from cutting of quality or from variation of package sizes.

It must be recognized, of course, that for the effective application of such standards as may be adopted, sales methods would need to become more informative than the kind we have been used to. There is a desirable pattern in the methods used to distribute industrial goods with emphasis given to information regarding the constituent materials, construction, and performance. It is my own belief that manufacturers and the advertising profession alike are missing an opportunity in not achieving voluntary change. If they would do it now, they might take advantage of a rising tide of skepticism and so further their own interests, quite aside from the public service involved. Experience of the Consumers' Counsel in trying to further this policy has not been very successful. The enlightened self-interest of which we used to hear a good deal seems not to function very effectively in this field. And consumers themselves have developed more passive skepticism than active support for constructive change.

Underlying other aspects of the work of the Consumers' Counsel is the basic research and analysis of marketing agreements and codes under the Agricultural Adjustment Administration. It is here that the staff in company with other experts of the administration expends its efforts most effectively. The form and construction of the marketing agreements and codes are subjected to searching scrutiny so that the purposes of the Act may be effectuated. In general, agreements and codes have been analyzed with a view to establishing their possible effect with respect to increasing the income of farmers, maintaining or increasing the real income of the consuming public, extending the efficiency of manufacturing and distributing processes, assuring adequate supervision by the Government in the interests of the entire community.

In the course of these studies it has been inevitable that the Consumers' Counsel should find itself wrestling primarily with such problems as price-fixing, spreads between the producer and consumer, and methods of bringing about more effective distributive processes between the farm and the city.

It has been recognized that raising the purchasing power of farm commodities in many cases may involve higher prices to consumers. Fair exchange prices, however, should not work a hardship upon anyone. In fact, they should benefit the community as a whole by improving the farm market for city goods and creating city jobs. For years now city consumers have bought farm products at low prices only by being subsidized by farmers. This is not good business even for the consumer. It threatens ultimately to dry up the sources of supply. Everyone has an interest in paying the farmers fair prices.

Fortunately it is possible in many instances to raise the prices of farm commodities without bringing about a proportionate rise in the prices paid by consumers for the same commodities. This is particularly true when the charges for bringing the goods from the producer to the consumer represent a high percentage of the final retail price. A small change in market price results in a large percentage rise in the price to growers because total marketing charges remain relatively fixed.

It is well known that growers of many products, such as grains and many vegetables and fruits, receive a greater return, within limits, for a small supply than for a large one. In other words, an excessive supply bears down so heavily on price that the growers receive exceedingly low returns. It is altogether fair that consumers should be asked in such instances to pay slightly higher prices so that the growers may receive much larger incomes. But the consumer has a right to expect that the addition to his food bill will go to the farmer and to no one else. For this reason, the Consumers' Counsel has advocated, as a general policy, reduction of spreads between farm prices and consumer prices wherever this can be achieved without interfering with efficient distribution, and has scrutinized codes and agreements to detect provisions which might result in governmental sanction of increased spreads. These spreads are comparatively wider now than they were before 1929 and before the War. Manufacturing and distribution took a steadily increasing share of the consumer's dollar between 1910 and 1929. In the case of milk the share increased from 56 percent to 62 percent; in the case of bread from 74 percent to 81 percent. On the average, the retail prices of foods increased nearly 70 percent during this period, whereas the farm prices of foods increased only 36 percent. After 1929 farm prices dropped much more than retail prices. The spread between country and town prices increased proportionately. Processors, distributors, and others hold a strong position in the economic system. They can continue to exact an undue share of the consumer's dollar if nothing is done to prevent it. Only effective support of such agencies as the Consumers' Counsel of the A.A.A. and the corollary Consumers' Advisory Board of N.R.A. can offset the power of organized producers. This is the opportunity of such organizations as your own.

It is perhaps somewhat unrealistic to expect that the opportunity will be seized to full advantage. There has always been a question about this, and a conflict over it within and without the emergency administrations. It seemed obvious that the consumers had interests at stake in what was to be done, but they were diffused, and without a strong tradition of support. Up to now, I think it has to be admitted frankly, much more for the public interest has been gained by the alternate method of trying to raise wages and farm incomes faster than prices went up. The object was to insure the continuity of the system by creating purchasing power which should be equal to the volume of goods times their price. Either method would be justified only by its results in this respect.

Perhaps the efforts which went into the building up of these governmental consumers' agencies will prove not to have been justified by results; certainly they have not been up to now in spite of some lesser achievements and in spite of an excellent record of criticism and protest which came to very little. All of us, who would like to see the experiment carried further, may be unrealistic; the whole attempt may prove futile. But some of us still remain, stubbornly perhaps, unconvinced. We still have hopes.

The hopes we have are based on the intangible foundation of proved rightness. These organizations may not have influenced policy greatly; but I think it is demonstrable that we should have been better off if they had. And that is something to go on. For a thing like that cannot be kept quiet. Many people come to know it. And as they do they may lend a more and more active support. Then, too, there is another consideration which has some weight. It may be that this is a movement whose growth is slow but formidable. It may become more so as time goes on and as the public comes to see how much is to be gained from it. This depends largely on whether the public is informed and organized for the purpose. The organization of industry into larger producing units has progressively weakened the position of consumers in the market. The time has come for them to organize if they are ever going to; they can still exert some pressure through the market, but also they can influence governmental policies. Groups like yourselves can do that. That is why I have insisted that you have an opportunity now such as you never had before. For myself I hope you will make the most of it.

XXVIII
BREAD OR CAKE *

IN the past two years I have had very little chance to talk to college students. Evidently I have forgotten how to go about it; for recently when I went up to Dartmouth, I failed to give them what was wanted. The editor of the paper there, on the morning following my address, wrote an editorial about it which was headed: "They asked for bread and he gave them cake." What I said to the students there was substantially what must be said to you too—that we were in the midst of active social change, that its direction depended not so much on what officials do as on what public opinion requires them to do, and that the responsibility for the future was largely theirs.

I was well enough aware that most students want direction rather than responsibility. They want to be told what to do rather than to be told that they must think about what ought to be done. Yet I believe profoundly that this is not only wrong philosophically, but also as an expedient. No one is going to lead the students of this country on a crusade for definite objectives. In the first place, not many would join and so it would fail; and in the second place, the objectives might be mistaken ones. The kind of crusade we need is not that sort: it is the less romantic but more permanent one of experiment with the materials of social management. I am afraid my student editor was wrong. What I offered was bread—the bread of hard work and responsibility—and what he wanted was cake—the cake of hullabaloo, brass bands, and easy reform. There isn't any such thing. What we have to

* Address delivered at Oberlin College, Oberlin, May 12, 1934.

offer your generation is the difficult discipline of social administration, the working out of plans and detail. And whether you like it or not that is what you will have to come to. Perhaps I can put it to you in another way. Liberal schools and colleges provide a focus for disinterested intelligence in dealing with the problems of life. Not many of these problems can be solved by intelligence alone but none of them can be solved without it. And there is a great deal more in my use of the word "disinterested" than might at first appear. Intelligence used for selfish ends is often worse for society than stupidity might have been. Such a center of intelligence as Oberlin is, has special duties and obligations. You represent Oberlin and you also represent the generation which will soon have to take part in the game which we are now playing. You have not invented this game and neither did we invent it; and should you come to the conclusion that the generations which have preceded you, have played it stupidly and clumsily, you will be justified.

However clumsy we are, however, you are in the position of substitutes still on the coach's bench, about to warm up to enter a game which is going none too well for the home team. But you enjoy one privilege which the athletic substitute does not share. You have the power to alter the rules within very wide limits, if you so desire, and if you are strong enough to do so. Every generation has that right and my generation is just now making some special efforts of that kind. We are trying to eliminate some of the gouging, slugging, ear-biting and general dirty work in the economic scrimmage. Speaking without metaphors, I should say that we are trying to break through the resistance to change which has been typical of the last few generations of Americans, and to shape wisely the changes which now have to be made. We are trying to turn over to you a social and economic organization in which you will each have your fair chance and in which the brutalities of human life may be softened and civilized to a degree which will permit people to live more humanely and will give creative intelligence its necessary place in our system of social management.

I should be the last to insist that we have succeeded in achieving this object or even that we are succeeding. Success is a purely relative term and what might impress me as being a magnificent achievement might impress you as being rather irrelevant or positively old-fashioned. It is for this reason that I desire to remind you that it will be within your power to change the rules to suit yourselves, before you too in turn become old-fashioned in the eyes of *your* successors. It is you who will have to decide whether the system, as you receive it, is to your taste. It is you who will have to judge our tree by its yield. We may think that we have produced a rather fine fruit, but when you come to eat it, if it tastes to you sourish and unpleasant, you will want to try some other form of political and economic diet than that provided by the New Deal, just as we are now rejecting the Old Order.

We were told in the days of the Old Order that certain rules were necessary. We were even told that they were beneficial to everyone, although that might at first seem strange, and that it was sacrilegious to tamper with them. We tried to do things that way and found that it was no longer possible. The things the Old Order said were true, proved false; the things the Old Order said would be beneficial to everyone, became calamitous to the entire nation; and so my generation came to the conclusion that, sacrilege or not, something had to be done to these Old Order ideas and institutions.

Perhaps we should not have tried to make American institutions work. There are quite a few, I know, who seriously consider that democracy, for instance, is a proved failure, but I personally do not see that we could have done otherwise than we did: to extend the democratic process to those areas formerly ruled by industrial autocracies, and to prefer human beings to the things which human beings use. Perhaps we should have sat back with folded hands and pious resignation, waiting for a new-fashioned revolution or for plain old-fashioned anarchy, collapse and famine, to sweep away in one great social deluge all of the outworn ideas and abuses which were and are still holding us back. It is history that we did not so choose and that the American people themselves decided, using their sovereign power through the instrument of President Roosevelt's administration, to have a New Deal in order to make our American institutions and beliefs work. And it is very strange to me, though perhaps familiar to students of abnormal psychology, that there are today in this country still a considerable number of irrational people who do not realize that something more than an ordinary presidential election took place in 1932, and who now are clamoring for a return to a kind of civilization which is as archaic as the oxcart and the windmill. We cannot possibly return to the old dead predepression order of things simply because some people don't feel quite at home in an era which is dedicated to the proposition that every American should be given a chance to obtain a decent living in a country which has solved the problem of scarcity.

Let me repeat as emphatically as I can that it will be up to you in your time to decide whether you want this thing we call the New Deal or even a Newer Deal which you will invent. There will be another political choice in 1936 and another in 1940; in these choices you will share the decision as to whether what is being done is suitable. Nobody else can decide for you whether you ought to prefer one way or another way. I find myself hoping, however, that in making your decision, you will not allow yourselves to be condemned to inaction and acquiescence by unctuous talk about posterity. I do not suggest that you should join the famous politician who asked, "What has posterity done for us?" but I should like to remind you that posterity has a habit of thinking for itself just as you—who were the posterity of whom our grandfather talked—are going to think for yourselves. If you do what you can in your time to better the lot of your countrymen, those who come after you will be as well looked out for as is possible.

In the process of choosing your path, I ask you to consider quite carefully the merits of the Old Order from which we have departed; you must judge whether they suit your needs and purposes. Perhaps you will want to go back instead of forward. But in this connection, I do not scruple to remind you that you represent the privileged classes of this country. No people in America have had better opportunities than college graduates. And yet, how did the Old Order treat your group when it was free to work itself out to its logical conclusion? Did it give employment to all? Did it give genuine opportunities? Did it offer security?

There is no better way of answering these questions than by appealing to the record, and projecting its application to your case; for the New World is only now struggling to be born; the conditions we hope to establish are not yet made. Is each of you reasonably sure of a job when you graduate? Is each of you convinced that you will have a satisfactory opportunity for the exercise of your talents? Is each of you certain that you will be allowed access to the kind of work you want to do? Are you sure of peace and security in illness and old age?

A survey of Oberlin graduates made in 1926 showed that

about 2 percent of them were without employment. What has been the situation at Oberlin since the Old Order came to its logical result in 1929? Seventeen percent of Oberlin men and women graduating in 1929 had found no employment within six months of graduation. Over 20 percent found no employment in 1930, 1931, and of the class which graduated in 1932, nearly 40 percent had found no employment by the time of the presidential election. Putting this another way, I am informed by your president that where ten years ago only three men of the Oberlin class which graduated in 1925 were listed as unemployed in November of that year, thirty-four men of the class of 1932 were unemployed in the November of the New-Deal election.

I wish that there were some way in which your elders could appreciate what it must be like to be an American undergraduate today, facing, unless there are great changes, a future of diminshing opportunity. At the time when I and my friends graduated, everything was quite different. The professions and the business world were still hospitable to us. The War took up any possible slack in the demand for our services; and with the 1920's, an era was entered on which seemed to offer an almost limitless market for well-paid advertising men, bond salesmen, stockbrokers, and for executives of banks, investment houses, and industrial concerns. We had no more technical knowledge than you will have when we emerged from the colleges of liberal arts, but we were able to complete our education with pretty good assurance that the world had a place waiting for us and that we could find that place without too much trouble.

The tales I have heard since the Old Order came to its crisis and degenerated into what seemed like permanent depression, suggest that the modern American undergraduate is profoundly disturbed by the haunting thought that all his

years of special training and all his privileged opportunities
may be wasted. He hears that some of the ablest men in the
classes just ahead of him have been vainly hunting work for
months and even for years, or he hears that they have been
forced to accept uncongenial employment at an unsatisfac-
tory wage. He has seen some of his classmates drop out of
college because their parents had lost their money or because they themselves had lost faith in the practical value of
education. He knows of girls who are qualified for teaching
positions, who discover that there are no salaries for teachers,
and of girls who are wanting to marry who must wait months
and even years because there is no money with which to
found a household. Yet college men and women have not
suffered the worst penalties of this depression. Bleak as the
world must seem to them, it is bleaker still for millions of
their less fortunate fellow citizens. You cannot escape the
realization that something rather appalling has befallen our
civilization, when the plenty which we are so abundantly
equipped to produce automatically causes nation-wide misery, suffering, destitution, and hopelessness, whether it has
come home to you through personal privation or only
through observation. You *must* feel the urge to do something
about it, for your fellows if not for yourselves. Life was
meant to be lived abundantly and to be enjoyed—not to be
drained away in the bewilderment of poverty and unemployment. We all of us have to face this terrible and baffling
paradox together and to find the means for its resolution.

So I ask you, very seriously, what do you propose to do
about it? There are some philosophers of doom who will
assure you that we ought not to try to do anything about it,
because, as was said in war time, it will all be the same in a
hundred years. Very true, but *you* won't all be the same in a
hundred years. You will not be here at all. You will be dead

and gone. Today you are of an age when the world should be opening out before you rich with opportunity. Are you going to let your elders tell you that it is your duty to starve through the years of potential plenty, when you should be enjoying the fullness of life? Will you let them convince you that Yankee ingenuity is a myth, or that there are regions of human enterprise which are exempt from its operations? Will you let them prevent you from establishing homes, bringing children into the world, and using your talents in the ways you desire to use them?

I hope you will pardon me if I answer the old war-time saying: "It will all be the same in a hundred years," with another war-time saying: "Once you are dead, you stay dead for a long, long time." That strikes me as sufficient rebuttal to the suggestion of passive fatalism.

Perhaps these war-time sayings are not so out of date as they must seem to you now, for all of us are engaged in another war today, a war against human misery, against poverty, against human stupidity. We have seen how four years of depression can inflict as much damage on a great and wealthy country as an enemy blockade. We have seen men drop dead in the bread lines from starvation—malnutrition, I believe they call it. We have seen the impulse toward human life blighted; young men and women have become afraid to establish families and to create those new American lives which we must count on if our race is not to die. We have seen strong men and devoted women numbed and palsied by the fear of loss of homes, of jobs, of fuel, and of food, the most elemental needs of life. It was these results of the Old Order which my generation thought intolerable. Were we wrong to undertake reconstruction? We think there was no alternative except social suicide.

The New Deal is the first great national counter offensive

in that war against human misery. The formal parade-ground tactics of the Old Order proved ineffective, and they were abandoned. Other methods are being tried and when one is found which works, even tolerably, its pursuit is pressed. Some of the things now being done or which may be done will undoubtedly prove to be mistakes. No claim is made of infallibility for present policies, no dogmas are preached. It is the essence of the New Deal that its practitioners are honestly trying to find ways to establish the security and abundance to which our resources entitle Americans. And we ask for tolerance on the plea that we are preparing the way for the more expert work which you may do.

We need your help. We feel that you are with us and that time is with us both. The World War was a desperate and a tragic era which I for one devoutly hope will never come again; yet it had one redeeming feature which is applicable to our present struggle: the gayety, the gallantry, and the love of life of the young men "who went abroad to die." Death in those days was very close and very real to the dearest friends of all of us. The friend with whom you were sharing life and dreams today might be blown to fragments tomorrow. Each kiss might be the last; and each moment the prelude to eternity. There came of this an outbreak of amazing vitality which has left a crown of unforgettable beauty upon the great tragedy of my generation. Many of my fellows lie buried in the fields of France; many were crippled in body or mind by the ordeal of war. But that, I think, was not a greater struggle, or a more disastrous one, than the one we are now in the midst of.

The vitality of youth then was deplored by hasty moralizers; those who were set apart from the struggle thought that young men and women of my age were wicked and irresponsible. This was a wrong judgment. For both moralists and biologists will, I think, agree with me that the fear of death is the beginning of life, and, I might add, that the fear of life is the beginning of death. My friends may have feared death too much in those days of war for their love of life to express itself decorously, but I am equally convinced that in the intervening period we have, as a nation, been too afraid of life for our civilization to be altogether strong, natural and healthy. These are matters which I suppose must be left to the psychologists and the theologians. But I think I may, out of that experience, appropriately point out to you that many of the great moments of civilization, the age of Pericles and the Renaissance in Italy, and in Elizabethan England, the revolution in France, the establishment of independence in America, were achieved by young men and women—often by mere children—who themselves were so convinced that life might be short that they were determined to live it magnificently while they were sure of its possession. The ordeal of war brings out the magnificent resources of youth; it plumbs the depths of that vitality which generations of strong ancestors have accumulated. The ordeal of depression ought to try your mettle in similar ways. And, unlike war, this trial of strength ought to deepen your reserves of experience rather than waste them in futile effort.

Today, I should like to see the young men and women of America realize the contemporary challenge to their vitality. The feeling which shook humanity during the War and which after the War reshaped the entire civilization of mighty nations is called for again. Will you let it take hold of you or will you wait for things just to happen—as you easily may. When I was a child there used to be repeated by the ancients a hoary formula that if you opened your mouth and shut your eyes they'd give you something to make you wise. In effect the faculties of some, at least of the universities and colleges I know of, still continue to treat students as though they were children—to maintain an academic tradition of unquestioning acceptance. If you will let yourselves, I am afraid you undergraduates of today can sit around your halls and campuses with your eyes shut and your mouths open without anyone bothering to put anything wise or otherwise into your mouths for you. Sometime—and better soon than late—you will realize that this fight is yours, and you will cease to wait for someone to show you what your duty is. You will go out and find it, making suitable preparation while you can.

There are some signs of awakening; but most Americans are still lost in the easy contemplation of the past or the engaging techniques of individual competition. Dr. Carlos E. Chardon, the distinguished Chancellor of the University of Puerto Rico, recently remarked to me that he considered the greatest single contrast between American and Puerto Rican students to consist in a difference in maturity. American undergraduates, he said, were nice-mannered and healthy boys and girls, but they were generally without ideas and without intellectual interests, whereas Puerto Ricans of the same age were in most mental respects men or women, interested in and able to discuss ideas and understand them. I do not, I think, wholly agree with Dr. Chardon's diagnosis, for it has been my experience that American students show sufficient vitality and maturity of decision when brought into contact with reality, whether that reality takes the form of an antagonist on the athletic field or the necessity for working one's way through college, or even in the physical sciences.

I feel free to make this statement because my own special field of study—the art of economics—is a conspicuous academic sinner against the light of reality. Here you have an art—or at best a descriptive science—which has been taught from textbooks and according to dogmatic assertions of principle for generations. One of the few really great books on economics, Adam Smith's *Wealth of Nations,* was written as a generalized description of what had happened when Europe moved out of the era of mercantilism and into the era of laissez faire. Instead, however, of accepting this book for what it was, it was converted by later and lesser men into a rigid economic dogma, as beautifully symmetrical in its architecture as was the theological system of St. Thomas Aquinas. Laissez faire was regarded as a final truth which had been revealed to Adam Smith and any facts which deviated from the principles which he had deduced were either suppressed, ignored or treated as insignificant exceptions. For generations, as a result, economic thought departed further and further from reality. Nonconformists were treated as unscientific heretics when they tried to point out that the rigid conceptions of the classical economists were no longer a true picture of what was really happening. However, as one of the social sciences, economics was subject to all sorts of taboos which no longer trouble the man with the microscope and the test tube. There was no chance for the economist to experiment. Economists could not investigate the truth or falsity of the protective tariff, the defects and advantages of the profit motive, the desirability of unemployment insurance. These were matters of public policy and public law and were properly outside the control of academic experimentation. But they were and are within the limits of observation of every student and teacher. It is government and industry (though these terms are not mutually exclusive, as they used to be) where experiments are carried on and where your reality lies—not in textbooks and not in the past.

How then, could a socially constructive education achieve contact with reality? The answer is, I think, quite obvious.

Education must be for a real life; it must be based, therefore, on actual observation and interpretation of contemporary data.

What about the marketing system in your own town? What about your own father's source of income? Who has even bothered to write the economic history of the American bootlegger or to inquire of the local dairy farmer as to the incentives which induce him to rise at four in the morning to milk his cows? What makes the nearest factory run? Has it a code to operate under and why? How are its prices fixed? Where does its policy-making occur? How about the local tax system? Where do you get your gas and your electricity? Why do you, as students, spend four rather delightful years engaged in no directly productive enterprise while millions of other young men and women start seeking full-time employment at the age of sixteen? Or, if you want to vary your material a little, you might inquire what race and what religion produces the best farmers in Ohio, what the best coal miners, and why? And why not consider Washington, where so many economic policies have come to focus recently, as the proper objective of an educational pilgrimage? Your teachers might take you there and show you how everything works—if they know.

I ask these questions in no unkind or captious spirit, but simply to point out that even in economics—ticketed as the Dismal Science—there is a huge and fascinating fund of knowledge concerning human motives and human behavior in seeking a living which has been scarcely developed. And I would also point out that through some such simple direct personal approach as that indicated above it would be both possible and easy to bring American undergraduates into early contact with the realities of the business system, of agriculture and of government.

In fact, I foresee the probability that this depression and this continuing crisis in our system of feeding, clothing and sheltering our people will compel you young men and women to ask more and more searching questions of your teachers, and better still, of one another. I can even foresee the day when the standard courses in economics and politics will be conducted with no textbooks other than those supplied by the daily newspaper, and when the students will examine the professor instead of the professor examining the students, and when the professor will be forced in self-defense to turn his students loose on the vast stores of unexamined and unexploited realities which lie before the humblest doorstep in this great and bewildered nation.

When that time comes, it will be as safe to question in the class room the eternal rightness of the business system and to examine critically the operation of the various governments under which people live, as it is to dissect a frog in the biological laboratory or to solve a problem in differential calculus on the blackboard. And when that time comes it will be your turn to carry into our public life some of the questions which the class room must always leave unanswered and to press for the answers through political action.

That, to my mind, is the greatest service which you can render to yourselves and to those which come after you—to love your country well enough to live for it and to live for and in it with that independence of private judgment, that hospitality toward all phases of reality, and that refusal to let yourself be bullied into acceptance of the unacceptable which we like to think of as American.

From no other section of American life can we look for help as hopefully as from the colleges. They are, as I have said, the greatest single focus for the application of disinterested intelligence to our problems. The young men and women of this country are the people for whom we are making this great effort which we know as the New Deal. To carry out the liberation of the American people from the dead weight of outworn ideas and obsolete institutions, we shall need you to join our struggle.

I say "you" advisedly. It is *your* problem. *You* are going to have to live in the real world sooner or later and to run it, no matter how pleasant it may seem to prolong on the campus your introduction to life. No sleep is so sweet as that which follows the hour when we should get up. Yet you must arise sooner or later and nobody but yourselves will have the power to decide the sort of world in which you are going to live twenty and thirty and forty years from now. You can't blame me or my generation if you don't like things then, for we will have passed from power long ago. You are the ones who must decide whether you like the way the New Deal is being run. Are you going to take what is given you, ask no questions, and be thankful that it is no worse? Or are you going to come over to Macedonia, take the conduct of the campaign in your own hands, and put your elders on the high shelf where they belong? In any case, it will be your world soon; and I would have you believe that the whole purpose of the New Deal is to see that you find a fair field and no favor to show what you can do in it.

XXIX
RELIEF AND RECONSTRUCTION *

IN the course of the last century a Russian priest invented a variant of the Christian religion which spread like wildfire until the police suppressed it; but its baleful influence hung over the Czarist court right up to the end of the Russion monarchy. This novel creed asserted that since repentance is one of the great Christian virtues, the most practical way of indulging that virtue was to sin in order that you might repent.

I am sometimes of the opinion that much of what is regarded as social-service work in the United States labors under a remotely similar influence; that it is predicated upon charity and that, inasmuch as charity is admittedly one of the chief great human virtues, there has been too little inclination on the part of social workers to eliminate the need for charity rather than minister to it. Certainly, so far as concerns the general community which supplies the funds administered by social-service work, this has frequently been true and there are great sections of unconscious but extremely potent public opinion which would be unwilling to see the things done which would be necessary for the institution of a social system in which the need for private and public charity were eliminated. The impulse which has, year after year and generation after generation, persuaded the people of this country to contribute millions of dollars for the support of charitable enterprises is one of the most generous of which our natures are capable. But the existence of

* Address delivered at the National Conference of Social Work, Kansas City, May 21, 1934.

kindness in the world in no way absolves you from your deeper responsibilities. You must in some measure devote yourselves to constructive thought as to how we can best prevent the American people from needing your services, except in rare and accidental cases.

I say this with the full consciousness that many of the relief measures of the present administration have been directed to precisely the sort of thing which a stable society would avoid. That is to say, except in so far as they have kept people alive who would otherwise be dead, have held together families which would otherwise have been broken up, and have maintained order and hope instead of chaos and despair—except in so far as our relief measures have accomplished these emergency purposes, they have hardly touched the real problem at all. This is not the fault of your devoted corps of workers, nor the fault of any of the rest of us. We have had, all of us, to accept conditions as they were and to do first things first. Relief needs are always pressing after a disaster; and reconstruction has to come later. But as time passes reconstruction has to be thought of; and no one is so well qualified to think of it as those who have seen the disaster at first-hand. What I would plead with you to do, therefore, as you go about your daily business of succoring the needy, is to devote your thoughts, at least, to the larger problems of rehabilitation.

What we have been able to do so far, in the way of substituting rehabilitation for charity, has not been much. I know, from many conversations with your workers how you have reacted against so limited a program. It is as though you found a starving man in ragged clothes on a park bench, took him to a restaurant and gave him a two-dollar dinner, then outfitted him from top to toe in new clothes, including a cane and a high silk hat, and said, "There!

because this man is now dressed as he would dress if he were well off, therefore he is well off." Public opinion, up to now, has prevented social workers from going much beyond this state in dealing with the fundamental economic and sociological problems set us by the breakdown of the Old Order. Here and there you may have succeeded in introducing a little permanent rehabilitation into the social system, but on the whole, our social-service work is still a hand-out on the giving end and an insufficient dole on the receiving end.

This was inevitable in a society which conducted its affairs on a laissez-faire basis. We allowed ourselves to be projected into an era of mass production and large-scale management without giving serious thought to the changed relationship of the individual to the system. It was assumed that it was the business of each of us to provide for his future and that of those for whom we had a responsibility. No consideration was given to the new conditions being set for living which made this an impossible task for millions of workers. New machines and processes were introduced to take the place of workers, and a policy was adopted in industry of managing prices by varying the rates of production of goods. These two, between them, left workers periodically helpless to carry out their old responsibilities.

The adoption of new machines and processes need not necessarily throw men permanently out of work. But it will do so unless other steps are taken to see that some of the gains made in this way are diverted to the workers. Those steps have not been taken; and, in any case, there was always temporary dislocation while the displaced workers were finding the new jobs made possible by the increase in social income which efficiency brought. For this dislocation no provision was made, either. And the total result of our increased efficiency, therefore, was to throw most of its costs upon one group and to secure most of its gains for another.

If Americans had seen this process clearly for what it was, their sense of sportsmanship, if nothing else, would have intervened. But these processes take place, in a laissez-faire system, so casually, and with so little thought of the relation of one thing to another, that before we realized it we had a growing group of displaced workers without jobs and without the hope of any. Even in boom times this had become a formidable problem; and when depression came the personal disaster involved was almost overwhelming. For then, also, the full results of the other policy I have mentioned made themselves felt. As the demand for goods failed, and prices fell, the situation was met by stopping production. People wanted just as many goods; there were just as many factories and just as many workers to make them. But the fact that each business unit had a responsibility to stockholders rather than to workers or consumers dictated the way in which the crisis was met. For all this I would not have you think that I impute blame to anyone. Nothing is further from my purpose. But I would have you consider whether in view of what happened great changes are not necessary in the system which makes us behave in these ways.

You know, as well as I do, that the disaster was not confined to industry as we usually describe it. It extended to rural America too. With that problem I have been in closer touch than with any other these past years; and I know that the suffering which has been imposed on farmers and their families, in spite of all you could do in the way of relief, is something which no really civilized society would permit to happen twice. The same forces were at work here in somewhat different ways. And here even more remote causes reached down into every farm home in the land, bringing the blight of poverty. Foreign markets failed; efficiency increased and made the work of thousands of farmers on poor lands unnecessary; machinery replaced horses and mules and threw more acres into the submarginal category. No one farmer, and no group of them, was able to gauge the effect of these great imponderable forces upon his own small operations. He only knew that his prices fell, that he could not buy the things necessary to support life. He felt a natural resentment, since he had worked harder than ever to meet the crisis and had done all the things we have always considered to be right. But the disaster came; and its coming again cannot be prevented by just tiding him over for a while. Rural life needs reconstruction along with industrial life.

This is the problem which is set for all of us. We are not too well equipped to meet it. You yourselves labor under special handicaps. The private charitable agencies which have been operating for years have failed to impress the dominant influences in our towns and cities with the need for skill, experience and wisdom in dealing with the social problems of the community. And they have failed to realize, perhaps because their interests lay elsewhere, that it is better to prevent disaster than to relieve it. As a result, when the breakdown of economic arrangements compelled the assumption of relief as a public responsibility too great for private charity, the appointed leaders of local relief were too often handicapped by a limited view of the work they were supposed to do.

One time, on a visit to a certain island in the West Indies, I was told of a curious belief that the voodoo doctors knew of certain unique drugs, so powerful that they gave the appearance of death. The victim, properly dosed, was then buried by the sorrowing family, after which the witch doctors came at night, opened the grave and restored the supposed dead man to animation. These living dead men were called "zombies" and they lived lives of complete apathy and complete docility. The higher brain cells no longer functioned and they were to all intents automatons, who did as they were told, asked no questions and were told no lies. In that way, the voodoo men got a supply of cheap and docile zombie slaves. Whatever the truth of this traveler's tale, there is a lesson for us in it. Use your imaginations for a moment and see whether American workmen under the Old Order were not expected really to behave like zombies. When new machines forced them out of jobs, they were expected to applaud the spirit of progress, and find other jobs—if they could. When the selfishness and shortsightedness of the Old Order led our industrial machine into periodic depression—into those surprisingly regular outbreaks of "bad luck"—the millions out of work were expected to resign themselves to industrial "bad luck," to hope meekly for the best, and to live on whatever charity was offered them. And if by the millions they huddled through the winter nights in flop houses, on park benches, in pitiful shacks pieced together from discarded tin cans; if whole families crowded together in one room in poorly ventilated, unlighted, unheated and unsanitary tenements; if farm families—a million and a half of them between 1921 and 1933—were forced off their land to whatever haven they could stumble into—if all this has taken place in America, as all of us know it has, what is it but economic regimentation of the most tragic sort? These millions have been expected to live like Haitian zombies— to ask no questions, to take what is given them, and to be thankful. It is desirable, therefore, to examine carefully the false beliefs which stand between us and effective social action.

One of these beliefs is that if we take care of the immediate emergency the future will take care of itself. Feed the hungry and succor the distressed, it is said, but by no means commit the un-American crime of facing the causes of our distress. Don't admit that, so far as can be seen, we shall have an acute relief problem for years to come. Just pretend that it will all be over in six months or at the most a year, and devote all available time and energy to the "here" and the "now" and trust that something will turn up—a war, a boom, a new invention, or something—to prevent us from the necessity of taking thought for the morrow.

This is the first fallacy and it suggests the second: the assumption that if the wheels of commerce and industry, as now organized, can be set going full speed, all our worries will be over. Without questioning the obvious necessity of restoring the going processes of industry to supply man's material needs and to employ human productive energy, it is possible to question whether that is not merely one of the important objectives for which we must work. We now know that there are millions of workers, formerly employed by industry, who cannot be reabsorbed by our present industrial system, assuming it to remain unchanged, even if the volume of physical production is brought back to the levels of the turbulent twenties. In 1932, I am told, industry could produce as much as in 1923 with one-third less labor. And this development has by no means stopped. We know also that the same situation faces many farmers on lands which are inefficient. The formula for fundamental social service is somewhat more complex than is suggested by the shibboleths which still dominate the social thinking of too many of us.

We shall have to be pioneers if we are to rise above this vicious circle. Courage and fortitude, as well as intelligence and experience, are essential to the new civilization which *may* be ahead of us, if we have the perseverance and the wit to conquer the ideas which now thwart us. These moral qualities prevailed when our wilderness was conquered, but then always there was great hope. "Oh, Susannah, don't you cry for me!" was the marching song of a generation of Americans who set out to conquer the West. Americans want no pity, no one crying for them. They want opportunity to use their energies and their talents. There has been recently a great recovery in national morale, thanks to the leader who has never lost his courage and faith, and who has always seen our problems in true perspective, even when others gave themselves to blind fatalism or panicky confusion. The new hope which has found its way into the hearts of our citizens must find its substantiation in a real program of reconstruction.

In the present confusion of thought there are two doctrines of despair which you must combat. I have suggested one of these—the apparent belief that what is known as "business recovery" is the one panacea. The influential people of many communities see things in that light and have asked that the jobless, like zombies, should hope for it. Yet all the while industry is making technological improvements at an undiminished rate. I find little evidence that the advocates of "business recovery" are weighing the consequences of technology; if they have any realization of what may happen, I have not heard of it. Furthermore, among those who are obsessed with the speciously simple "recovery" formula—attractive because it appears to avoid the necessity both for thought and for reform—there seems scant recognition of the human deterioration which has been going on with increasing speed among the unemployed. With the fatal consequences to the bodies and souls of people who revolt from a prolonged social and economic catastrophe, the mere salvaging of the producing and distributing process may have little meaning for a dangerously large number of our people. And this proportion is so considerable as to threaten the social composition of our entire civilization.

My second major observation relates to what may be called "social recovery," broadly represented in the Federal Emergency Relief Administration and its state and county units. In many instances, local administrations—good, bad or indifferent—have followed on the heels of previous confusion or even chaos, combined sometimes with maladministration and socially destructive influences. Subsequently it appeared that the obstacles to a program of "social recovery" by the relief units—outside of their own shortcomings—were sins of omission and commission which had to be rectified if progress was to be made.

Sins of commission can be charged against the community on three counts. One is a hangover from old attitudes toward social service, which denied the need of skill, experience and ability. The second is subversive political influence which may blight the quality of relief personnel and subordinate stable policies to partisan advantage. The third is the demoralization which arises from the first two factors and which not only prevents the creation of competent organizations but produces a feeling of insecurity and fear where courage, continuity and confidence are needed.

The sin of omission lies particularly in the lack of comprehensive thinking. This is largely due to the attitude which prevails in many communities. Both city and county governments have one eye and one ear turned toward the local taxpayer and the other eye and ear toward business interests. The sanctity of property rights is interpreted as the sacred right of the individual to private advantage over others if he can get it. Thus all the dominant influences of the community combine in the sin of omitting measures to promote well-being in reconstruction.

It seems very plain to me that there has been an over-emphasis on business recovery and on pure relief, necessary as both are. It is, however, the prevailing idea of many people in all communities that nothing else matters very much. This is not universal, for every community has its quota of workers for the New Deal, but these are scattered and are too often obsessed with some sort of thirty-day panacea for solving everything without the necessity of thought. The problems—both physical and psychological—which we face are too formidable to be met by any panacea. Survival of our present civilization does not depend on advantage in any particular kind of industrial operation. Its reconstruction, however, cannot be achieved without the goods which we are equipped to produce and habituated to employ. It is for you to help supply the immediate and extensive social engineering required by a great period of transition, locally as well as nationally.

In spite of all the difficulties its workers have labored under, the Federal Emergency Relief Administration stands out in my mind as the foremost of all the recovery agencies. Through it the administration of President Roosevelt has been able to make good its belief that no American ought to starve; through it the administration has been able to liquidate some of the worst results of neglect in the hard years of depression; through it most of us hope to see the beginning of a program which will insure once for all the security of American lives and homes. It has done much more than it was strictly charged with doing. It has not been afraid of unconventional procedures; it has not stopped to ask whether what had to be done met anyone's preconceived

ideas about how it ought to be done. It has been the right
hand of the President in the rescue work of disaster.

The Civil Works Administration represented something
new in relief work; it gave jobs and income to fathers of
families by the million who had not had either for years; and
it carried out works of reconstruction which changed the
country physically as it had never before been changed in a
like time. The Surplus Relief Corporation helped us in the
Department of Agriculture to solve the paradox of want in
the midst of plenty. It made doubly certain that our program
of crop reduction should not take place in a land where anyone went hungry. Among the unconventional things which
were done, not least in its ultimate effect on the American
spirit, I think, was the rescue of artists and the dignification
of their work. The country is richer for what was done in
this way, just as it is richer for what was done to make the
countryside and the cities more beautiful. For the impulse
which was not afraid to risk Philistine criticism in a good
cause, we all of us ought to be thankful.

All these, and many other lesser acts of social kindness,
stand to the credit of the Relief Administration; but most
of all it has served as notice to all that government belongs
to the people and that when they are in need, it is government's duty to come to the rescue. Furthermore, it has shown
that there is at the disposal of government energy, intelligence and imagination, vast resources of each, ready to be
used when the need arises. You want no thanks for your
own services in this great crisis; but what thanks a single
citizen can give you, I am proud to convey. In my opinion
you have rescued our nation from the dishonor of inaction
in time of need. So that if the trend of my appeal to you on
this occasion is for further efforts, efforts of a new and even
less conventional sort, it is not because in any sense I would

belittle what you have done; it is because what you have done shows how much you can do in the effort which must come for reorganization of the system which brought this disaster upon us all.

I would see you enlisted as soldiers not in a new cause but in an old one. I would ask your loyalty not to a new faith but to an old one which for a while has been lost to sight. This administration is struggling to return to a lost democracy; it is trying to do it through a discipline of groups which oppress the individual. We stand face to face, today, with a clear choice and all of us have to take sides. Either we are to have a closed system or an open one. Either we are to give people access to income which they have earned as a right, or we are to give them pittances as charity. Either we are to permit industry to manage its affairs so that workers and farmers suffer continual small disadvantages and periodic great ones; or we are going to see to it that industry is so managed as to provide continuous employment for all and to distribute purchasing power which will enable the public to buy its goods.

The opportunities for a reorientation of social work will be numerous in the years to come. Their nature is foreshadowed by the demands which already have appeared. The move for the decentralization of industry and the establishment of new communities linking agriculture with industry will require the most delicate judgment concerning the practicality of proposals and great tact in organizing local initiative. Rural rehabilitation is part of your program for the current year. If you can find ways to transform the hopelessness of stranded populations on submarginal lands into hope for the success of newly conceived ventures, and do it for any considerable number of families, you will have demonstrated the idea I have been trying to put to you. Hitherto you have had to be content to bring these people an uncertain support for what they know to be a hopeless economic effort. If you can furnish practical ideas and persuade them into actual being you will have substituted reconstruction for relief.

This is a peculiarly satisfactory kind of effort. There is something physical to show for it when it is done. And if meanwhile some readjustments in the economic system can take place which will establish the freedom and the security of these communities, we shall all have reason for pride. No more is needed for this than to establish a fair exchange among our various producing groups so that each can exchange its products with others on such a basis as will do no injustice to any one of them. This would provide for continuity of operations, for then none would be unable to purchase the products of others. That, as well as the physical rehabilitation of communities, is something for which you need to work.

The Agricultural Adjustment Administration has been criticised for its policy of limitation. Its reductions have not been carried beyond what would be needed for a liberal use of agricultural goods in this country. But if it had, this criticism would come with poor grace from the industrial leaders who taught it to the farmers. Industry meets every critical situation by reducing production; it freely limits the supplies of goods to protect prices. Industrial production during the depression fell off sometimes to half, in some instances a third, or even more, of predepression volume. Farmers actually increased theirs. And now that they have taken a small leaf out of the industrial copy book and followed the maxim there written down, there are howls fit to wake the ghosts of our forefathers. Limitation is necessary for industry; for farmers, they say, it is un-American.

We who are working for the farmer might be willing to make a bargain with industry to stop limitation if industrialists will do it too. Of course they will not do it. It is right, in a way, that neither should. I say, "in a way," because if we are to have order in industry and agriculture too, there will have to be arrangements made so that only those things are produced which are wanted. This may, on occasion, involve limitation; but it is even more likely to involve expansion. A different kind of mechanism is needed for expansion, however, and one which seems not to have so great an appeal to immediate self-interest. It really would have, of course, if we had succeeded in bringing the interests of all into concord with the interest of each, for then we should have that fair exchange of which I have spoken. But all this is something to be worked out over considerable time. It is, I believe, inherent in the future operations of N.R.A., just as it is in A.A.A. This means that flexible mechanisms have already been brought into existence through which justice is available to all when we are ready for it.

Your part in it is a vital one. It will not be possible to gain the time necessary for agriculture and industry to work out a program for continuity and equal exchange unless those who are suffering from past maladjustments are cared for. And it will not be possible to work out such a program at all unless it is understood and interpreted by you and unless you are willing to join in working for it actively.

Our problem is a tremendous one and I do not think that it is even acknowledged to exist at all, in many responsible circles of our economic life. I shall put it to you as in one of its worst aspects as bluntly as I know how. What I refer to is the problem of those who have come of age economically since the sins of their fathers were visited upon them in the form of the present depression.

Every year about 2,400,000 Americans reach the age of eighteen and thereby become available for the purposes of our economic system, whatever these purposes may be and whatever form that economic system may take. To make room for these nearly 2,500,000 young able-bodied Americans, 1,500,000 people in this country reach the age of forty-five, the age at which our economic system begins to tighten its qualifications for workers.

As to the fate of the men and women over forty-five, you have one problem of relief—the care of old age, and this is serious enough. But what about the extra 900,000 youngsters for whom no places have been provided by the resignation or obsolescence of their elders?

Since 1928, nearly 5,000,000 more Americans have come of working age than have passed out of industry from age or disability. I am informed that the distinct tendency has been to reëmploy those who were employed in 1929 and who lost their jobs during the depression. This is fortunate for these men but it has concentrated unemployment among those who are over eighteen and under thirty.

That this is true is suggested by the figures of the Federal Emergency Relief Administration, which is now caring for over 3,500,000 persons between the ages of sixteen and thirty-four. There are, it is true, some 300,000 in the C.C.C. camps who are satisfactorily situated. But in spite of this the condition is still serious, since this cares for only a small percentage. Evidently we are faced with the alternatives of making rapid readjustments in our social and economic system which will enlarge its capacity to absorb the young, or of risking the consequences of idleness among millions of them. We have no problem more serious than this and the social-service workers of America must help us solve it, without political violence, social demoralization or economic chaos.

This is not an issue which can be deferred until some theorist can work out a neat solution. It is terribly urgent. Men live by more than bread alone. They demand jobs: that is to say, not only reasonable security in receiving their bread, but the sense of being useful to and of being used by society. We cannot indefinitely stave off this demand for food and work. But we have done too little to prepare the public mind for the necessity of meeting this demand.

In this you have the greatest opportunity which has ever faced a single professional group of Americans. The Agricultural Adjustment Act and the N.R.A. are available to you, as examples of how the community, working democratically through a multitude of face-to-face discussions and practical adjustments, has moved forward into new economic areas. As social workers, whose job it is to make people's lives easier, you must help the community move forward into new social conceptions. The old era of passing around the hat and waiting for the upturn is as dead as the one-horse plow and the hansom cab. You are now working within a new framework. The method to be used is one of overhead planning, with the initiative and the force coming to the centers of coördination from all over the country. You are right on the firing line and little can be done in Washington unless a great deal of the initiative and all of the action comes from you. You have been given ample opportunity especially through the decentralization of the relief organization. Over against this everyone is aware that you are under the strain of attempting to do in a hurry what should have been done forty years ago: to establish security against the various risks of society, especially illness, old age and unemployment. You have had to improvise institutions which have been maturing in other countries for the last two generations. It will be necessary to reinforce some of your efforts with legislation and to obviate many of your problems by appropriate industrial and agricultural controls, and to transform your volunteer army into a corps of seasoned fighters against misery, with ample supplies and strong reinforcements. I think you can count on help in these ways.

This transformation will mean that some of the romance of social service will be lost, along with some of the inefficiency which is associated with improvisation. We must get rid of the oversimplified notion that face-to-face relationships with those who are insultingly described as "the deserving poor" are sufficient, without any sense of the general situation which produces poverty, whether deserved or undeserved. We must modify the old idea of a personal salvation and case work, in which it is said to be sufficient to adjust the individual to a society which itself needs to be changed and is changing. Your task is not only to help the individual but also to assist in attacking the causes of his distress.

In fact, it has always seemed to me arrogant to assume that we have any right or power to change people at all. People are pretty much the same, with respect to their basic wants, urges and passions, as they were five thousand years ago. What changes is our institutions. Men establish ways and means by which they satisfy these wants, these needs, urges and passions. These institutions take many shapes and forms and constitute the organized milieu of society. When we talk of social change, we talk of changing these institutions, not the men who use them. When we speak of the need for social change, we mean that these institutions are failing, that they do not provide effective instrumentalities by which the urges, wants and desires of people are satisfied.

The essence of the New Deal is that it recognizes and gives expression to the people whose wants are going unsatisfied, because of the failure of the industrial and political institutions which they have established in the hope of satisfying those wants. Historically, political leadership does little more than guide people whose institutions fail, when the people press against these failures in their attempt to recapture arrangements that formerly satisfied their basic needs.

In other words, the New Deal is attempting to do nothing to *people,* and does not seek at all to alter their way of life, their wants and desires. It finds them hungry, in need of clothing, shelter, being denied the good things everywhere existing around them in abundance. The obvious situation is that these people call for a redirecting of the management of the institutions and organizations through which they feel they should be able to obtain a portion of these good things that they see lying around everywhere. Therefore, what is demanded of us in America today is the making over of the institutions controlled by and operated for the benefit of the few, so that regardless of their control they shall be operated for the benefit of the many. In all this there is no thought or need to change the individual so that he may conform to some pattern or be fitted to some industrial scheme about to be created. The reverse is true: that the industrial scheme shall be made over to fit the individual and supply his wants. What the Old Order describes as "rugged individualism" meant the regimentation of the many for the benefit of the few. The social mission of the New Deal has a somewhat higher standard of individualism—it believes in freeing the many from the regimentation of the few.

There, it seems to me, is the angle of attack for the social-service workers of this country, to sublimate the moral force of personal charity into a sense of social responsibility, and to abandon thought of any exclusive personal mission to be or to do good.

The chief aim of social work under the great governmental

program now under way ought always to be concentrated on helping people to help themselves—to take advantage, for the reconstruction of American life, of those springs of individual initiative which are so native to the American culture. Citizens must be made to feel themselves a part of a great civil movement which has as its object the creation of a better America for themselves and for those who will succeed them.

The most you can do for people is to discipline the institutions and forces which are inimical to the individual and so to provide freedom for action. You cannot forever go on providing subsistence for the idle at government expense. This will never be more than subsistence and it will eventually kill the thing we are trying to foster.

You may say that as social workers this is not your task, that you are merely parts of a machine for the rescue of the civilian wounded. This is too narrow a conception of your task and your duty. You will never be through with it if this is your only effort. You must understand what is afoot of a reconstrutive sort, and you must bring your patients out of your care into the free world again. This is their nation and it will be the kind of nation they make it. It is your duty to make them understand it. You can do no more for them than give them the health and courage to take their part. You cannot do their job for them; but you can make them understand that they have a job.

A free man on his feet, presented with opportunity to work for himself and those for whom he is responsible, will rise to the occasion well enough. If men had not always done that we should not be here today. The industrial system has been turned into an autocracy which was well on the way to killing this impulse in men. It must be shown that this cannot be tolerated. This is where our duty lies: the rescue of men from oppression. If we can do this our present rescue work will become unnecessary. As social workers this is where your ambitions should lie, no matter how seriously you take your immediate work of binding up wounds.

The challenge is an open one to our society. The opportunity is great. The time is now.

INDEX